Troy on Display

Also published by Bloomsbury

Troy: Myth, City, Icon, by Naoíse Mac Sweeney
Priam's Gold: Schliemann and the Lost Treasures of Troy,
by Caroline Moorehead
Homer's Iliad and the Trojan War: Dialogues on Tradition,
by Naoíse Mac Sweeney and Jan Haywood
Digging the Dirt: The Archaeological Imagination, by Jennifer Wallace
Sir Arthur Evans and Minoan Crete: Creating the Vision of Knossos,
by Nanno Marinatos

Troy on Display

Scepticism and Wonder at Schliemann's First Exhibition

Abigail Baker

BLOOMSBURY ACADEMIC
LONDON • NEW YORK • OXFORD • NEW DELHI • SYDNEY

BLOOMSBURY ACADEMIC
Bloomsbury Publishing Plc
50 Bedford Square, London, WC1B 3DP, UK
1385 Broadway, New York, NY 10018, USA
29 Earlsfort Terrace, Dublin 2, Ireland

BLOOMSBURY, BLOOMSBURY ACADEMIC and the Diana logo are trademarks of
Bloomsbury Publishing Plc

First published in Great Britain 2020
Paperback edition published 2021

Copyright © Abigail Baker, 2020

Abigail Baker has asserted her right under the Copyright, Designs and Patents Act, 1988, to be identified as Author of this work.

For legal purposes the Acknowledgements on pp. x–xi constitute an extension of this copyright page.

Cover design: Terry Woodley
Cover image: Heinrich Schliemann, *Ilios: The City and Country of the Trojans*
(London: John Murray, 1880), figures 235 and 236.
By kind permission of Newcastle Lit & Phil.

All rights reserved. No part of this publication may be reproduced or transmitted in any form or by any means, electronic or mechanical, including photocopying, recording, or any information storage or retrieval system, without prior permission in writing from the publishers.

Bloomsbury Publishing Plc does not have any control over, or responsibility for, any third-party websites referred to or in this book. All internet addresses given in this book were correct at the time of going to press. The author and publisher regret any inconvenience caused if addresses have changed or sites have ceased to exist, but can accept no responsibility for any such changes.

A catalogue record for this book is available from the British Library.

Library of Congress Cataloging-in-Publication Data

Names: Baker, Abigail, 1983– author.
Title: Troy on display : scepticism and wonder at Schliemann's first exhibition / Abigail Baker.
Description: London : Bloomsbury Academic, 2019.
Identifiers: LCCN 2019011538| ISBN 9781788313582 (hb) | ISBN 9781350114296 (epdf)
Subjects: LCSH: Troy (Extinct city)–Antiquities–Exhibitions. | Schliemann, Heinrich, 1822-1890.
Classification: LCC DF221.T8 B35 2019 | DDC 939/.21–dc23 LC record available at
https://lccn.loc.gov/2019011538

ISBN: HB: 978-1-7883-1358-2
PB: 978-1-3501-9136-5
ePDF: 978-1-3501-1429-6
eBook: 978-1-3501-1430-2

Typeset by RefineCatch Limited, Bungay, Suffolk

To find out more about our authors and books visit www.bloomsbury.com
and sign up for our newsletters.

For Geraldine, who got me interested in old things

Contents

List of Figures	viii
Acknowledgements	x
Part One Introduction	1
1 Troy and Truth	13
Part Two Putting Troy on Show	29
2 Bringing Troy to London	35
3 Making Sense of the Trojan Collection	45
4 How Schliemann Displayed His Treasures	61
Part Three Schliemania?	95
5 Visualizing Troy	99
6 The Appeal of the Primitive	115
7 Laughing at Schliemann	125
8 Weighing Up Ancient Troy	131
Part Four Troy's Place in History	137
9 The Other Homeric Question	141
10 How Old Was Troy?	151
11 Who Were the Trojans?	161
Part Five Troy's Legacy	177
12 Jane Harrison's Odyssey	181
13 Arthur Evans's Labyrinth	189
14 Dream and Reality	197
Notes	205
References	241
Index	259

Figures

1. 'Dr Schliemann's Trojan Antiquities at South Kensington', *Illustrated London News*, 1878 — 3
2. Helen, Paris and Hector in classical garb and pose — 4
3. Schliemann's finds from Mycenae on display in Athens — 38
4. Map of the South Kensington Museum (*c.* 1878) — 39
5. Exhibition in the South Court of the South Kensington Museum, *c.* 1876 — 40
6. A typical case design — 40
7. Stratigraphy diagram showing the depths assigned to different phases — 48
8. An eccentric arrangement of pots on shelves — 50
9. The trench cut under the temple — 51
10. Sophia Schliemann wearing the jewellery from Troy: 'the parure of Helen' — 53
11. Plan of Troy, clearly marked with Schliemann's trenches and the various structures he had identified — 55
12. Screens used for displaying drawings and photographs at South Kensington — 57
13. Plan of Schliemann's exhibition at South Kensington — 63
14. Drawings of spindle whorls from Troy showing their inscribed decoration — 67
15. Decorated terracotta balls, including *glaukopis* and swastika designs — 68
16. The *glaukopis* vase Schliemann found in the 'House of Priam' — 72
17. Skull from Troy, clearly not reconstructed by an expert — 73
18. 'Shield' which Schliemann claimed was used to cover Priam's Treasure — 76
19. Gold diadem with decoration that Schliemann saw as owl-headed Athena — 79
20. Gold vessel termed *depas amphikypellon* by Schliemann — 80
21. Assortment of pots from Troy, including the kind called *depas amphikypellon* today — 81

22 Objects from 'Priam's Treasure', including the 'key', hanging from strings	83
23 Star objects from the 'Treasure of Priam', including the 'key' and 'shield'	84
24 Apollo Metope from Troy	85
25 Pottery from Troy, including a double jug	87
26 Pottery from Troy, including a one-handled goblet like ones found at Mycenae and Tiryns	89
27 Pottery from Troy, including Schliemann's heavily reconstructed 'chimaera'	91
28 'Neo-Greek costume', *Harper's Bazaar* fashion plate, 1881	101
29 Trojan pots in the Hews and Company catalogue [c. 1877]	102
30 Frederic Leighton, *Captive Andromache* (1888)	103
31 Dante Gabriel Rossetti, Study for *Troy Town* (c. 1870)	104
32 Herbert Gustave Schmalz, *Queen Zenobia's Last Look upon Palmyra* (1888)	106
33 John Collier, *Clytemnestra* (1882)	107
34 Print of John Collier's *Clytemnestra* (c. 1914)	108
35 Frederick Sandys, *Medea* (painted between 1866 and 1868)	109
36 The first tableau from *The Tale of Troy*. George C. Warr and Walter Crane, *Echoes of Hellas* (1887)	112
37 William Bell Scott's sketches made at the Trojan exhibition	116
38 Pitt Rivers's 'Realistic Degeneration' diagram	158
39 'At the British Museum – A Peripatetic Art Lecturer', *The Graphic*, 1881	182
40 Map of the palace at Knossos (1921)	191

Acknowledgements

This book began as the last chapter of my PhD thesis to be written. It could easily have been the whole thing if I had tackled it first. As a result, it owes much to the support team who helped me throughout my PhD and to the full funding I received from the Arts and Humanities Research Council (AHRC). First, Caspar Meyer, without whom this book would not have been written. He gave me invaluable feedback on it as it evolved from a PhD chapter to a full book and kept me going through some difficult times both personally and professionally. The feedback and support of my examiners, Caroline Vout and Lindsay Allen, helped me identify the areas of this project that were unique and worth expanding. Birkbeck was an excellent environment for study and I want to thank all of the colleagues and friends who helped make it that way.

Early advice from Leslie Fitton helped me navigate the sources on Troy. Andrew Shapland kindly read a draft of this book and provided valuable suggestions. I have also had some useful conversations with Victoria Donnelan in the final stages. I am privileged to have been able to help them with the British Museum's forthcoming exhibition on Troy and look forward to seeing the results.

Much of this book was written while working on the AHRC-funded Ashmolean Latin Inscriptions project. While the subject matter is largely unrelated, I could not have found the time to write this without Alison Cooley taking an interest in my wider development. Working on such a publicly and theoretically engaged project has made this a better book and I am grateful for the interest taken by my colleagues in the Ashmolean and Centre for the Study of Ancient Documents.

This project has been a wonderful opportunity to talk to scholars in a range of disciplines about their work. I was glad to talk to Alexia Petsalis-Diomidis about Thomas Burgon's status as an early 'Homeric' archaeologist. Ioannis Galanakis was extremely helpful in getting to grips with Arthur Evans's museum work, and took the time to give a wonderful tour of the Ashmolean's archival holdings. Greg Woolf gave me useful feedback on an early version of this project. I am grateful to the people who commented on versions of this research presented at the Institute of Classical Studies Classical Archaeology Research

Seminar (London, 2015) and The Classical Association Annual Conference (Reading, 2013), especially Kate Nichols for asking such interesting questions.

Publishing with Bloomsbury has been a pleasure. Early editorial guidance on this project from Alex Wright helped me work out the final structure of the book. Alice Wright then took over the project and has been extremely helpful and reassuring as I navigate the process of publishing my first book. Lily Mac Mahon has provided editorial support and kept things on track.

The research itself would have been impossible without the expertise and assistance of museum professionals, archivists and librarians, including Emmalee Beddoes at Worcester; Carolyn Cruthirds from Museum of Fine Arts, Boston; the staff at the V&A archive, Newcastle Lit and Phil and the Cambridge University Library.

It has been a strange time to be writing about race in archaeology and the ways fiction can seep into truth. It has been especially hard to treat swastikas as a historical phenomenon when they were appearing in graffiti on my street. It is important to acknowledge that these issues are dangerously real, especially for those who do not share my privileges. I have been especially glad of my friends and family throughout this process. Conversations with Jen Grove, Alex Wardrop and Marie Almond kept me feeling human in the final stages. Martin O'Leary has helped me in so many ways: taking care of me, reading drafts and helping me work through my ideas. My love and thanks to my parents, Peter and Ellen, who have been incredibly supportive.

Part One

Introduction

In 1871, Heinrich Schliemann dragged Troy from myth to the headlines by announcing that he had discovered and excavated the city. It has been a topic of controversy ever since. Troy was an ambiguous site: a meeting point between fact and fiction with an untrustworthy excavator and novel and complex archaeological evidence. Seeing real objects that were (purportedly) from the site of the Trojan War changed people's perception of the ancient world, provoking heated debates on everything from aesthetic principles through Aryan theory to the gold standard. In this book, I explore how encounters with the objects from Troy allowed people to evaluate the evidence for themselves and come up with a diverse range of solutions to the problems that Troy posed and how these new approaches were felt far beyond the mound in Anatolia where they started.

The public's first chance to evaluate Schliemann's (often fantastical) claims against the material evidence came in 1877, when the exhibition of Schliemann's Trojan collection at the South Kensington Museum (now the V&A) opened. It became an instant sensation. Visitors poured into the museum's recently completed South Court, drawn by what Schliemann claimed was the treasure of the Trojan royal family, miraculously preserved from the city's famous fall. They picked their way through the far more modern objects (including glass, porcelain, metalwork, musical instruments and chimneypieces) that shared the temporary exhibition space. At the heart of the exhibition, they found two cases of glittering treasure, as expected. However, the exhibition as a whole seems to have surprised its public (and disappointed many of them) by being very different from what they had imagined. Visitors encountered case after case of strange-looking pottery, crumbling metalwork, stone tools and thousands of spindle whorls. We can get a sense of what they saw from the image of the best 'non-treasure' items (which actually included a silver vase) published by the *Illustrated London News* two weeks after the exhibition opened (Fig. 1).

This was not just an exhibition that struggled to live up to its own hype, it also had to live up to the imaginary Troy, drawn from Homeric epic and centuries of visual and poetic receptions. Homer was much admired and discussed in Victorian London, even before Schliemann's announcements. It was common for Victorian writers to recall Homer's central place in their childhood imagination and how they gained literary appreciation with maturity.[1] While the literary importance of Homeric epic was uncontested, it was subject to a range of debates about its origins and mode of creation, described as the Homeric Question. This had begun in the late eighteenth century, when the German philological scholar Friedrich August Wolf argued that the Homeric epics had

Fig. 1 'Dr Schliemann's Trojan Antiquities at South Kensington' from the *Illustrated London News*, 5 January 1878 (two weeks after the exhibition opened). © Getty Images, 3403064, Hulton Archive/Stringer.

been composed orally and written down at a much later date, including interpolations from other sources.[2] There was much resistance to this idea in nineteenth-century Britain (discussed in Chapter 1) because of Homer's foundational status for Greek literature and continuing influence. While they were not usually accepted as a straightforward representation of history, the *Iliad* and *Odyssey* were still regarded as the best evidence for the early culture of Greece.[3] Schliemann's collection was welcomed as another possible source of information in this debate, one that might provide a concrete starting point for the story of Troy and a set of known facts to counter the uncertainties of the textual scholarship. There was more at stake in the Homeric Question than individual readings of these poems: Homeric epic was used as evidence for the origins and value of Greek art, literature and culture and was used as an analogy for the reading of the Bible. As a result, the question of what the Trojan exhibition meant for readings of Homer was key to how critics assessed its value.

Before Schliemann, attempts at imagining Troy usually derived from Classical Greek imagery. For example, Flaxman's illustrations of the *Iliad* (Fig. 2) draw heavily on the costumes, objects and compositions in red figure vase painting. Schliemann's archaeological Troy was far more difficult to pin down. It represented centuries of habitation that we now know span from about 3000 BCE to the Roman period.[4] The artefacts that Schliemann associated with Homeric Troy were, by Victorian standards, strangely shaped and simply made. Schliemann found few examples of what we might describe as representational art and nothing like the detailed decoration vividly described in Homer and

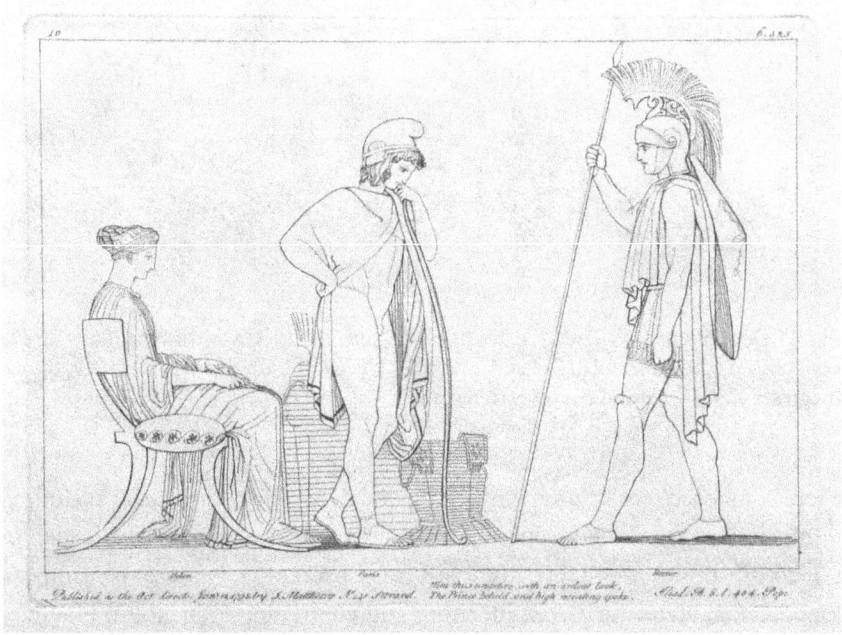

Fig. 2 Helen, Paris and Hector in classical garb and pose. *The Iliad of Homer Engraved by Thomas Piroli from the Compositions of John Flaxman* (Rome, 1793). © Foto H.-P. Haack, 2008-04-18.

imagined by artists ever since. While Schliemann's collection troubled old images of Troy, it offered no single clear replacement.

The gap between Schliemann's Troy and the public imagination is most strikingly illustrated in visual terms, but its scope was much broader. It made unquestioned assumptions about the past visible and opened up scope for new interpretations of the site's age, cultural and racial origins. These, in turn, demanded re-evaluation of pre-existing world histories to enable Troy to take its place in them. Troy became an important site for the central questions of nineteenth-century archaeology: imagining European origins; exploring the roots of religion and myth; tracing the beginnings of art; and questioning dating systems. It placed the roots of classical culture in a very unclassical context.

This book is about the point of crisis at which people who knew only the imagined Troy of text encountered Schliemann's material Troy and the role of the museum in shaping these encounters. Schliemann carefully crafted his exhibition to emphasize the objects and ideas that were most important to him and presented the whole as incontrovertible proof that he had discovered Homer's Troy. The exhibition was a carefully constructed representation of Schliemann's theories and I explore what it means for real objects to be used as material evidence for fantastical claims. It was also a rich spatial experience, which allowed new approaches to ancient Troy that used its materiality to ask and answer new questions about the past. Troy's materiality married romanticized legend to the stuff of everyday life. This paradoxical combination proved challenging to represent in the Victorian media (such as painting and theatre) that thrived on reconstruction, but it inspired new engagements that searched for different kinds of value in Troy's strange objects and joked about modern life through an ancient lens. Material analysis of Troy by archaeologists, anthropologists, metallurgists and many more produced new readings of the site, many of which were sceptical of Schliemann's Homeric claims. But even supposedly 'scientific' approaches were not immune to irrationality and mythmaking, and I explore how the search for a material and rational approach to Troy created new myths that shaped both disciplinary and public archaeology.

People have been examining the importance and effects of Schliemann's discoveries continuously since they were announced. There have been several recent examinations of his intellectual contribution. Marchand has shown how Schliemann shook confidence in philological approaches to the ancient world and set the parameters for the later practice of archaeology.[5] Gere's study of the so-called 'Tomb of Agamemnon' demonstrates how the popular fascination with Schliemann's material gave it a cultural impact far beyond the academy.[6] In such work, the more photogenic, less contested material from Schliemann's later excavations at Mycenae tends to receive more attention, but there have been some useful recent examinations of the importance of the site of Troy. Mac Sweeney has produced a helpful overview of the history of the site from the Bronze Age to the present.[7] Bryant Davies has considered the city's cultural significance in the nineteenth century, with a particular interest in popular receptions and performance.[8]

I am also interested in Troy's impact on a wide range of audiences but focus on the objects collected by Schliemann at Troy, with a particular interest in the museum as a venue where Schliemann's finds were encountered and interpreted. Collections of Schliemann's letters to museums begin to show how these institutions shaped his theories and allowed him to communicate with colleagues and the public.[9] However, there has been no close examination of the exhibitions themselves and their wider cultural impact. The contribution of museums and temporary exhibitions to thinking in Classics is generally undervalued, although there have been several recent demonstrations of their importance for cultural history and classical reception studies.[10] Museum exhibitions may have been overlooked because they are ephemeral, although other forms of classical reception that are time-limited are studied – compare the thriving field of performance studies.[11] This book shows how we can explore the experience of museum visitors as an instance of classical reception, where texts and objects come together in surprising ways.

The history of museums is a thriving field.[12] Since the New Museology's critique of the power structures embedded in the museum, many of these histories are interested in more than just how these institutions came to be.[13] They can be important works of intellectual, social and disciplinary history in their own right. Witcomb has noted that such histories tend (under the influence of Foucault) to be preoccupied with how museums exercise power and constitute the nation. There is no question that museums can play a hegemonic role, but there is often more going on under the surface. She calls for a more complex version of the history of museums as places where tensions between high and popular culture, rational and irrational could be explored.[14] This book answers this call in a number of ways. There is no better figure to explore the conflicts between rational and irrational than Schliemann, with his idiosyncratic readings of archaeological evidence, based on a profound desire to prove fiction true. Schliemann was viewed as irrational by many of his peers and the many different approaches to the Trojan collection cannot be understood by reading the museum as a top-down enforcer of high culture. Instead, the Trojan exhibition allows us to explore the many possible meanings that can emerge from contact with ancient objects in such an institutional context.

Studies of temporary exhibitions are comparatively rare outside the literature on international exhibitions. Haskell has sketched the history of Old Masters exhibitions and explored how their ephemerality gives them a particular rhetorical impact and public appeal.[15] Pearce (in her work on William Bullock's Egyptian Hall) has shown how temporary exhibitions outside the sphere of the national museums could prove highly influential.[16] Temporary exhibitions were an important part of the nineteenth-century experience of art and archaeology. Their ephemerality allowed their organizers to experiment with different approaches and make a case for the value (both in market and intellectual terms) of their collections. Schliemann was no exception, and we will see how he used the exhibition at South Kensington both to demonstrate his theories to as broad a public as possible and to appeal for help from experts who might improve his understanding of his collection.

The temporary exhibition at South Kensington is important to study for a number of reasons. It was the much-anticipated first public display of an influential and controversial collection and generated a wide range of responses (both in Britain and internationally) that show archaeology's intellectual and cultural role. It was also used by Schliemann to appeal for help from London's experts in understanding his collection, and to develop ideas that became part of the collection's permanent display at the Royal Museum in Berlin. As it turns out, Berlin was not the collection's final home. Most of the treasure was removed during the Second World War and thought destroyed before its high-profile rediscovery in the 1990s.[17] But even the plainer archaeological material (perhaps because of its plainness) has been split into other study collections.[18] Apart from being a rare moment of apparent unity in the collection's turbulent history, the London exhibition is also important because its nature as a temporary exhibition allowed it to do different things. It was temporary, flexible and attracted attention from a wide range of people. There was scope for the exhibition to voice ideas that were not yet part of the mainstream and make a bid for the inclusion of both objects and ideas in the prestigious spaces of permanent museum galleries. Studying temporary exhibitions gives an insight into how new sites and new ideas are evaluated and adapted to become part of the archaeological mainstream.

Schliemann saw exhibiting his finds from Troy as a way to win over his doubters and prove his theories in a large public forum, but his audience was not interested in passively absorbing his messages. This book explores responses to the objects from Troy, using ideas about museum interpretation drawn from the

New Museology, which sees visitors as active participants in building meaning.[19] While nineteenth-century models tended to be more didactic, this does not mean nineteenth-century museum visitors always behaved according to expectations.[20] Schliemann was well established as a point of controversy before the exhibition opened, so the exhibition was bound to extend and deepen that controversy. Schliemann characterized London as very welcoming to his ideas and gave this as the reason he chose to exhibit there, but that does not mean that the audience for the Trojan exhibition was uncritical.[21] In fact, it was the scope for debate that drove much of Schliemann's popularity. Visitors used their experience of the exhibition to come up with their own explanations of the archaeology of Troy or redeployed Troy in a range of contexts, including home design, humour and debates about international policy.

This kind of active participation reflects the dynamic model preferred by classical reception scholars. For example, Martindale (following Jauss[22]) calls for a model of reception that depends on a present engaging actively with the past allowing each to shape the other.[23] However, this model of textual reception does not account for the additional layers of complexity introduced by museum exhibitions. An exhibition appears to be one of our culture's most direct encounters with the past – allowing its visitors to see ancient objects first-hand and make their own judgements. However, it is a heavily mediated experience that uses a range of interpretive methods (selection, arrangement, labelling, images etc.) to produce a reading of those objects. It is also a more social experience than reading tends to be in our culture and was open to many interpretive communities. Nineteenth-century museums (especially South Kensington) were never conceived as the final stage in the process of interpretation, rather they were somewhere people could encounter (see, draw, write about, compare, discuss) objects from the past and feed these encounters into their own ideas, tastes and creations.[24] My model of reception will need to be attentive to a wide range of different sources in order to understand the Trojan exhibition's full impact. Accordingly, it reads far more like the sort of cultural history that Martindale dislikes, but I am not doing this to seek some sort of 'Geist' but to show the complexity and diversity of possible experiences of the past and out of a belief that insight is not limited to the big names of the literary canon.[25]

This is not to say that we will not encounter some important figures in this history. Former (and soon-to-be) prime minister William Ewart Gladstone and Austen Henry Layard (the excavator of Nineveh and one of Victorian London's biggest archaeological celebrities) both played an active role in bringing the exhibition about.[26] Gladstone also famously had a public argument with poet laureate Alfred, Lord Tennyson about the relationship between Schliemann's Troy and Homer's Troy.[27] This was a fashionable debate and we will explore how a range of important figures (Gladstone, Pitt Rivers, Pater, Müller, Newton etc.) contributed to it. Two detailed case studies (Chapters 12 and 13) will show how Arthur Evans and Jane Harrison used the popularity and accessibility of this debate to draw attention to their own theories.

The book is divided into five parts. This first section summarizes the state of knowledge about Troy before Schliemann, covering debates about the location of the site, the value of Homer as a source on Greece's early history and the range of textual and authorship debates caught up in the 'Homeric Question'. It discusses the controversial status of Schliemann as an influential figure known (even in his lifetime) to lie when it was most convenient for him. Finally, it discusses why Troy, with its deeply layered archaeology and role in both history and myth, is so rich for thinking about how we engage with the past.

The second part of the book, 'Putting Troy on Show', looks at how Schliemann used the Trojan collection to draw attention to his discoveries and make the case for his theories, and how he managed anxieties about people taking the wrong message from his collection. Chapter 2 explores Schliemann's early experiments with displaying his finds and his attempts to find a permanent home for his Trojan collection in a major European museum. It asks why Schliemann chose South Kensington for his first exhibition and explores the incongruity of displaying archaeological finds in a space designed to encourage a specific (and contrasting) model of taste. Chapter 3 looks at the interpretive media used in the exhibition such as labels, photographs and plans and considers why these show an unusual interest in relating the objects back to their archaeological context. Chapter 4 goes through the contents and spatial layout of the exhibition and the way that objects were carefully grouped to explore particular themes. I explore the effects of this arrangement through visitor responses. This detailed examination of the exhibition shows how it brought together archaeological evidence and Schliemann's theories to make a powerful rhetorical tool. I argue that this is as worthy of critical and historical exploration as any of Schliemann's (much-discussed) books.

Having established what Schliemann was hoping to achieve, and his methods, the third part explores the idea of 'Schliemania', considering the cultural impact of the enthusiasm for Schliemann and his finds in the immediate aftermath of the exhibition. Expectations were high that artists would visit and be inspired by the Trojan exhibition and Chapter 5 explores the extent to which this can be seen in representations of Troy. It covers examples from fashion, home décor, paintings, poetry and drama. Schliemann's finds were challenging because they did not fit easily with prior representations of ancient Greek life and did not offer a complete enough alternative to replace them. I argue that the few examples of art that did reproduce finds from Troy used these anxieties to achieve their effects, with Troy emerging as a way to bring foreign influences into the visual language of the classical. Chapter 6 then looks at another angle on artistic engagement with the strangeness of Troy by considering attempts to admire objects from Troy despite seeing them as 'primitive'. I show that Troy gave people an excuse to look for beauty in new places and show how this resonated differently with the ideas of the aesthetic movement and colonialist thought.

Not all engagements with Troy were serious, and Chapter 7 looks at some of the jokes that were made about the Trojan collection. The contrast between simple objects and grand descriptions that challenged artists also proved fruitful for making bathetic jokes that could critique Schliemann or use Troy as a lens for distorting or clarifying contemporary social practice. There were also questions about whether Troy might shape contemporary life, and Chapter 8 considers why the Royal Mint became interested in the weight of some silver objects from Troy and how bankers and economists fed this into debates about monetary policy. The Troy that emerged from these debates had little in common with Schliemann's Troy or that of Homer but proved useful for considering how nations relate to each other and where systems of value come from.

The fourth part of the book considers the questions about 'Troy's Place in History' that were up for debate at the time of the Trojan exhibition. The biggest question was still whether this was Homer's Troy, and Chapter 9 considers the challenges of comparing Schliemann's Troy with the rich descriptions of objects in Homer. There was a complex interplay of scepticism and belief in seeing real objects through epic, and I consider the distancing mechanisms used to entertain Schliemann's ideas without seeming credulous and what these tell us about how different audiences were supposed to approach Homer. While there were no firm answers to the Homeric Question on display at South Kensington, people hoped that the objects would tell their own story. Chapter 10 looks at the difficulties presented by Troy's unprecedented depth and complexity and how these inspired a range of competing accounts of its development. I explore how Schliemann's attacks on the three-age system aimed to complicate models of technological development and stake a claim for Troy as an important early site with lessons for wider archaeology. A competing narrative of technological development was also emerging from anthropological uses of evolutionary theory, and I show how

Pitt Rivers challenged Troy's stratigraphy and used the site to tell a story of degeneration.

Narratives of progress and decline in the nineteenth century relied heavily on ideas of racial difference to explain differences in culture, so Chapter 11 looks at attempts to assign a racial and cultural identity for the people of Troy. I argue that previous explorations of this topic have been too preoccupied with the idea of Troy as Aryan, and that a wide range of different racial theories were applied to Troy's objects and human remains. The question of whether Troy was Western or Eastern had long been debated but took on a new dimension in the light of European imperialism. The material from Troy came at a perfect time to offer new answers, based on new forms of expertise. The skulls attracted particular interest and I explore how these generated a range of readings of Homer's Trojans, from ape-like to Aryan. Material culture also seemed a promising way to connect the Trojans to other known peoples, and I explore how Troy's objects were used to link it into broader narratives about the origins and transmission of human culture. While the materials studied and techniques used by these approaches vary widely, they all used the veneer of objective analysis of material evidence to make modern identities and power structures seem natural.

The fifth part of the book looks at Schliemann's legacy in the lasting appeal of ancient stories in public discourse on archaeological discovery. Jane Harrison identified Schliemann as a game-changer who finally attracted the attention of classicists to material evidence and got them asking anthropological questions about ancient life. Chapter 12 looks at Harrison's early career, lecturing to the public in London's museums. She told the Homeric stories on Greek vases and used this to communicate contemporary theory on mythology and iconography to a broad audience. Her work used enthusiasm for Homer after Schliemann to make a case for a different relationship between ancient objects and ancient literature that was attentive to the realities of ancient life. While Harrison was re-evaluating the objects already in London's museums, Schliemann also shaped expectations for new archaeological discoveries, and nowhere more so than Knossos. Chapter 13 looks at how Arthur Evans manipulated those expectations to draw attention to the first exhibition of his finds from Knossos, while managing to avoid much of the scepticism that Schliemann faced. I consider discourses of authenticity and plausibility in the reception of Knossos and how even Evans's replicas were seen as authentic experiences of a lost mythical city in the way that Schliemann's genuine artefacts rarely managed.

Chapter 14 concludes by looking at how Homeric resonances are used by museums today to attract public interest and communicate ideas about the ancient world. The exhibition *Troia: Traum und Wirklichkeit*, which toured a number of museums in Germany in the early 2000s attracted international attention for renewing controversy over whether Hisarlık was really Homer's Troy.[28] This controversy echoes debates over the first Trojan exhibition in a much changed archaeological and political context. I argue that part of the appeal of sites like Troy is the way they bring different uses of and approaches to the past together in ways that inevitably generate friction. Despite the heated opposition to using romantic literary narratives to understand real archaeological finds, many museum exhibitions set up a contrast between 'dream and reality', using the appeal of such approaches while claiming to get at the real facts behind the myth. This dichotomy between hard facts and evocative legend continues to be compelling more than a century later when dealing with the tricky epistemology of material culture. The fact that Troy is still a contested site today could be seen as a failure of Schliemann's mission. Certainly, the material from Troy never achieved the iconic status of the gold masks from Mycenae or the wall paintings of Knossos, despite the long-standing fascination with the city as represented in Homer. But the way it continues to be debated shows its deep influence of Schliemann on our ideas about the past. Many of these ideas can be directly traced to the debates following Schliemann's first exhibition. The Trojan exhibition proves to be a valuable way to get at a number of oppositions in our relationship with the past: fact and fiction; public and professional; verbal and material; ancient and modern; reason and emotion. This book works to complicate some of these dichotomies and explore the importance of the museum as a site where these issues meet.

1

Troy and Truth

In July 1877, Schliemann wrote to *The Times* complaining of an article 'which by the abundance of false statements in it, throws into the shade all that has yet been written against me in any country'.[1] While there had been much scepticism about Troy, this particular attack had struck a nerve. The 'libel' in question was an evaluation of Schliemann's claims by comparing them to the site of Troy itself. It was written by William Simpson, an artist who worked for the *Illustrated London News*.[2] He had travelled to the site of Schliemann's Trojan excavations in the height of the controversy in 1877. He made detailed drawings of the site and purchased objects found by locals.[3] On his return, he published a full report in *Frasers Magazine*.[4] He celebrated Schliemann as an exceptional excavator, who could claim excellence in archaeology because of his instincts and energy: 'if Agamemnon's Sceptre has been or is yet to be found, no one can show a better right than himself to be its possessor'.[5] However, he concluded that Schliemann had let his imagination get the better of him and that this site could not be the Troy of Homer. He described the idea as 'something in the light of a joke' and said that Priam's palace looked more like a pigsty. Simpson was only an amateur archaeologist and, while his platform as a journalist and an artist may have carried some weight, the particularly threatening feature of the article must have been its direct, eye witness engagement with Schliemann's discoveries.

Schliemann had notoriously thin skin and hated being criticized.[6] He also carefully manipulated press coverage by inviting his supporters to refute criticism and was not above paying for good reviews.[7] In this case, he called on his friend, the Oxford philologist Friedrich Max Müller to write an article in his defence.[8] Another 'esteemed friend' of Schliemann, Bertram Fulke Hartshorne also waded into the debate (possibly after similar begging) to describe his visit to Troy and agreement with Schliemann.[9] However, there may have been more in Schliemann's reaction than a knee-jerk response to criticism; he also used the disagreement to generate interest in his collection. Schliemann's rebuttal of Simpson led by announcing that he would display his Trojan collection to the public in London, boasting of its great age and the unusual objects it contained: 'the ruins of four successive prehistoric cities, with immense archaeological treasures, which will soon be shown at South Kensington Museum. I ask the civilized world if I stand in any need to engage Mr. Simpson, as my master to teach me archaeology'.[10]

It is unclear how many of Schliemann's readers stuck around for fifteen paragraphs of tediously detailed argument about the exact nature of Trojan building techniques; certainly much of this was cut when other papers reprinted this letter.[11] Schliemann presented his finds as his main weapon in this debate, positioning his exhibition as a way for many more people to view his discoveries and judge his conclusions for themselves: 'I thought the most eloquent and crushing answer I could possibly make to them would be the exhibition of my Trojan collection in London.'[12]

In fact, the exhibition had been planned for some time: Schliemann had made a promise to Gladstone that he would bring his collection to London at least a year before Simpson's attack.[13] Schliemann framed this decision as both a gesture of gratitude to his supporters and a final refutation of his opponents.[14] This placed the Trojan collection at the heart of the debate about the site of Troy and how it related to the city described in Homeric epic. As a public exhibition, it showed Schliemann's confidence that his conclusions about Troy would seem self-evident from viewing the finds. It presented the materiality of Troy as its strength; something accessible to common sense and so vividly real that it spoke for itself. At a time when philology and comparative mythology were framing the problem of Troy as a scholarly exercise that should involve close reading in the original language and comparison with other texts like *Ramayana* (an approach favoured by Simpson), Schliemann offered the possibility of a Troy rooted in material objects that people could see and understand directly.[15]

In many ways, this book is about how Schliemann's collection failed to be an 'eloquent and crushing answer' to his critics. The site it came from is known as Troy today, but this took a long time to be accepted and its relationship with the Troy of Homer remains problematic. Only a few visitors to the exhibition agreed wholeheartedly with Schliemann that his finds were evidence of the factual truth of the *Iliad*. Those who did, like the correspondent for the New Hampshire paper the *Independent Statesman*, highlighted its find-spot, not any intrinsically Homeric quality of the material:

> The Doctor defended his position with much vigor, and what is a nut his opponents never cracked is, that no one of them can question that he found the

articles on exhibition in this museum, and also at Athens in the places which he says he did and the value of the articles to the antiquarian and the historian speak for themselves.[16]

For most people who saw it, the Trojan collection raised more questions than it answered. Being able to see objects from Troy for themselves gave people a new body of evidence to enrich debates about the site, which had previously been fuelled by travellers' accounts and readings of the classical texts. The people of London were now able to experience the objects from Troy for themselves and draw their own conclusions about life in this ancient city. While debate about where Homer's Troy really was rumbled on, Schliemann was successful in shifting the terms of the debate and introducing a new body of evidence.

This shift from a focus on texts to a focus on objects reflects broader trends in nineteenth-century culture. Approaches to the past that depended on literary records were being displaced by disciplines that specialized in 'reading' objects (including archaeology, natural history and geology) which were deepening time far beyond known history.[17] Schliemann's role in archaeology's challenge to literary history is somewhat ambiguous. His obsession with Homer could make him seem part of an earlier tradition that trusted the authority of text, but he focused on excavation and largely disregarded literary and philological scholarship. Schliemann's archaeology challenged the dominance of philology by developing techniques to 'read' objects that would compete with texts.[18] The Trojan exhibition showed objects that might not only serve as evidence in their own right, but also cause people to re-evaluate the text of Homer. It reached a broad audience with varying degrees of knowledge of the classics and encouraged them to engage with the collection in their own terms.

Schliemann's insistence on the ability of his collection to speak for itself could be infuriating. At its core was a circular argument, as Simpson had pointed out:

> Dr Schliemann tries hard to make us believe that no one ever doubted the Iliad or the existence of Troy. The old authors may be consulted by anyone, and the accuracy of this statement can be easily tested. That Ilium was a real city he pretends to prove from the fact that he has actually explored for it and found it, and that it is Troy he has discovered he established by asserting that it is so.[19]

There is no question that Schliemann fell prey to this kind of reasoning. He would cheerfully describe a face vase as representing owl-headed Athena on the basis of it having been found at Troy, then later use having found such items at the site as conclusive proof that the site was the Troy described by Homer.

Maurer has described such arguments as a set of 'reality effects' that were sufficient for Schliemann not to pursue the facts further.[20] For all Schliemann's talk of evidence (and we will see him using many of the cutting-edge discourses of nineteenth-century archaeological evidence such as stratigraphy and photography) his biggest claim required a leap of faith and raised questions about exactly what would constitute proof.

The discovery of Troy was not a single breakthrough by Schliemann, but the product of centuries of speculation and exploration. The debate was about much more than the question of where excavators should dig. It also meant questioning what sort of truths one could look for in an epic poem. This chapter looks at the traditions of visiting and writing about the sites identified with Homer's Troy and how these earlier engagements shaped responses to Schliemann's discoveries. Much was at stake in identifying a real archaeological site with an epic poem and many doubted that Troy would ever be found, so it is worth exploring this process. Schliemann's character and actions have also been a source of controversy and we must explore the implications of these debates for our understanding of Troy. I argue that Troy, with its untrustworthy excavator, archaeological complexity and combination of truth and fiction is an unusually fruitful site for thinking about what fascinates us about the past and questioning the methods we use to understand it.

Finding Troy

For Schliemann to announce that he had discovered Troy, it needed first to be lost. This was not the case with Mycenae (another famous site that Schliemann excavated) where local tradition, corroborated by comparison with ancient authors, had been able to guide interested travellers to the right place for centuries.[21] By contrast, Schliemann's claim to have discovered Troy revived a long-running debate about exactly where the site was. Landmarks mentioned by Homer (such as Mount Ida and the islands of Imbros and Tenedos) left no doubt that the Troy described in the *Iliad* was somewhere in the region known as the Troad, in north-west Anatolia.[22] Travellers had visited the area since antiquity to experience something of the world of Homer for themselves but by Schliemann's time there was no certainty about the location of the city or whether there were any ruins to find.

The destruction of Troy has been one of its defining features since ancient times. As a result, it was seen as a place that was easier to visit in the imagination than in reality.²³ Lucan described Julius Caesar visiting the site of Troy to find that even the ruins were destroyed.²⁴ Lucan's Latin phrase to express this (*etiam perire ruinae*) became a way of lending ancient authority to the idea that if Troy had existed, it must be long gone.²⁵ However, despite there being little to see, there was still a tradition of visiting the area to experience its absence. Caesar was already following in the footsteps of Xerxes and Alexander the Great, who had both taken a break from their military campaigns to pay their respects to this previous great war and assert their own place as heirs to its combatants.²⁶ Modern travellers continued this tradition of visiting the Troad, often self-consciously emulating earlier and more famous visitors. For example, the British architect Charles Robert Cockerell, visiting the Troad in 1810, stripped naked and ran around (what he believed to be) the tomb of Patroclus, directly emulating Achilles and Alexander the Great who had both done the same.²⁷

Foreign travellers looking for Troy before the nineteenth century might be taken to one of several ancient sites in the Troad, depending on where their ships landed. Later sites which had more impressive and more classical-looking above-ground ruins, like Alexandria Troas (with its suitably grand ruins of Roman baths) or Yenişehir (a city founded and then abandoned by the Emperor Constantine in the fourth century CE) were favoured above the sites that later became serious contenders for Homer's Troy.²⁸ Detailed topographical arguments about which sites were the best candidates for Troy began in the eighteenth century. British traveller Robert Wood visited the area in 1742 and closely examined its landmarks as features of the Homeric poems, considering how they might have changed since, but he did not identify a particular site as Troy.²⁹ The French Ambassador to the Sublime Porte, the Comte de Choiseul-Gouffier commissioned a more detailed series of investigations into the area, which included the earliest documented excavation (at the site traditionally identified as the burial mound of Achilles) and highlighted the two main contenders for Troy: Hisarlık and Pınarbaşı.³⁰

Bryant Davies describes the nineteenth century as bookended by two debates over Troy, the first (in the late eighteenth and early nineteenth century) was a debate over whether or not Pınarbaşı was Troy, the second was over whether Schliemann had actually found Troy at Hisarlık.³¹ Many travellers and antiquarians investigated the relative merits of the two sites, based on how closely their landscape (especially the rivers and springs) fitted with the one described in the *Iliad*. By the time Schliemann had started excavating at Troy, this debate had largely settled in favour of Pınarbaşı. Even Schliemann, on his first visit to the Troad, went looking for the site at Pınarbaşı. He was won over to the idea of Hisarlık as Troy by Frank Calvert, a local landowner whose trial investigations at the edge of the site had proved promising, and who mistakenly thought Schliemann might be an ideal excavation partner.[32]

Today, prevailing archaeological opinion is that Calvert was right. If any site can be identified with Homer's Troy, it is the site at Hisarlık, which was the only major settlement in the area in the period that most likely inspired the epics.[33] Later inhabitants of the site knew it as *Ilium Novum* (New Troy) and believed it was the site of the conflict described by Homer. Archaeological investigation since Schliemann has revealed that Bronze Age Hisarlık was a trading centre in the sphere of influence of the Hittite Empire. Hittite records describe a site called Wilusa (similar to *Ilios*, one of Troy's ancient names) in north-western Anatolia, which fits the site. Other details in Hittite inscriptions allow scholars to find out more about the political history of Wilusa and some go further to describe them as proof of the Trojan War.[34] However, while the site broadly fits with the city described in Homer and there certainly were conflicts at Hisarlık, no single event neatly lines up with the siege and destruction of Troy.[35]

Finding a city named *Ilium* that might have inspired later legends in roughly the right place was not the only challenge. The question of whether this was Homer's Troy has proven far more difficult to answer. It meant measuring an archaeological site against the events, people and objects described in the *Iliad* and *Odyssey* and the broader cultural expectations set up by them. These poems were known to be some of the earliest produced by Greek culture, which meant that Troy occupied an important place at the start of the Western literary canon. The Homeric epics were seen as works of outstanding literary quality that were profoundly influential on everything that followed (both classical and more recent). They were also the earliest known documents of Greek culture and were often searched for clues about the origins of this civilization and, by extension, of all European civilization.

In his influential 1846 *History of Greece*, George Grote explained why he chose not to treat Homer as a historical document or to try to pick fact from fiction:

> I describe the earlier times by themselves, as conceived by the faith and feeling of the first Greeks, and known only through their legends – without presuming to measure how much or how little of historical matter these legends may contain. If the reader blame me for not assisting him to determine this, – if he ask me why I do not draw aside the curtain and disclose the picture, – I reply in the words of the painter Zeuxis, when the same question was addressed to him on exhibiting his master-piece of imitative art: 'the curtain is the picture.'[36]

Grote references an incident described by Pliny the Elder about a painting competition won by deceiving a human opponent with an image of a curtain so realistic that he asked for the curtain to be pulled back and the painting revealed.[37] For Grote, the realism of Homer was not a sign of some underlying truth, but part of the artistry of the work and there was no sense in trying to pick history from poetry. Grote was pushing back against a long tradition of using Homer as a historical source. Attempts to document early history often pieced together information from the Bible with ancient literature like Homer to create chronologies in which the fall of Troy was an important event.[38] While literal readings of Homer were looking less plausible by the nineteenth century, there was very little to replace it as evidence for the early history of Greece, and so Grote still included the Trojan War as myth. Archaeology offered another possible source, but was easiest to contextualize with reference to literature. In 1844, the merchant and antiquarian Thomas Burgon visited Mycenae and identified the zig-zag and spiral decoration of the Bronze Age pot sherds he saw on the ground as distinctive features of 'the Heroic and Homeric ages'.[39]

Today we have much more information about life in the Mediterranean before recorded history. The question of whether there could be some underlying truth in Homer that might be reflected in archaeological discoveries is more marginal, but continues to be asked. The culture described in the Homeric epics is now seen as mostly a product of the period around 700 BCE, but there are a few objects in the text that seem distinctively Bronze Age, such as Meriones' boar tusk helmet.[40] Textual scholarship on Homer has shown how the epics progressed through a series of stages from flexible oral poetry to fixed text, and Snodgrass notes that this makes Homer a 'moving target' on which it is extremely difficult to pin any particular archaeological find.[41]

While these changes to our understanding of Homer are products of the 1990s, the Victorians had also had their readings of Homer destabilized in ways that made pinning down Troy both difficult and appealing. In 1795, Friedrich August Wolf published *Prolegomena ad Homerum*, which argued that the Homeric poems were products of an oral tradition, put together by a later compiler. The immediate debate among Wolf's colleagues was not about whether or not this was correct, but whether his ideas were original and whether he used the right methodology to arrive at them.[42] However, there was a backlash later from scholars who believed that the poems showed a unified composition that would be impossible for oral poets. This backlash was particularly strong in Britain, and the controversy (known as the Homeric Question, although really a cluster of questions about the identity of 'Homer' and the conditions and methods of composition) was still active when Schliemann made his announcements.⁴³ Schliemann was hailed as defeating the scepticism of Wolf and his followers, despite not having much to say about the composition of the Homeric epics. The anxieties about a complex process of composition involving many participants were less about close textual scholarship than uncertainty over the literary and historical value of the *Iliad*, and these anxieties could be allayed by the idea of a clear historical truth behind the epic.

Archaeology was not the only discipline that was looking for the underlying truth of the Homeric epics. Another destabilizing force in the understanding of Homer were nineteenth-century theories of language and religion. Friedrich Max Müller (who held the chair of Comparative Philology at Oxford) read stories of the Greek gods as allegories of nature, generated by properties of early language.⁴⁴ In this reading, Homer preserved traces of an earlier society, but it was not the literal truth of the events described. Instead, the names and actions of the gods represented an earlier common mythology, shared by Aryan ancestors and more clearly seen in ancient Indian texts.⁴⁵ For Müller, the conflict of East and West in the siege of Troy was an allegory for the movement of the sun across the sky. Troy was useful for debating the origins of human culture and processes of cultural change.⁴⁶ Despite his theoretical differences with Schliemann, Müller was involved in analysing the finds from Troy and arranging them for public display (see Chapter 3).

Schliemann's discoveries added new questions and uncertainties. However, like the debates over how to understand the poems, which can be traced back to antiquity, this made them fruitful for thinking about the relationship of truth and fiction, history and literature. In the nineteenth century, these were particularly fraught issues because of the doubt thrown on the Bible by recent scientific discoveries and close textual analysis. Homer (known in Victorian cliché as the 'Bible of the Greeks') was inevitably caught up in these anxieties over the relationship between text and truth:

> The contested ground Troy occupied was that between truth and lie, reality and non-existence. Whereas few doubted the actual existence of biblical cities such as Sodom and Gomorrah (whatever their opinions as to events said to have occurred there, or where the cities' remains might be) a host of scholars doubted that Troy 'had any existence, except in the brain of Homer'.⁴⁷

Because many imagined Troy as having no basis in reality, it could be used by sceptics as an analogy to show the difficulty of looking at the Bible as historical truth. Schliemann's discoveries reversed this significance, making archaeology into a science that might offer definitive proof of faith. The connection between Homer and scripture was made particularly clear in the writings of Gladstone, who thought that Homer contained truths about human nature in the same way that the Bible contained divine truth. Gladstone believed that humankind had gradually deteriorated since expulsion from the Garden of Eden, and so early events in human history were documents of a time when there was less sin in the world.[48] These ideas hinged on believing in the Trojan War as a historical event (and the *Iliad* as a faithful document of the characters and events represented) so the discovery of Troy seemed a convenient confirmation and Gladstone proved a powerful ally for Schliemann. Gladstone had a heated debate with Tennyson about this in 1877 at a dinner to celebrate Schliemann. For Tennyson, Schliemann's historical Troy was too small and drab and threatened to undermine the beauty of the imagined city. Such debates about whether Schliemann had really found Troy were often actually about other things, in this case, the disagreement was both personal (working out their feelings over their deceased mutual friend, Arthur Hallam) and about whether the *Iliad* was better read as a fictional work of literature or as a historical record.[49] Finding Troy meant figuring out whether a work of literature could really be related to a mound in Anatolia and (if so) how to read each in the light of the other.

The myth of Schliemann

Modern scholarship on Schliemann is deeply divided on the extent to which we should trust him. Several things he wrote in his diaries and in the press cannot possibly be true and this throws into doubt all his claims that cannot be independently verified. Schliemann centred his character and biography in the way he presented his work: his books on Troy included an autobiography as the first chapter, as if Schliemann himself was one of the most relevant facts about the site.[50] This has set the agenda for the study of his work and there have been many biographies of the man since, covering everything from a collection of love letters to character assassination.[51] While this book is not another biography, Schliemann's strong personality clearly influenced how his discoveries were received. To understand why this was the case, it will be valuable to look briefly at Schliemann's background and why he is such a controversial figure, whose character, behaviour and extraordinary claims complicate the study of Troy to this day.

Heinrich Schliemann came late to archaeology, after making his fortune trading commodities internationally. He emphasized his humble beginnings, born in 1822 as the son of a clergyman in the village of Kalkhorst in Mecklenburg-Schwerin and how circumstances prevented him from pursuing his education and forced him to take a manual job in a grocer's shop.[52] When an injury forced him to leave that profession, he learned bookkeeping and English (the first of about fifteen foreign languages in which Schliemann became fluent).[53] He gradually worked his way up to become a wealthy independent trader. He was then able to use his fortune to retire and travel, and took up the interest in archaeology that was to make him famous. This biography reads like the rags-to-riches stories that were popular at the time, and these themes probably influenced Schliemann's choices about which facts to include and how to present them.[54]

Schliemann achieved worldwide celebrity as a result of his excavations at Troy: begun without a permit in February 1870, and quickly shut down.[55] He began the first officially sanctioned excavations at the site in late 1871, cutting a massive trench right through the centre of the mound, working quickly in a rush to get to the earliest levels where he was sure he would find Homer's Troy. He returned to the site every year until 1873. The most famous objects from the site, the so-called Treasure of Priam, were found (perhaps too conveniently) just a couple of weeks before the excavations were set to finish.[56] The press eagerly covered his finds and public appearances, generating interest from a broad public. Schliemann's claims were controversial everywhere, but he found the English (primed by the accounts of previous traveller-archaeologists) less hostile to him as a successful amateur.[57] By the time of the Trojan exhibition, Schliemann was already excavating at Mycenae (begun in 1876) and often coverage of the exhibition ran alongside discussion of his more recent discoveries, such as the gold 'Mask of Agamemnon'.[58] Schliemann actively courted press attention, with regular letters to *The Times* announcing major finds.

The doubts over Schliemann have deep roots. In his lifetime, he admitted to lying about the conditions of his discovery of the Trojan treasure: including his wife, Sophia Schliemann, as a witness, despite her being in Athens at the time of the discovery.[59] He was also successfully prosecuted by Turkish government for not sharing his finds with them (as stipulated in the terms of his permission to excavate) and smuggling the treasure out of the country whole.[60] Many of Schliemann's contemporaries were sceptical about whether his finds were as ancient as he claimed, or even genuine at all. Further doubts were raised at the height of Schliemann's London success when his former cook accused him of forging the treasure.[61]

Schliemann's character inevitably ends up being relevant to our understanding of the sites he excavated. He repeatedly retold his own rags-to-riches story, and the idea of his great astuteness, hard work and luck became an important part of his appeal as a public archaeologist.[62] Newspapers and magazines eagerly retold Schliemann's account of his success, often holding it up as a model for people (especially children and the working class) to emulate.[63] Aside from Schliemann's tendency to make his archaeological work all about him, and his skill in crafting a life story as appealing adventure narrative, there is another reason that Schliemann's biography and character get mixed up in trying to understand his work as an archaeologist. Schliemann was far from the ideal of the neutral, detached observer that archaeology has often held up as the best way to produce accurate data. His work (from selection of sites to excavate through to minor decisions on what to call objects) was clearly shaped by his love of Homer and his desire to prove these stories true. Because of the irreversible and unrepeatable nature of archaeological investigation, an excavation that has not been recorded accurately (or is deliberately fraudulent) can mean a massive loss of information about the ancient world and a set of questions we are frustratingly unable to answer.[64]

Schliemann is just such an unreliable excavator. Renewed interest in him as a major figure in the history of archaeology in the 1980s and 1990s brought a more critical perspective to Schliemann's account of his life story and his discoveries. As a result, many of the achievements he was celebrated for in his lifetime have since been questioned. While he is often called the discoverer of Troy, Allen has demonstrated that Frank Calvert believed Hisarlık to be the site of Troy and convinced Schliemann to excavate there, but was cut out of the mainstream story of the discovery thanks to Schliemann's reluctance to share credit. To obscure this unethical conduct, Schliemann may have concocted the story that finding Troy had been a childhood dream of his, which he wrote in his own autobiography, but his papers show little evidence of this interest before 1868.[65] A number of passages in his diaries have been demonstrated to be false, although it is possible that these were intended to be language exercises.[66] He has also been accused of more serious archaeological frauds, especially fabricating Priam's Treasure out of smaller finds.[67]

Archaeologists reflect with horror on the speed and technique of his excavations. He used levers and battering rams to remove large chunks of earth in his earliest seasons of excavation.[68] In doing so, he passed quickly through the levels of Troy that are contemporary with the height of Mycenaean civilization (and hence the most likely candidates for the Trojan War as described by Homer). However, many of Schliemann's contemporaries treated archaeology as mining for art objects, whereas the excavation at Troy was conducted with far more of an interest in smaller finds and anything that might shed light on life as described by Homer.[69] Because of this detailed interest in life at Troy, Schliemann became a pioneer of scientific analysis of metals, pot sherds, organic material and human and animal remains in archaeology.[70] The apparent contradiction of science and fantasy working together at one site makes sense because of Schliemann's defensiveness in the face of critique and eagerness to find any evidence that might prove his detractors wrong.

Schliemann's willingness to court the public has been seen as suspect in its own right. He has become an important model for stories about fictional archaeologists who know an important truth, but are doubted by the establishment before eventually proving it to the world.[71] This archetype laid down by Schliemann does not stay in the world of fiction, also shaping public expectations about how archaeology should be conducted and challenged. Schliemann's loose relationship with the truth and love of a good story generated a sort of myth of his own which can prove challenging for archaeologists:

> Archaeologists who wish to make the broad public aware of the enormous differences between their subject and the counterfeit versions that throng popular literature and the mass media have a grim and not altogether pleasant task before them. First, they must disown some of the most glamorous legends of their past, precisely those that begat widespread interest in archaeology in the first place. Schliemann and similar intellectual swashbucklers must be cut down to size.[72]

Attacks on Schliemann seem personal because, for those of us trying to make sense of the past through partial and fallible sources, they are. It is telling that Schliemann's crimes against archaeological epistemology have received far more attention than acts that are actually much more abhorrent. For example, he admitted what would today be called rape of his first wife.[73] Schliemann continues to haunt archaeologists as a figure who can dramatize both the desire to know about the past and the fear that that desire might lead us astray. These concerns were already active at the time Schliemann's discoveries were made. To return to the article by William Simpson with which we started this chapter:

> Imagination is a very important qualification for an archaeologist to possess; without this he becomes only a chronicler of facts – a mere writer of catalogues – and must be wholly without the power of seeing the value of the discoveries he may have made... But in proportion to the strength of this power, a counterpoise of judgment is necessary, otherwise the imagination gets loose and runs riot.[74]

To get from the scraps of everyday life found in most excavations to meaningful information about the past requires both careful analysis and imaginative speculation. With professional archaeologists today taking a greater interest in storytelling and acknowledging the difficulties of the ideal of neutrality, it is worth reflecting on Schliemann as someone who embodies some of the discipline's most challenging contradictions and (through his work to court a wider audience) shaped some of the biggest debates of the formative years of archaeology. In working on the impact of viewing the Trojan collection, I am less interested in evaluating what sort of a man (unreliable narrator, liar, fantasist, father of archaeology) Schliemann was than in exploring how his eccentricities provoked debate about what we can know about the past and who can participate in that knowledge. I will return to some of these questions when discussing Schliemann's impact on public archaeology today in the final chapter of this book.

Reception and archaeology

Jorge Luis Borges's thought experiment on reading, writing and historicity describes a modern author, Pierre Menard, who has attempted to reproduce Cervantes' Don Quixote exactly, thus transforming it into a modern work with a new significance. The text Menard has produced, while indistinguishable from Cervantes' original also contains traces of Menard's previous work: 'I have reflected that it is permissible to see in this "final" Quixote a kind of palimpsest, through which the traces – tenuous but not indecipherable – of our friend's "previous" writing should be translucently visible. Unfortunately, only a second Pierre Menard, inverting the other's work, would be able to exhume and revive those lost Troys'.[75]

The metaphor of drawing these traces out as excavating the successive cities of Troy is almost certainly meant to play on the contradictory character of Schliemann: both diligent scholar and deceptive fantasist. Schliemann, in excavating and explaining the material from Troy, put his own interests and preoccupations into the site. Just as Schliemann's claims to have discovered Troy are still disputed, we are meant to ask ourselves whether Menard could really have reproduced the Quixote exactly without transcribing, and whether he could have added to its meaning without changing its text. Troy, Don Quixote and all other cultural touchstones will inevitably be reshaped by their readers and rewriters and we are haunted by the question of whether this exercise is creative or fraudulent.

The idea that archaeological stratigraphy resembles the layered rereadings of texts across long spans of time is one that also crops up in the writings of Classicists. Martindale has attacked the idea that subsequent receptions of a text are 'accretions' that build up over the text and must be stripped away to restore its meaning (since what is left, no matter how well corroborated by the evidence, will not contain all of the ancient understanding).[76] Butler has advanced a version of the layered meanings metaphor that uses the cross-section of the layers of Troy from Schliemann's book *Troy and Its Remains* (see Fig. 7 in Chapter 3 of this volume) to reflect on the ways in which we can view the many layers of the past together and envisage the working of time itself. Troy is a deeply ancient site that was lost but, thanks to its place in the classical literary heritage, never forgotten. As such it is an unusually rich place for thinking about how the cultures of Greece and Rome have been used to engage with the much less familiar material that came before them – the deep time that informs Butler's term 'Deep Classics'.[77]

Troy is not a text, but it is (perhaps more than any other archaeological site) shaped by relationships with text; primarily the *Iliad*, but also all the numerous ancient and modern texts that deal with the Trojan War. When the public encountered the material Troy for the first time through Schliemann's Trojan collection, they had to reconcile it with a rich textual tradition. This material Troy was a complex, layered site that was never conceived as a coherent text. It is the debris of millennia of life that must have carried countless ancient meanings and has been reinterpreted several times since. The process of imagining this past, often with reference to Homeric poetry and broader expectations set up by the classical world, makes this a complex and important site of classical reception, in which text, object and complex cultural expectations come together to try and form a coherent view of a past reality. The fact that this view of reality often claims to be objective makes it no less a construction of modern archaeologists.

If literary scholars sometimes imagine themselves peering at stratigraphy (whether by neat cross-section or complex peeling back of layers) to understand the ways in which a history of reading shapes understanding of a text, archaeologists often see their work as containing elements of storytelling. Simpson's assertion that archaeology needs imagination to go beyond listing facts and make sense of the value of its discoveries shows the nineteenth-century roots of this phenomenon.[78] However, these ideas have been particularly influential in archaeology since the 1990s. Shanks and Tilley argued that the need to convert archaeological information from material into a publishable text builds a fundamental break into the discipline, and explored how storytelling is an unavoidable product of trying to make sense of a series of events in this way.[79] The discovery of an archaeological site is only the first step in an ongoing process of understanding it. The idea that Troy is as much invented as discovered is a common observation in work on the cultural impact of the site.[80] Schliemann used his first museum exhibition to tell the story of Troy, but his will not be the only construction of the site we encounter. While Schliemann wanted the last word on the meaning of the site, many members of his audience engaged in their own terms and came to their own conclusions using the objects from Troy. The long history of fascination with (and controversy over) Troy meant that a public that was suspicious of Schliemann's inventions but fascinated by the possibility that a well-known story might really be true were able to discover the site for themselves through its objects.

Part Two

Putting Troy on Show

In the week before Christmas 1877, 14,355 visitors came to the South Kensington Museum. Londoners were enjoying some additional leisure time because of the upcoming holiday and *The Times* reported on how people chose to spend it. There were pantomimes, plays, a circus, a lecture on torpedo warfare (with real torpedoes) as well as London's zoo, museums and galleries. South Kensington was not the most popular entertainment – its numbers were eclipsed by Sanger's circus, which claimed to have sold out 20,000 seats for its Roman chariot races and mock battles that week.[1] But South Kensington's visitor figures were nearly double those for previous years.[2] The recently opened exhibition of Schliemann's finds from Hisarlık accounts for this massive increase in interest. *The Times* described the finds from Troy as 'the principal attraction' at the museum.[3] There was strong interest from the press, both in London and far beyond.

The enthusiastic press coverage of the Trojan exhibition demonstrates the level of interest it generated and preserves many details about the layout, contents and interpretation of the exhibition. The chapters in this section explore the first public encounters with Schliemann's Trojan collection, from the earliest visitors to the excavation site through to Schliemann's donation of the collection to (what was intended to be) its permanent home. It focuses on the first public museum exhibition of the collection held at South Kensington between 20 December 1877 and early January 1881. I argue that this was the most important stage in working out Schliemann's presentation of these objects and in deciding their place in the public imagination.

This section builds on recent work on museums as more than just a series of texts, object and images, to treat the museum visit as an integrated, embodied experience. While much of this experience of historical exhibitions is lost due to the partial nature of the sources, we can still get a more complete sense of an exhibition by considering all the factors that shaped it. Work on the history of museums is beginning to reflect this complexity. Bennett has described an 'exhibitionary complex' in which museums' architecture and display techniques shaped visitor behaviour and ideas in order to constitute a citizen body.[4] Leahy has written about the embodied nature of museum experience from the nineteenth century to the present and the way that museums expect (but do not always effectively enforce) particular methods of moving and viewing.[5] Meyer has written about how vitrines transformed people's experience of Greek vases by altering the ways in which they could be encountered and understood.[6] Candlin's work on museums and touch demonstrates the changing ways in which social status has dictated the kinds of sensory interaction that museums allow.[7]

In-depth histories of particular exhibitions have also recognized the importance of space, architecture, juxtapositions with other material and a range of other factors that shape museum experiences. Bilsel's book on the Pergamum Great Altar is rooted in the architectural layout of its display in Berlin, which encourages visitors to interact with the architecture and elides the modern building with the ancient art displayed in it.[8] Nichols has discussed how reconstructions of historical environments at the Crystal Palace could be experienced as paradoxically authentic by visitors.[9] Unlike these examples, Schliemann's exhibition was not an immersive reconstructed environment, but I want to argue that its display techniques were equally important for constructing an experience of the ancient world. Detailed exploration of museum exhibitions allows us to consider the things that distinguished them from other ways to experience antiquity. Given how many different experiences of the past were on offer in the nineteenth century (including novels, dioramas, explorers' accounts, circuses, lectures and many more) a sense of the distinctive appeal of museums allows us to take them seriously as a medium in their own right.[10] Schliemann certainly saw exhibiting his collection as an important tool in getting his work recognized and (as we will see) put a lot of work into getting the objects seen in an arrangement that would communicate his ideas.

While Schliemann's impact through his books and public appearances has been widely recognized and has a massive literature, there has been very little exploration of his exhibitions. Easton's account of the Trojan collection traces its history of display, including a brief discussion of the London exhibition.[11] Fitton's publication of Schliemann's letters held by the British Museum offers an insight into his dealings with museums, and is especially useful for understanding the decision to bring the collection to London.[12] The most in-depth exploration of Schliemann's museum work is the publication by Saherwala, Goldmann and Mahr on the history of the Trojan collection. This publishes a series of Schliemann's letters from Berlin, but also gives a narrative history of the collection from Schliemann's earliest attempts to find a home for it to after his death.[13] While the collection's movements and Schliemann's contacts with museum professionals are well documented, these accounts do little to explore how the collection itself was displayed and what effect encountering artefacts from Troy in a museum context had on a broad public. Schliemann's museum exhibitions played a crucial role in publicizing and understanding his collections. In the chapters that follow, I explore Schliemann's innovative approach to displaying his collection and lay the groundwork for understanding the debates that it provoked.

Looking closely at this exhibition allows us to resist the tendency to assume that we know what nineteenth-century museums were like. There is good reason to make this assumption – many of the most famous museum buildings that we still visit were constructed at this time. Some displays (like the Pitt Rivers Museum) appear little changed since this period, while others (like the British Museum's Enlightenment Gallery) have been recently made to evoke past display.[14] It is easy to imagine similar spaces a couple of centuries ago, celebrating historical architecture (particularly classical or gothic), filled with dark wooden cases, slightly overfilled and under-explained, peered at by well-behaved, smartly dressed visitors (a vision supported by idealized nineteenth-century images such as Fig. 5, in Chapter 2). By considering the context, layout and interpretation of an actual exhibition in detail, there is an opportunity to test some of these assumptions. We will see a version of the nineteenth-century museum that is superficially similar (plenty of dark wooden cases and ornate architecture) but more experimental and contingent than we tend to assume. This will reveal some of the assumptions from the present that we tend to project back on museums. In doing so, I hope to challenge the teleology that can haunt museum histories.

Examining these factors can be difficult because museum exhibitions are ephemeral and records are patchily preserved. For example, all of Schliemann's letters to the South Kensington Museum now only exist as summaries in the letters book.[15] There is also the difficulty of evoking complex spatial experience through words on a page – it is hard enough to fully describe museum exhibitions that we have visited but it becomes particularly tricky in the case of past exhibitions that we can only experience indirectly through the accounts of others. However, for exhibitions like Schliemann's that had a sizeable social and intellectual impact there is a good range of evidence to work with and good reason to try to understand them. A number of helpful documents survive about the Trojan exhibition, such as Schliemann's careful record of the South Kensington case layout and the series of visitor guides published in *The Times*. By bringing together a range of sources, I will create an impression of Schliemann's South Kensington exhibition that (while it is inevitably imperfect) gives a detailed sense of why this exhibition was so widely discussed and what it was trying to achieve. This is not an attempt to get at a past as it really was (which would be impossible), so much as a process of collage, bringing together a range of receptions. This builds a composite picture of the exhibition that gives a sense of its context, spatial layout and interpretation, without obscuring the interests and agendas of the sources from which it was drawn.

Chapter 2 explores why the Trojan collection (rather than the site of Troy) was the main focus of public interest and what opportunities there were to see it before the first museum exhibition. It considers why the first Trojan exhibition was held in a museum that was primarily dedicated to modern design and how the context of South Kensington shaped the display. Chapter 3 then considers the forms of interpretation that helped visitors make sense of the collection and what impression of Troy these were designed to give. Chapter 4 explores the Trojan collection itself and how Schliemann arranged it in the available space (both at South Kensington and its permanent display in Berlin) to emphasize certain objects and ideas. Through the course of these chapters, I will explore the exhibition's scale, the development process and how it was promoted to experts and the wider public. I consider the range of media and approaches Schliemann used to ensure that this was not just a neutral display of objects, but a careful demonstration of his own ideas about the site of Troy.

2

Bringing Troy to London

Seven years passed between Schliemann's first excavations at Troy and the first opportunity to see his finds in a public museum, and public interest remained high throughout. Going to see Troy itself was an option for those who were wealthy enough to travel, and Schliemann welcomed interested visitors to his excavations several times, including on the day he discovered Priam's Treasure.[1] However, after Schliemann had illegally removed the treasure, the welcome for foreign visitors was much less warm. The antiquarian William Borlase, who visited the site in 1875, did so under armed guard (to protect the antiquities, not him) and described one group of travellers who were not so lucky: 'Even the country people, jealous enough of foreign intrusion before had been aroused to aid the Government in preventing strangers without passports from approaching Hissarlik, and, shortly before our arrival, a yachting party, who had landed at Besika Bay with the innocent object of "doing Troy" had been compelled by villagers to return to their boat.'[2]

Borlase described these new difficulties in visiting Troy as a direct result of the way Schliemann conducted his excavations. Borlase was contributing to a public controversy about Troy by giving his own opinion of site and excavator, which was far from positive. He went on to discuss Calvert's role in the discovery and described feeling 'taken-in' by Schliemann's grand descriptions and disappointed by the reality.[3] Individual visits to Troy like this could have an outsize impact on the public consciousness because of the question of whether Schliemann could be trusted.

Despite legal and ethical problems over the treasure's removal, it was now mobile in ways that made it much more accessible than the site. This meant that Schliemann's Trojan collection was now his best hope of presenting tangible evidence to the public. This chapter traces how Schliemann began to feed public hunger for information about his discoveries through small displays in private spaces while he looked for a permanent home for his collection. It begins with Schliemann's early experiments with displaying his discoveries in private contexts, asking what motivated these displays and how the public responded. It also considers Schliemann's search for a permanent home for his collection and why he chose to have a temporary display in London first. It concludes by looking at the context of South Kensington, asking why the Trojan collection was displayed in an institution dedicated to design, not archaeology and how this shaped the resulting exhibition. These exhibitions had to cater to a public who, like Borlase, were keen to see Schliemann's discoveries but critical of his methods and conclusions. By asking who was allowed to see Schliemann's finds and under what conditions, we can begin to understand how Schliemann negotiated this tension.

Schliemann's early displays

While South Kensington was Schliemann's first official museum exhibition, it was not the first time the Trojan collection had been displayed to the public. Schliemann had already created a display of his finds from Troy at his house in Athens and thrown this open to the public in an attempt to silence his doubters. This informal exhibition was visited by 'large crowds of curious [people]', who were eager to see Priam's treasure in the year of its discovery. By the next year, Schliemann had invited all of Athens to verify his claims by visiting.[4] As with the London exhibition, he framed this decision as a response to a particularly vehement critic (in this case, the Greek archaeologist and collector Athanasios Rhousopoulos).[5] As Schliemann put it: 'Thus I have been obliged publicly to invite all Athenians to come to my house to convince themselves with their own eyes of the atrocious calumnies of that foul fiend.'[6] It is unclear how many people took Schliemann up on the offer or indeed whether he followed through on his rhetoric, but this display also became publicly accessible in another way. Photographs of this display were published as part of the album to accompany Schliemann's first book on Troy: *Atlas Trojanischer Alterthümer*.[7] These images give a sense of how Schliemann presented his collection and, as we will see in Chapter 3, were probably an important part of the London display in their own right.

By 1877, Schliemann was becoming serious about displaying his collection in museums. His new finds from Mycenae were the property of the Greek state, but Schliemann retained some control over how they were displayed. Even before permanent display space in a museum was found for them, the highlights were exhibited to the public in the Athenian Bank.[8] An image from *The Graphic*

(Fig. 3) shows this display: an informal arrangement of trays on a single table, without much space for visitors. While this hardly counts as a full exhibition, it shows Schliemann's eagerness to show his finds, and how strong the public demand was to see them. One of these early viewings was reported on by the British Consul at Piraeus, Charles Merlin, in a letter to Charles Newton, keeper of Greek and Roman antiquities at the British Museum:

> The gold ornaments and treasure, as they call it, from Mycenae have been on view this week ... the room was so crowded with the ladies of the diplomatic corps that I could not examine them as closely as I wished. What I saw of them however impressed me with the opinion that they are very different from anything I have seen up to this time – whether of the <u>very great</u> antiquity Schliemann claims for them I am not able to judge ... whenever the period was, gold must have been extremely abundant ... Schliemann is evidently very jealous lest people describe them before his work is published ... it is a pity he is so vulgar in his manners and gives his opinions as if there is no one who knows anything but himself.[9]

Schliemann wanted his finds to be seen and admired, while also wanting to retain control over their interpretation and publication. Displaying his finds to the public risked losing control of the narrative. In the exclusive early displays, he was able to control who saw his collection, and set conditions on their access. William Simpson (before his spat with Schliemann in *Fraser's Magazine*) saw the Mycenae display in Athens as an artist for the *Illustrated London News*, but he had to sketch the objects from memory afterwards.[10]

Schliemann was also trying to find a suitable place to display his collection from Troy during this time. He frequently changed his mind about where it should go, with attempts to donate or sell it to institutions in Greece, Italy and France.[11] In 1876, he had approached the British Museum about displaying his Trojan collection there for a year, to fulfil a promise to Gladstone. He inquired whether he could use the rooms emptied by moving the museum's Natural History collections to the site in South Kensington now known as the Natural History Museum.[12] The British Museum declined the offer because they did not have space. Instead, the exhibition was offered to the South Kensington Museum, which accepted.

Schliemann used his collections to secure favours from governments and influential individuals.[13] The London exhibition was a clear example of this – Schliemann described it as both fulfilment of a promise to Gladstone and a gesture of thanks to Layard for helping to obtain a permit for further excavations

Fig. 3 Schliemann's finds from Mycenae on display in Athens, *The Graphic*, 16 June, 1877. By kind permission of Cambridge University Library.

at Troy.[14] Gladstone's political power and Layard's diplomatic influence must have made them important allies for Schliemann as much as their interest in archaeology. Schliemann knew that exhibiting his collection could build good will and increase the perceived value of his finds. A temporary exhibition in London would allow a broader public to see the objects (which Schliemann saw as proof of his controversial claims) and gave him a new medium for expressing his ideas, with substantial institutional authority. To understand how the South Kensington Museum lent its authority to Schliemann's collection, we must look closer at this context.

South Kensington

The South Kensington Museum is known today as the V&A. By the 1870s it was well established (although still growing) in the same site as the V&A stands today. It had started as a collection of teaching aids for the School of Design in the 1840s. It soon expanded its remit to teach the appreciation of design to consumers, in order to create a demand for better products. It was also a small element of the wider educational work of the government's Department of Science and Art and so had much stronger educational priorities than other museums in London.[15] Because of this educational aim, it was open to a broad public, with opening hours and conditions designed to maximize accessibility to the working class.[16] At the time of the Trojan exhibition, entry cost sixpence, but was free on certain days.[17] There was no additional charge for the Trojan exhibition.

Schliemann's collection was displayed in the South Court: a large temporary exhibition space for small objects, opened in 1862 and extended in 1869-71.[18] Fig. 4 is a map of the South Kensington Museum made at about this time, showing the South Court on the right-hand side. The South Court in the 1870s was a new, purpose-built temporary display space, reflecting contemporary architectural and museological fashions. Fig. 5 shows the part of the South Court that held Schliemann's exhibition, a couple of years before the exhibition arrived. It was a large hall with a glass roof, held up by metal columns. The glass was important for allowing in light, since the museum did not install electric lighting until 1883.[19] The space was broken up by a colonnaded corridor to make it feel suitable for displaying smaller items.[20] It was filled with mahogany cases, lined with 'Turkey

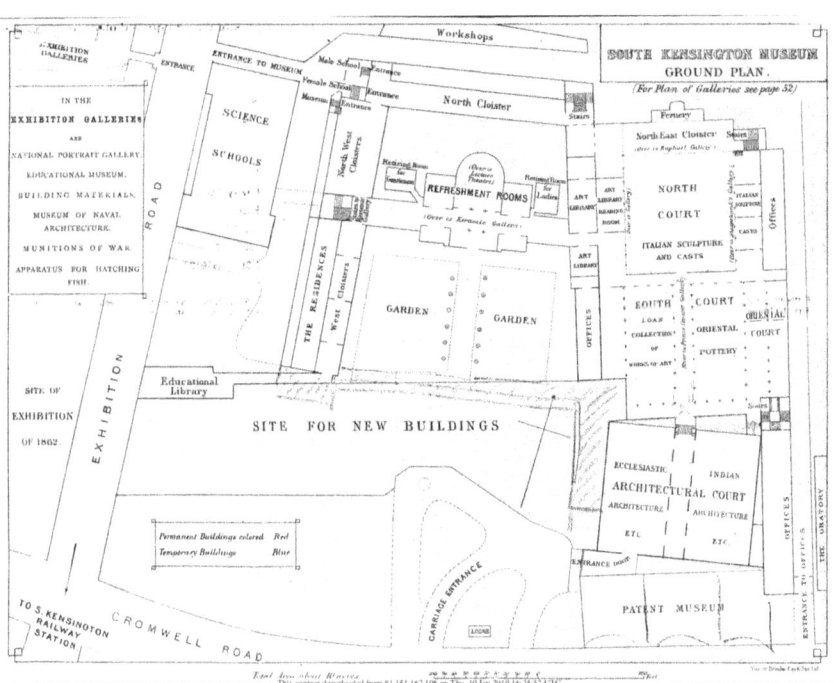

Fig. 4 Map of the South Kensington Museum (c. 1878) the South Court is on the centre right. South Kensington Museum, *A Guide to the Art Collections of the South Kensington Museum: Illustrated with Plans and Wood Engravings* (London: Spottiswoode & Co., n.d.), Durham University Library GreyPam926 (https://www.jstor.org/stable/60226562), reproduced by kind permission of Lord Howick.

Fig. 5 Exhibition in the South Court of the South Kensington Museum, *c.* 1876. John Watkins. © Victoria and Albert Museum, London.

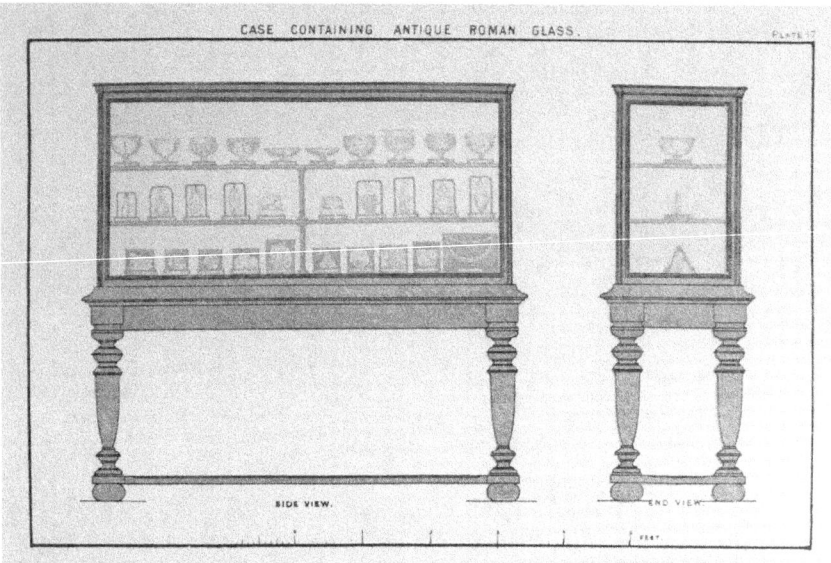

Fig. 6 A typical case design as shown in Science and Art Department of the Committee of Council on Education, South Kensington Museum, *Drawings of Glass Cases in the South Kensington Museum, with Suggestions for the Arrangement of Specimens* (London: Vincent Brooks, Day & Son, 1876) plate 17. By kind permission of the Bodleian Library.

red cloth' and specialized fittings to optimize the display of different types of objects (Fig. 6).[21] The walls were richly painted and gilded, and a canon of mosaic portraits of famous artists looked down from the alcoves high up on the walls.[22] This integrated display scheme was intended to have an educational, as well as aesthetic, effect. It showcased the styles and artists valued by the museum, but none of these had a clear connection to the unnamed craftsmen of Troy.

The display was smaller than Schliemann would have liked. He had asked for two rooms in which to display his whole collection when he first approached the British Museum. While the British Museum did not have facilities for temporary exhibitions, this was a speciality of the South Kensington Museum. It grew out of a culture of large international exhibitions and sought loans of important collections both to supplement its permanent holdings and to generate interest from collectors and visitors.[23] Schliemann's collection was just one of a number of disparate groups of objects on display in the South Court. Rows of cases continued beyond the Trojan exhibition, containing a variety of different objects, including glass, pottery and porcelain and a mixture of other materials and styles.[24] Many of the objects on display had been acquired by the museum from recent international exhibitions or loaned by private individuals. There were small loan collections of metalwork and a wide range of other items including a violin, a collection of carved pipes and Wedgwood-decorated chimney-pieces.[25] While there was no clear break in the layout between Schliemann's collection and the rest of the South Court, there must have been a strong visual contrast with the Venetian glass, Sèvres porcelain and other fine modern decorative objects on display.

The sharp contrast of ancient and modern was noted by visitors (as we will see in Chapter 6). There were some calls to move Schliemann's collection nearer to similar objects, such as those from Cyprus on display elsewhere in the museum.[26] However, this was far from the only odd juxtaposition in South Kensington at the time. There were Anglo-Saxon antiquities in the Persian Court and, across the road in the exhibition galleries, one could see the National Portrait Gallery, munitions and apparatus for hatching fish.[27] South Kensington had pulled together a variety of collections without a clear conceptual link. Some of these were described as discrete museums within the museum, such as the Museum of Patents (adjoining the South Court), which displayed models of mechanical and industrial innovations 'illustrative of the progress of national invention'.[28] The place of ancient material in this diversity was ill-defined. The British Museum was the main focus of such collecting in London. South Kensington did not make a priority of collecting ancient material and 'scrupulously avoided' classical art.[29] But in practice, many ancient items did make it into the collections.³⁰ The proportion of ancient objects on display was higher in the nineteenth century, given South Kensington's focus on loans.³¹ A visitor in 1878 would have been able to see special exhibitions of antiquities from Palestine and the collection of General Lane Fox (later known as Pitt Rivers) as well as Schliemann's Hisarlık finds.³²

While loans had started out as a way of supplementing the museum's small founding collections, this was less necessary by the late 1870s. In fact, the South Kensington Museum was running out of space. The museum's annual report for 1878 says of Schliemann's loan: 'the extent of this collection necessitated the further crowding together of the cases in the loan court'.³³ A comment like this in an annual report to a funding body is clearly pointed. Overcrowding was an issue throughout the museum and it was already in the middle of a major process of redevelopment. South Kensington could have made the same excuse as the British Museum regarding available space, which shows that the Trojan exhibition was worth the effort to cram into an already crowded space. The overcrowding meant that Schliemann had to edit down his collection for the exhibition. The exhibition was only about 5 per cent of the Trojan collection: just under 4,500 objects.³⁴ This was still a large exhibition by the standards of South Kensington.³⁵ Other loan collections in the space only occupied a single case, or part of one.³⁶ By comparison, Schliemann's took up approximately twenty-five cases (numbers in reports varied depending on which displays were counted as discrete cases). This took up a substantial section of the large hall.

While Schliemann's collection had to be edited to fit into the space, he still tried to ensure that the exhibition would be representative of his collection as a whole. *The Times* described it as 'strictly typical in its character, and in other respects as well is the flower of the whole'.³⁷ This paradoxical statement indicates (going by what we know of what was on display) that Schliemann tried to represent all different kinds of material from the collection, but picked out the best examples, rather than trying to make it statistically representative. About a fifth of his 5,000–6,000 spindle whorls were on display, which must still have seemed an impressive number.³⁸ The whole of the most famous part of the collection, 'Priam's treasure', was exhibited and Schliemann took special care to ensure that 'every symbolic form' would be represented.³⁹ While there was heavy emphasis on the treasure and symbolic objects, there were plenty of examples of plain, functional pots and implements to give visitors a general sense of the objects in use at Troy. These plainer objects were not just padding. As we will see in Chapter 4, many of these object types were heavily theorized by Schliemann and were important to his claims for the archaeological importance of the site.

The contrast between the plain archaeological objects that made up most of Schliemann's collection and the highly decorative objects that the South Kensington Museum prioritized was stark. We will explore the question of whether anyone took design inspiration from the Trojan exhibition in Chapter 5, but it is clear why South Kensington was not Schliemann's first choice. The Trojan collection stood out, even among the eclectic South Court loans. He needed to find and articulate an alternative value system that would make these objects meaningful to visitors. He needed the Trojan exhibition to make the case for Hisarlık as the Troy described in Homer and cover his more eccentric theories about the city's iconography and history.

This was a considerable challenge. As we have seen, there was already an active debate about whether Schliemann was a fraud, whether he had excavated the right site and whether there could be any truth to the Homeric epics. Displaying the finds from Troy left them open to interpretation by other people with competing theories, so Schliemann needed to use every resource available to him to make his arguments. Unlike the displays in his home and in the Athenian Bank, Schliemann would not be present to give his own account of the objects to visitors. However, the move from a private domestic space to a state-of-the-art temporary exhibition gallery brought new opportunities. Schliemann made full use of the space at South Kensington to show his finds off to their best advantage and to communicate his own view of their meaning and purpose. To understand how he did this, we must now turn to the interpretive techniques used by Schliemann.

3

Making Sense of the Trojan Collection

At the beginning of December 1877, Schliemann announced to *The Times* that he had arrived in London to arrange his Trojan collection for exhibition and that he had 'made such progress in his task during the short time he has been engaged in it as to enable him confidently to look forward to the opening of his Trojan collection in ample time for the sightseers who will throng the museum during the Christmas holydays'. Despite Schliemann's early confidence, this was a difficult task. He was deeply involved in the process, emphasizing that his collection was arranged by his own hand with such care and energy that he was suffering from exhaustion when it was finished.[1]

The process of arranging the Trojan exhibition was not just a matter of fitting nearly 4,500 objects into fewer than thirty cases, although this must have been a challenging task in itself. Schliemann needed to communicate a complex archaeological site through decontextualized objects which (contrary to his boasts) did not speak for themselves. Museum interpretation was seen as a powerful tool for public education in the nineteenth century and Schliemann was keen to make full use of the potential of the medium. While he was far from a member of the museum or archaeological establishments, his relentless focus on proving himself meant he was more keen on museum interpretation than many of his contemporaries. The exhibition at South Kensington used many familiar interpretive techniques (such as descriptive labels and singling out unusual objects) which are best understood by looking at how they worked on the specific objects in question (as we will do in Chapter 4). In this chapter, I want to look closely at two unusual approaches used by Schliemann: putting the depths objects were found at on object labels and displaying photographs alongside archaeological material. We will see how these interpretive techniques (which were used throughout the exhibition) related objects in the exhibition back to their archaeological context. This allowed Schliemann to gloss over some of the problems with the collection and stress that its importance lay, not in the intrinsic qualities of the objects, but in the place where they were found.

Order and chaos

The South Kensington Museum's aim to reach and educate audiences from all social classes made interpretation and supplementary information particularly important – Henry Cole (the museum's first director) described such work as transforming a museum 'from a mere unintelligible lounge for idlers into an impressive schoolroom for everyone'.[2] However, South Kensington's arrangement generally resisted the preference for displays laid out in historical order. It was originally arranged by material, but spaces like the South Court brought together many disparate kinds of objects and critics found them a confusing jumble.[3] Given this lack of an overall system, Schliemann was free to come up with his own approach for the Trojan exhibition.

Chronological displays were a popular option for building a coherent story out of a collection, with roots in attempts to displace the elite values that had previously defined art and shift the emphasis onto history after the French Revolution.[4] This was the preferred approach in the British Museum (Schliemann's first choice for the exhibition), which had undergone debates about the relative merits of aesthetic principles and grand narrative histories over the course of the nineteenth century and settled on the latter.[5] Museum displays that emphasized the passage of time and ideas of progress were becoming widely used on all kinds of material, including natural history, geology, archaeology and anthropology.[6] However, such displays presented a problem for Schliemann, who had not yet resolved his understanding of the various historical phases of Troy.

Schliemann wasn't working alone on this task – *The Times* notes the assistance of museum staff members Mr Laskey and Mr Thompson.[7] A Mr Streatfield was also involved.[8] Schliemann's carefully cultivated networks allowed him to gain influential supporters, bring together other people's expertise and improve and lend authority to his published work.[9] Networks have received more intense study in recent years, thanks to the new analysis techniques allowed by the digitization of nineteenth-century print media.[10] But they are harder to understand in the fleeting social and professional spaces created by the museum, which often leave little trace. The clearest example of Schliemann using the connections made through the press and his correspondence in the museum is his collaboration with the philologist Friedrich Max Müller. Schliemann had seen an article by Müller criticizing the attribution of the treasure to Priam in 1873, and started a correspondence. Müller was interested in the finds and became convinced that this was Troy, but not by all by the claims that went with it.[11] He encouraged Schliemann to bring the collection to London and reassured him about the suitability of South Kensington. Müller came to London to help Schliemann arrange the exhibition and to untangle some of the problems Schliemann had been having with the stratigraphy of Troy.[12]

> When Dr Schliemann exhibited his Trojan treasures at the South Kensington Museum, Max Müller spent some time in London helping him to arrange the things – an arduous task, for, as is well known, though he had the scent of a truffle dog for hidden treasures, he had little or no correct archaeological knowledge, and Max Müller found the things from the four different strata which Schliemann considered he had discovered at Troy in wild confusion – though he maintained they were all carefully packed in different cases. One day when Max Müller was busy over a case of the lowest stratum, he found a piece of pottery from the highest. 'Que voulez-vous?' said Schliemann 'it has tumbled down!' Not long after in a box of the highest stratum appeared a piece of the rough pottery from the lowest. 'Que voulez-vous?' said the imperturbable doctor 'it has tumbled up!'[13]

This is told as an example of Schliemann's lack of archaeological knowledge. The long-term implications were certainly clear to Müller who said that Schliemann 'destroyed Troy for the last time'.[14] Schliemann's self-confidence in his own theories meant that he was keen to find irrefutable evidence to bolster them but willing to believe irrational things rather than question his pet theories, with frustrating results for collaborators like Müller. However, Schliemann was working hard to resolve these difficulties in the exhibition's arrangement and come up with a coherent vision of Troy in spite of the complexities of the site and the failings of his excavation technique. He drew on the expertise of people like Müller to fit his confusing collection into the accepted theories of the archaeological mainstream. Schliemann's tendency to draw on local expertise means that we should probably look at the exhibition's interpretation as a collaboration between Schliemann, the South Kensington Museum and the various contacts that Schliemann made.[15]

In their search for a system of arrangement that reflected the recorded excavation results (incongruities included), Schliemann and Müller decided not to depend too heavily on dating. They grouped similar objects together in cases and gave each object a descriptive label that listed the depth at which it was found, relative to the other objects. Archaeological stratigraphy is not found in flat layers of even depth: the ground of the site would have been uneven to begin with, would have been reshaped by uneven distributions of deposited earth and further complicated by later activity (e.g. digging a pit and depositing rubbish). The depth at which an object is found is therefore meaningless without detailed excavation records. Without such records the stratigraphy of the site of Troy proved extremely difficult to understand and was not resolved until the 1930s.[16]

Schliemann seems to have used depths on object labels to sidestep the difficulties he was having with firm dating. He gave visitors the information he had about objects, without making guesses about dating that he couldn't support (or opening himself to the criticism that would result). Visitors could still get a vague sense of where objects were found in relation to one another and could check against Schliemann's depth ranges for the various phases of the site to get a relative age (Fig. 7). Visitors had to work hard to keep track of phases of the site

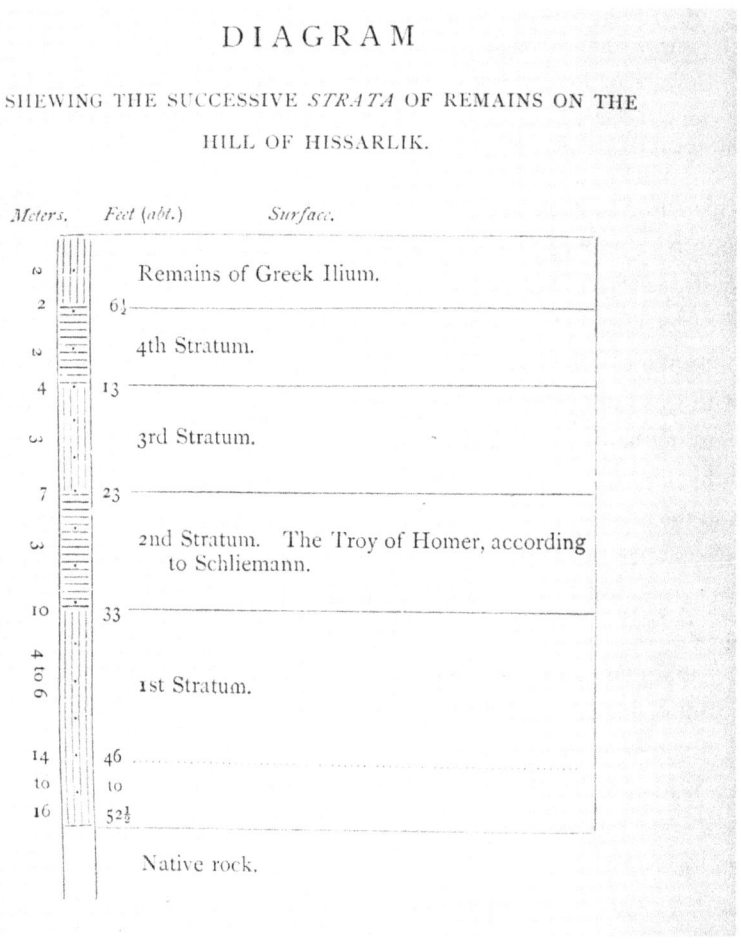

Fig. 7 The stratigraphy diagram showing the depths assigned to different phases. Heinrich Schliemann, *Troy and Its Remains: A Narrative of Researches and Discoveries Made on the Site of Ilium, and in the Trojan Plain* (London: John Murray, 1875), 10. By kind permission of Newcastle Lit & Phil.

and their boundaries, and the result was not an accurate representation of the site's chronology. Responses were mixed, with some visitors finding these depths helpful and others struggling to make sense of the history of the site or calling for a complete rearrangement on chronological lines (see Chapter 10).[17]

However, while the depths quoted on labels were not really useful for dating objects, they had rhetorical effect. They gave the impression of a scientifically rigorous excavation, in which the find-spot of each object was recorded, analysed and fed into the excavator's conclusions (however misleading this impression might have been). They also gave a sense of the scale and complexity of the site. The sheer amount of earth that Schliemann had to move to get to the earliest levels served as evidence for the deep antiquity of Troy and its distinctive character as a mound that had been occupied and built up over many phases.

Images

While the objects from Troy were the main focus of the Trojan exhibition, Schliemann also exhibited photographs and other images that he had made in the course of his excavations. This was an innovation. Photographic exhibitions had been taking place for several decades and the first photographic exhibition at South Kensington was in 1858.[18] However, these were exhibitions in which photographs were the main attraction, not a form of museum interpretation. Schliemann's photographs seem to have been the first to be used alongside archaeological artefacts to shape their meaning and give context to an exhibition.[19] To understand why Schliemann used photography in his exhibition, we need to understand what his images were like and what kind of information about Troy they were designed to convey.

Photographs had been used as a tool for archaeological recording almost since their invention. Their ability to elide past and present and to record visual information with apparent objectivity seemed perfectly matched to archaeology.[20] Schliemann enthusiastically adopted photography to showcase his excavations and collections. He published albums of photographs from Mycenae (taken in 1876) and Troy (published 1874).[21] These contained direct photography of the sites and finds from them, as well as photographic reproductions of paintings, sketches and plans. The albums were intended to complement Schliemann's published accounts of the excavations, although they were sold separately and in fairly small editions.[22] The photographs allowed Schliemann to show off his finds in person and could be bought and studied by enthusiasts.

Fig. 8 Image from *Atlas Trojanischer Alterthümer* showing an eccentric arrangement of pots on shelves. Heidelberg University Library, Heinrich Schliemann, *Atlas Trojanischer Alterthümer*, Tafel 54 – CC-BY-SA 3.0.

Schliemann was not a pioneer of archaeological photography – many of his contemporaries were doing similar work, and Schliemann's images do not have the clarity and detail necessary for good archaeological documentation.[23] There are no photographs of objects in situ in *Atlas* and little indication of scale in the landscape images, apart from the figures. Depths and find-spots were written onto photographs of the objects, as if as an afterthought. Schliemann's

Fig. 9 A photograph of the trench cut under the temple, framed to look picturesque and emphasize the scale of the trench. Heidelberg University Library, Heinrich Schliemann, *Atlas Trojanischer Alterthümer*, Tafel 113 – CC-BY-SA 3.0.

photographs were intended to communicate an overall impression of the site of Troy and the value of his collection, not a detailed record of the process of excavation. Most plates in *Atlas* show objects in large groups to maximize the amount of the collection represented. A few of the larger or more important objects (including the one piece of architectural sculpture he found and some items from the treasure) were photographed individually or from different angles. Other images in the album were concerned with the topography of the site of Troy. These included maps and plans and paintings of the surrounding landscape and direct photographs of the site.

Both archaeology and photographs often rely on the idea that they merely represent reality as the excavator/photographer discovered it. In practice, neither is as neutral or clear in its representations of the past as it might claim to be.[24] Even at first glance, there is much subjective interpretation in Schliemann's photographs. Many of the objects show signs of reconstruction (e.g. Fig. 8); sketches, plans and paintings were all processed through the interpretation of their artists; and all of the images were also extensively annotated. Even without these direct interpretive interventions, Schliemann's photographs had clear rhetorical aims. The images of the surrounding landscape are a direct response to debates over whether the site of Hisarlık corresponded with the Troy described in the *Iliad* (Taf. 179 even has a direct quote from the *Iliad* written on it, identifying it as Bateia, where the Trojan troops formed up in Book II of the *Iliad*).[25]

Photographs of the site provide context for the objects and assist with visualizing Schliemann's excavations. In doing so, they fit with a tradition of picturesque images of landscapes and ruins that both represent the idea of 'Oriental' landscape and demonstrate the power of Western technologies (such as photography and archaeology) to frame and analyse it.[26] Several of Schliemann's photographs (e.g. Fig. 9) were composed to show the volume of earth moved by the excavations: centring the voids of the large trenches without showing any archaeological features. This emphasizes the achievement of the excavators and the deep antiquity of the site. While the images are framed to demonstrate the effort expended in excavating Troy, they do not show Schliemann's workers. This may be because the photographs were taken when the site was not being actively excavated, but it also reflects Schliemann's general unwillingness to share credit for his discoveries.[27]

Schliemann made extensive use of these photographs to promote his discoveries, especially to influential people. In 1877, he met Dom Pedro II, Emperor of Brazil, in London and showed him his Mycenae albums.[28] He also sent copies of the photos away to archaeologists who he hoped would support his theories or purchase his collection for their museums.[29] The photographs served as visual aids to support Schliemann's talks: when he spoke at the Society of Antiquaries in March 1877, he exhibited his photographs on the walls.[30] Archaeological images were also a staple of the London press (particularly the *Illustrated London News*) and, while they mostly preferred to commission their own images, Schliemann's collection attracted particular interest. Schliemann seems to have actively encouraged London's illustrated newspapers to reproduce his photographs. He gave an interviewer from *The Graphic* the famous photograph of his wife Sophia Schliemann wearing a diadem that he insisted belonged to Helen, which they dutifully reproduced for their readers (Fig. 10).[31] Images like this one did much to capture the public imagination and shape people's enthusiasm for and expectations of the exhibition. We can see direct evidence of this in one review of the exhibition:

> The excellent illustrations given in the English version of Dr. Schliemann's work ... represent one of the Hissarlik diadems as set up by the discoverer himself, and the other as it might have appeared on the head of a Trojan lady. The hint has given rise to the very natural suggestion that a lay bust thus decorated might not be unwelcome at South Kensington.[32]

Fig. 10 Sophia Schliemann wearing the jewellery from Troy. 'The parure of Helen', *The Graphic*, 20 January 1877. By kind permission of Cambridge University Library.

Modelling the jewellery was a dramatic way to reconstruct the past in the present and it had a massive impact. In this case, the photograph seems to have offered a sense of connection with the past that was missing from the display of the actual objects. We will see further examples of the effect this photograph had on visitor expectations and experiences in Chapter 5, with discussion about how designers and fashionable women would respond to the exhibition. While the Trojan exhibition was the London public's first opportunity to see these objects, it is important that people already knew the collection through countless reproductions in the press.

Schliemann's decision to include his photographs in the exhibition itself was probably a response to public enthusiasm for these images in other contexts. However, putting images into an exhibition of the real objects gave them a new role: acting not as stand-ins for the collection but as interpretation of it. Some visitors struggled to make sense of the layout and stratigraphy of the site of Troy and complaints were voiced in the previews of the exhibition. On 17 December (a couple of days before the public opening), *The Times* complained of difficulty in understanding the layers of Troy without a plan of the excavation:

> The visitor cannot but be struck by the various stages of civilization shown in the diverse objects apparently belonging to one period; delicate gold ornaments and silver goblets, graceful vases of fine terra-cotta and lyres of ivory, side by side with stone, flint and bone implements as rough as any found in the Swiss lacustrine dwellings. It is difficult without very detailed plans of the excavations to account for these incongruities.[33]

Museum records show that a few days after this report (on 29 December), Schliemann added 'sketches and photographs' to the exhibition.[34] Some images must already have been on display before this date, since a report from the private viewing before the exhibition's opening (published 21 December) states that: 'On the walls of the large apartment in which these antiquities of Troy are displayed are hung a number of photographs, plans, and sections, with explanations in French and German, of the several operations he conducted here during the period already mentioned.'[35]

Photographs were part of the exhibition from before its opening and were intended to fill in gaps in the understanding of the site, thus making the collection more intelligible to visitors. Plans indicated levels, ancient landmarks and the nature of Schliemann's excavation and so could act as direct explanation of information about locations and depths on the labels. Fig. 11 is one such plan, with Schliemann's trenches and the various structures he had identified clearly

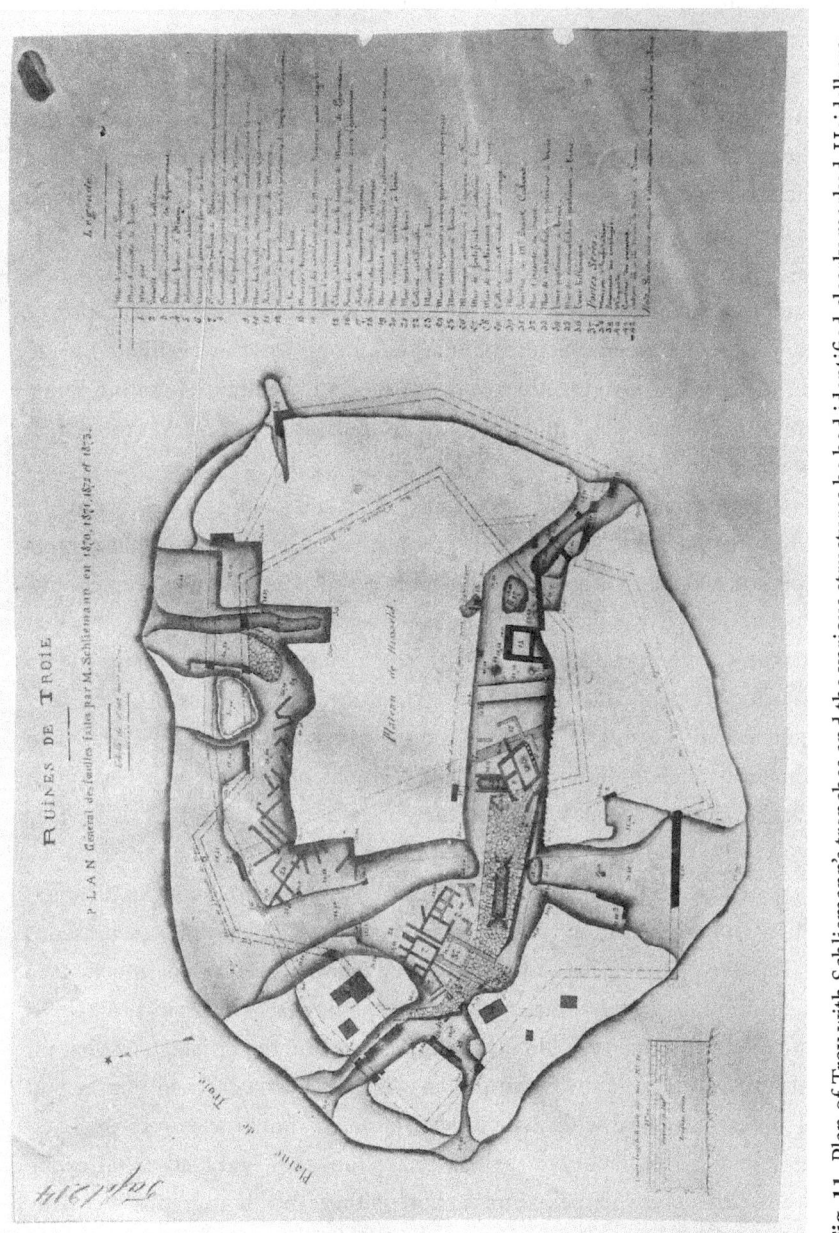

Fig. 11 Plan of Troy with Schliemann's trenches and the various structures he had identified clearly marked. Heidelberg University Library, Heinrich Schliemann, *Atlas Trojanischer Alterthümer*, Tafel 214 – CC-BY-SA 3.

marked. The annotations on the images could provide additional information to those who spoke French and German.[36] Regardless of whether visitors could read these annotations, they show a detailed approach to the site that made Schliemann's work appear more scholarly and methodical and showed off his use of photography itself as a modern recording technique. Demonstrating rigor was an important strategy for Schliemann as an outsider trying to secure his place in archaeology. It complemented his interest in scientific and technological approaches to recording and investigating his finds from Troy and made those approaches immediately visible to South Kensington's visitors.

The South Kensington Museum's annual report for the year 1878 lists photographs as an integral feature of the exhibition and gives some indication of how they were displayed: '[Schliemann's finds from Troy] are exhibited in 25 cases in the South Court, together with two pieces of sculptured marble, and a selection from 129 drawings and photographs illustrating the excavations which are shown on screens.'[37]

This is in line with the guidelines for displaying such images laid down by the South Kensington Museum (Fig. 12). Screens had multiple leaves that visitors could peruse, allowing for more images to be displayed in a smaller space. While we do not know exactly which photographs Schliemann used, this makes clear that the focus was on the excavations, rather than the images of objects that made up the majority of *Atlas*. This makes sense, since the other images in *Atlas* were photographs and illustrations of the collection, which visitors could see directly in the exhibition. Showing drawings and photographs of the site itself had much more interpretive potential. It allowed the objects to be seen as part of a wider context. As with the depths on the labels it stated a direct connection between the objects and the earth they had come from, as well as the surrounding landscape.

In the Trojan exhibition, photographs became another kind of museum object. They were a new technology that vastly expanded the kinds of information that the exhibition could contain. Photographs allowed Schliemann to exhibit not only the finds from Troy, but also its landscape and the visible marks left on it by his excavations. It allowed him to answer critics who claimed that he had dug in the wrong place with detailed evocations of how the terrain matched Homer. It enabled audiences to see the excavations they had read about in the papers and to visualize Schliemann's version of Troy. The photographs and plans emphasized the importance of context for making sense of archaeological material, particularly for this collection, which attracted interest not because of the intrinsic qualities of the objects but because of their links to a famous city from ancient literature.

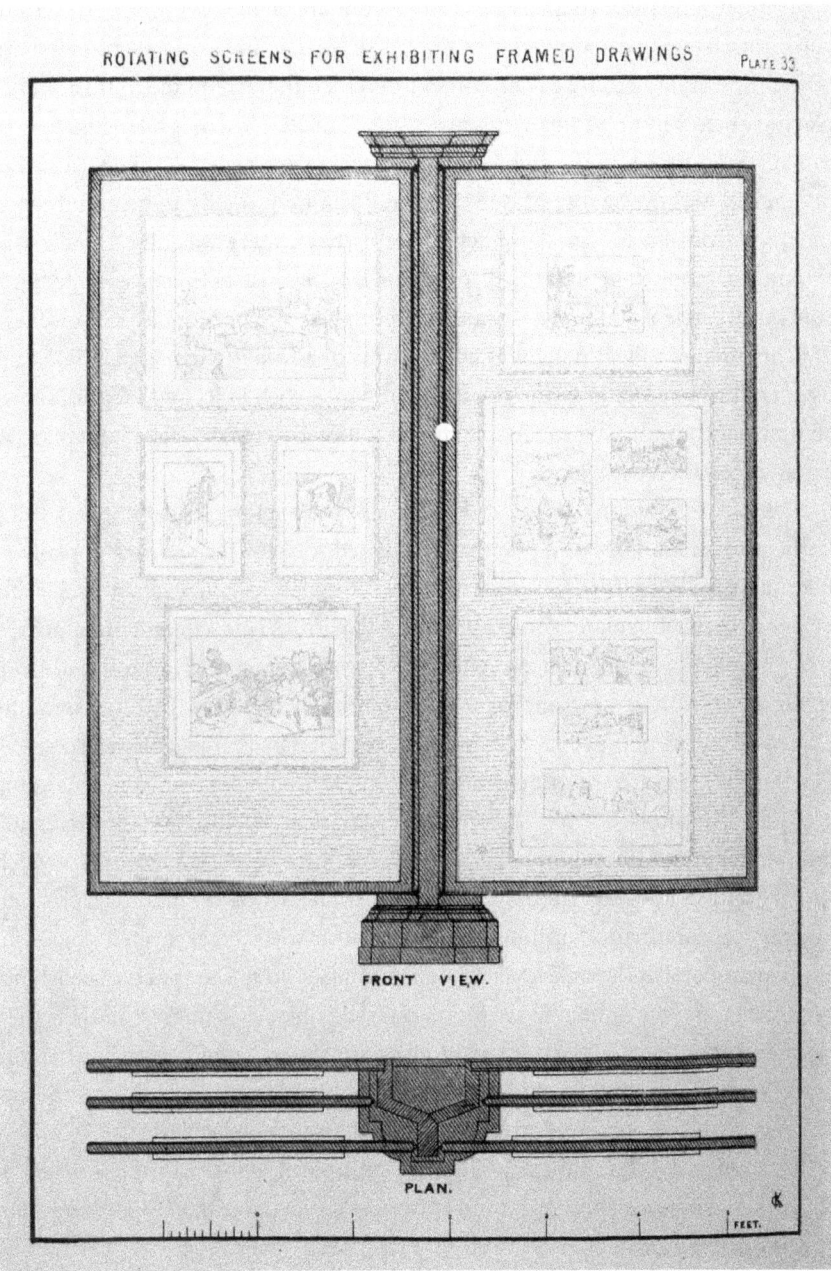

Fig. 12 Screens used for displaying drawings and photographs at South Kensington. Science and Art Department of the Committee of Council on Education, South Kensington Museum, *Drawings of Glass Cases in the South Kensington Museum, with Suggestions for the Arrangement of Specimens* (London: Vincent Brooks, Day & Son, 1876), plate 33. By kind permission of the Bodleian Library.

Context remains a sticky issue for museum archaeologists today. Surveys of current archaeological displays in museums stress how archaeologists understand objects' meaning because of the context in which they are found, but the act of placing objects in museums strips away this context.[38] There is a long history of this sort of critique: in the eighteenth century, Quatremère de Quincy (drawing on ancient authors) wrote of how art could not be properly understood when removed from its context.[39] By Schliemann's time, there was much interest in evoking lost context in museum displays, often by reconstructing the architectural context of ancient sculpture.[40] Smaller objects like the pots, tools and jewellery of Schliemann's collections could not be contextualized in this way. Schliemann's use of plans, photographs and the depth at which each object was found, shows an unusual commitment to relating his exhibition back to the site of and his own experiences as an excavator.

The use of photography to do this had its own rhetorical effect. It was still a fairly novel technology and one that purported to show the world as it really is. Like the depths on labels, this was a body of apparently neutral and scientific evidence that Schliemann could use against the critics who thought his approach irrational. Schliemann's concern with being seen as a good excavator made him experiment with a new approach to museum exhibitions that stressed the excavated nature of his collection and tried to root it in its archaeological context. Placing two important nineteenth-century technologies for understanding antiquity (the museum and the photograph) side by side has an interesting cumulative effect. Photographs showed the world beyond the museum to which the exhibition alluded. The museum space transformed the photographs into objects for examination and invited comparison with the excavated objects in Schliemann's collection to deepen understanding of both. The apparent neutrality of photography, and the role of photographs as objects of interest in their own right seems to have worked to make this innovation seem somewhat natural, since there is not much discussion of these images in reports of the exhibition. However, the emphasis on context and the process of excavation is widely reflected in responses to the exhibition. In grounding Schliemann's collection in this way, the photographs, maps and plans worked to make the Trojan exhibition specifically Trojan.

The Trojan exhibition was shaped by Schliemann's technical and technological approach to his collection – he used quantitative approaches, external expertise and the most up-to-date methods of recording and displaying his finds. These, in turn, shaped the version of Troy that visitors encountered – making a nondescript hill (that was far from the grandeur of the imagined Troy) into a modern archaeological site, defined by its depth and complexity in which even simple objects are part of a complex, layered history. The desire to relate the collection back to the place where it was found was not just about neutral archaeological evidence. The emphasis on landscape reflects the detailed topological debates that were involved in the search for Troy (see Chapter 1). It positioned the Trojan collection as an answer to a long-running debate about relating landscape to text, and showed off Schliemann's achievements as an excavator. The result was a paradoxical mixture of the objects' status as evidence that forms part of a larger archaeological assemblage and their role as small parts of the literary Troy that people knew and loved. This combination of archaeological rigor and literature seems contradictory but was central to Schliemann's thought. It presented the objects on display as evidence (rather than works of art or curiosities) in ways that had important implications for audience reception of Troy.

4

How Schliemann Displayed His Treasures

In 1880, the South Kensington Museum asked Schliemann to remove his exhibition, which had been taking up nearly half of their temporary exhibitions gallery for more than three years by the time it left.[1] Schliemann had already quietly made arrangements to give the collection to the Royal Museum in Berlin in his will and had been looking into displaying it there sooner.[2] It was initially displayed in the Museum of Decorative Arts (from 1882 to 1885), before moving to two purpose-built rooms in the Museum of Ethnology.[3] Schliemann and his discoveries were receiving recognition from the German archaeological establishment, after many years of his theories being dismissed by them.[4] However, it is also a sign of acceptance of Schliemann's collection into the grand narrative of a major museum. To understand what role Schliemann wanted his collection to play in this narrative, it is important to look at how the objects were to be displayed in their new home and how Schliemann managed the transfer.

As with the exhibition in London, Schliemann took an active, personal interest in how his collection was to be displayed. He reviewed the plans carefully with his own architect and (when the museum was complete) was personally involved in arranging his collection.[5] One of Schliemann's stipulations for the new display in Berlin was that it reproduce the case layout from South Kensington. Schliemann's involvement in the fine detail of arranging his collection has been seen as an example of a patron using his power to meddle in the work of the museum and defy the systematic arrangement preferred by professionals.[6] Not all of Schliemann's contemporaries agreed with his arrangement (as we will see in Chapter 10) but they generally agreed that this was an arrangement with a clear method and interpretive agenda. As one reviewer of the London exhibition put it: 'Gold work and pottery are alike in admirable preservation and the lessons to be learnt from them are not involved in the mystery of half-effaced inscriptions, but written large by the light of intelligent and scholarly arrangement.'[7] This chapter looks at the arrangement of the display at South Kensington and Berlin in the light of Schliemann's theories to show that, while it was idiosyncratic, the display of the Trojan collection was carefully arranged to make the case for a particular vision of ancient Troy.

This close examination is possible because of the care Schliemann took to preserve his arrangement between London and Berlin. In the process of packing up nearly 4,500 objects for transport, Schliemann created a plan of the exhibition that records its layout at South Kensington (see Fig. 5, in Chapter 2).[8] This plan was intended to help reproduce the arrangement when the collection arrived at its permanent (or so Schliemann intended) home in Berlin. It shows the architectural structure of the gallery, with cases arranged in three rows, and includes measurements of cases and notes about other aspects of the installation (e.g. 'Pedestal for marble slab', 'The South Kensington Court is 48 feet × 53 feet').[9] On its own, Schliemann's gallery plan does not give much more information than we can determine from images of the South Court at this time (compare Fig. 13 with Fig. 5, an image of the same space, showing a nearly identical case layout). However, the plan gives the case numbers, which can be matched up with descriptions of the contents of the cases in published accounts of the exhibition at South Kensington to give a surprisingly complete picture of the arrangement of the collection. This gives us a glimpse of the exhibition at South Kensington as visitors would have seen it, but it also lets us explore how Schliemann crafted the journey through this space in a way that told a story about the site of Troy through the objects themselves.

In this detailed exploration of the arrangement of Schliemann's collection, I consider what the display was designed to communicate and why Schliemann was so keen to preserve the arrangement in its new home. I explore the contents of the exhibition in roughly the order that visitors would have encountered them if they entered through the south entrance. This focus on spatial layout can reveal the interpretive potential of object groupings; why some displays grouped similar objects from all periods of the site, while others focused closely on one period; why some cases were cluttered, while others contained only one object; and how strange combinations of objects (such as showing skulls alongside face pots) conveyed Schliemann's ideas about Troy. This draws together discussions of the exhibition from a range of sources, alongside Schliemann's own writings and images to give a sense of how layout and juxtapositions of objects allowed Schliemann and his collaborators to shape visitor experiences. This is not an attempt to make a perfect reconstruction of the Trojan exhibition. Because of its sources, it is inevitably coloured by the interests and biases of visitors, but it is precisely those interests that allow us to study the exhibition's effects.

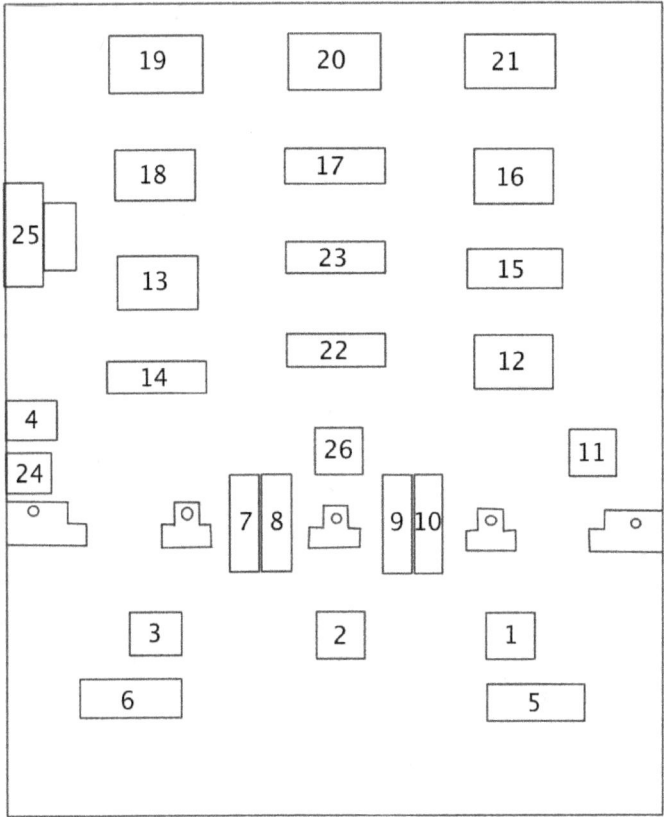

Fig. 13 Plan of Schliemann's exhibition at South Kensington, numbers indicate case numbers. After a plan drawn by Schliemann, in Berlin, printed in Geraldine Saherwala, Klaus Goldmann and Gustav Mahr, *Heinrich Schliemanns 'Sammlung Trojanischer Altertümer': Beitrage Zur Chronik Einer Grossen Erwerbung Der Berliner Museen* (Berlin: Spiess, 1993), 17, Abb.5.

Cases 1–3 and 5: introductory material

A newspaper correspondent from New Zealand described the first object he encountered in the exhibition:

> we may first observe, on our right hand, advantageously displayed in a large glass case by itself, the most important vase in the large collection of similar vessels... It is a splendid vessel of terra-cotta, an indescribably brilliant brown in hue, with a throat thrice the circumference of its base, the upward spring from which is noble, and consummately adapted to the poise of a majestic top-weight. Without a single feature directly borrowed from animal life, the tutelar goddess of Troy,

with owl-face, a woman's breast, a necklace, and a regal belt or scarf, stands unmistakeable and authentic in poetical force of suggestion.[10]

This was a large and dramatic vase that could fill a whole case on its own, draw the eye and make a strong impression on visitors. It set the scene for an exhibition that was full of unusual pottery, but Schliemann was displaying it as more than just a pot. This pot was one of the type (e.g. Fig. 16) that Schliemann called *glaukopis* after a Homeric epithet for Athena (γλαυκῶπις Ἀθήνη).[11] Schliemann proposed a translation of this epithet as owl-eyed or owl-faced rather than the more conventional grey-eyed or bright-eyed. He believed these vases showed a woman with the head of an owl, and took this as proof of his 'owl-faced' translation, although there was no corroboration of his decision to associate them with Athena.[12] This resulted in a circular argument in which these must be owl-faced Athena because of Homer, and the site they were found at must be Homer's Troy because of the owl-headed images:

> The first conclusion to be drawn from this is that when civilization advanced Minerva got a human face and her owls face was metamorphosed into the owl, her favourite bird, which, <u>as such</u> is unknown to Homer. The 2nd conclusion is that all these owls faces on gobelets idols and vases confirm Homer's statement that Troy existed and that Minerva was its πολιουχος θεὰ. The 3rd conclusion is that Troy existed on the premises which I am excavating.[13]

This interpretation of these objects was not widely accepted, but the debates that it provoked drew a lot of attention to these objects, as did their prominent placement in the exhibition.[14]

Schliemann was proposing a new and radically different image of the Homeric Athena. Placing an example at the entrance of the exhibition foregrounded the possibility for this material to change how visitors imagine Homer's characters. These were pivotal objects for Schliemann's understanding of the site. By reading them as representations of Athena, he could interpret them as evidence of religion (which he had trouble finding elsewhere). The identification as Athena linked Troy with the Greek tradition, and aligned his reading with the *Iliad*, in which Trojans are described praying fruitlessly to Athena.[15] This also gave Troy characteristics associated with very early religion: animal-headed gods and stylized imagery of them. This placed Troy at the start of Greek religion.

This vase was a challenging choice to start the exhibition. Any important archaeological display was expected to contain images of the gods, but this was far from a standard representation of the Greek gods. It was a plain vessel, without the idealized beauty that one could see in the marble statues at the

British Museum. Its place at the front of the exhibition makes this seem a deliberate challenge: this object was not aesthetically beautiful by the standards of the time and was radically different from how people had imagined Troy. It set an agenda for a vision of Troy that was older and stranger than expected and made claims for the roots of classical civilization in a very unclassical object and inspired debates about the evolution of art (see Chapter 6).

The neighbouring cases contained other large vessels. These demonstrated the scale that potters could work at and underlined the simplicity of the first vase:

> Several cases are devoted to vases and jars of considerable size, the fragments of which have been collected and pieced together with remarkable success. Interspersed with these are handmill stones, 'craters' for mixing wine, one of which is 2ft in diameter, and in the second case from the entrance the keystone of a door of the first city of Troy, found at the depth of 40ft.[16]

These objects were probably grouped together at the start of the exhibition because of their size. As well as being visually impressive, it also established the scale that Trojans were capable of working at. It implied skilled craftsmen, agricultural plenty and a lavish elite lifestyle (requiring a two-foot wine vessel). The keystone evoked the scale of the architecture as well as the depth (both literally and temporally) of the absent site. These objects represented several distinct phases of the site: *The Times* review describes the vases in cases 1 and 2 as chosen to 'illustrate the Homeric Ilium and the supposed Lycian Troia', which is to say, the Troy Schliemann identified with the *Iliad* and the city that replaced it.[17] The keystone represented the earliest level – the phase before Homeric Troy. So, the early cases had already represented the full span of Schliemann's pre-classical Troy.

Alongside these was a case of smaller objects dedicated to 'Homeric Troy'. *The Times* describes a Homeric case that contained 'ivory lyres and flutes, a lion-headed sceptre-handle of fine crystal, combs of stone, terra-cotta brush-handles, copper weapons, and stone and bone implements of all kinds'.[18] This was clearly a prestigious group of material, but densely enough packed that no single object caught reviewers' eyes. This is often the point at which reviews broke down into long lists, such as this one from the *Manchester Weekly Times*, which seems to elide the 'Homeric Troy' case with the small finds cases that followed it. 'Of discs, balls, hammers, axes and other stone implements of prehistoric times; small idols, in stone, bone, ivory, and wood; terracotta brush handles, stone beads, buttons, seals, stag horns, saw knives, vertebrae of sharks, bone needles for knitting, embroidering, and netmaking, there are numerous specimens, amounting to several hundreds.'[19] The need for such lists is obvious for reporters who wanted to capture the number and diversity of objects in the exhibition. These cases seemed to span the full range of Trojan life: encompassing natural curiosities, tools, religious objects, practical and decorative items. This diversity seems to have bewildered many visitors and challenged the categories and narratives that helped make sense of archaeological material. As a result, any messages Schliemann may have been trying to convey with this material, beyond its links to Homeric Troy are impossible to tease out of accounts of the cases.

Cases 6–10: small finds

Next were four cases, crammed between pillars, containing at least a thousand spindle whorls, as well as stone tools and other small finds. These were less impressive than the large vases at the beginning of the exhibition and not as glamorous as the treasure still to come. However, they were central to Schliemann's theories about Troy. Large numbers of spindle whorls were found at Troy, including many with inscribed decoration. Because very few objects from the early levels of the site were decorated, Schliemann read a lot into these markings. He believed he saw letters in the inscribed surfaces and hoped that someone might be able to decipher them.[20] The first *Times* report about the exhibition stressed that 'these were not used for spinning, hardly any of them showing traces of friction or usage, but were votive offerings'.[21] As with the *glaukopis* vases, objects were stripped of practical function to elevate them into objects of religious value:

> Dr Schliemann himself regards these discs as votive offerings to Athena Ergana. Vast numbers of them were found in all the Trojan strata and their designs are infinitely diversified. All the devices are taken to be of a more or less religious character, solar and stella [*sic*] types being the most common. It startles one to meet so frequently with the sacred symbols of the oldest Vedic faith, such as the hitherto unexplained *rosa mystica*, the *soma*, or Indian tree of life, and the ever-recurring *suastica*.[22]

Schliemann used the spindle whorls to argue that Trojans were an Aryan people. The presence of the swastika was used to imply a shared culture with other places that used this motif, including India (as above) and Germany. It took on its modern connotations in the light of Schliemann's racial theories and Chapter 11

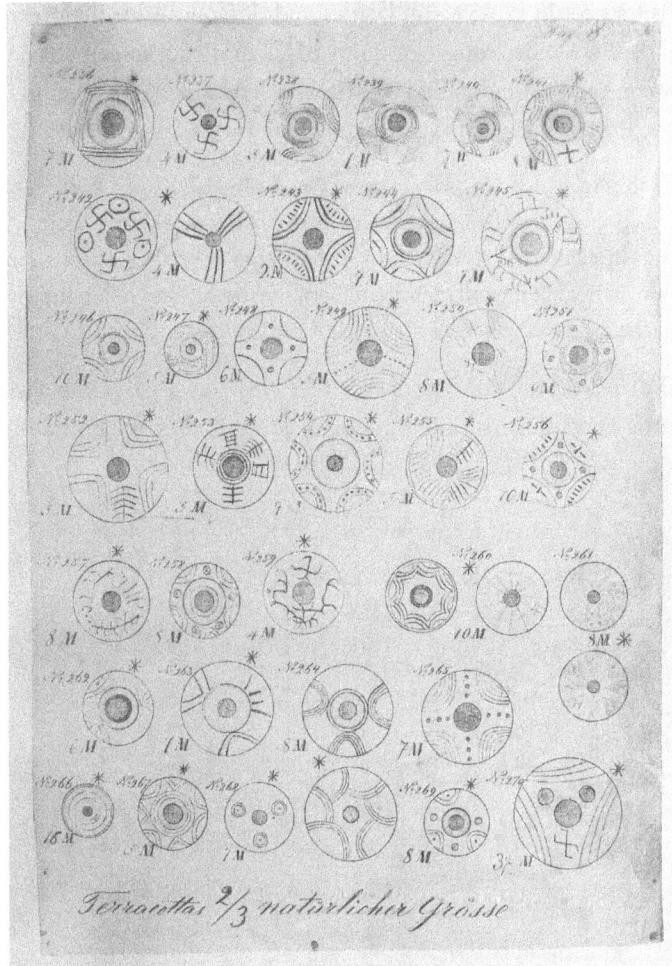

Fig. 14 Drawings of spindle whorls from Troy showing their inscribed decoration. Heidelberg University Library, Heinrich Schliemann, *Atlas Trojanischer Alterthümer*, Tafel 8 – CC-BY-SA 3.

will explore how the South Kensington exhibition raised interest in this topic.[23] To underline the importance of these as symbols, Schliemann's arrangements emphasized decoration over function: 'Specimens of these whorls almost fill one case; they are arranged according to their patterns.'[24]

Schliemann brought these small objects together in large numbers, using repetition to give visual impact. On their own it might have been easier to dismiss their decoration, but drawing together many examples of each kind allowed Schliemann to make a visual argument about the significance of their motifs. Visitors could explore similarities and differences for themselves, while always guided by Schliemann's taxonomy of decoration. He seems to have taken special care to pick out individual whorls with outstanding decoration and raise them above the main level of the case to ensure they were visible on all sides:

> One which is suspended in order to show the whole design upon its outer surface is described thus: 'The Ilian Minerva, in form of an owl, with two hands (one of which has three fingers) rising to heaven, having to her right a wheel symbolical of the sun, to her left the full moon, and between the sun and moon the morning star. On the reverse, the hair of the goddess is distinctly engraved' No. 257[25]

This kind of terracotta ball with a face (Fig. 15) was a particular favourite of Schliemann's and informed his arguments about Trojan religion and celestial

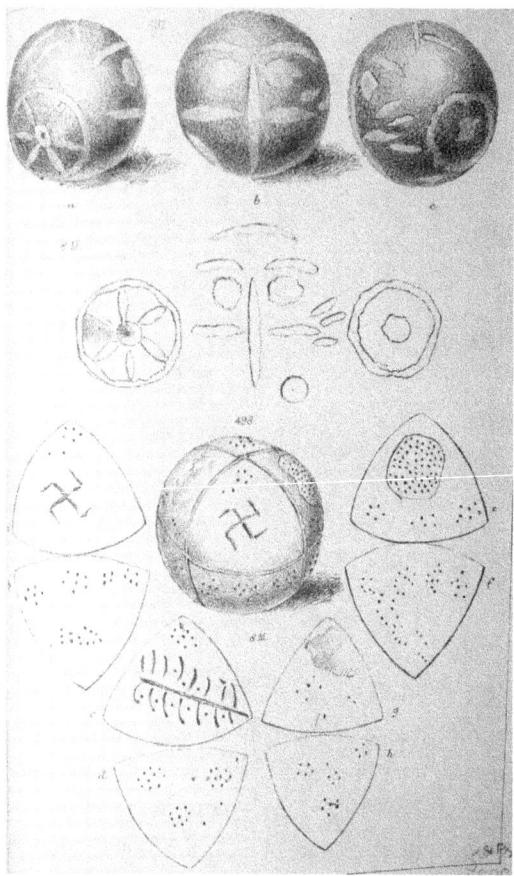

Fig. 15 Decorated terracotta balls, including *glaukopis* and swastika designs. Heinrich Schliemann, *Ilios: The City and Country of the Trojans* (London: John Murray, 1880), plate 52. By kind permission of Newcastle Lit & Phil.

symbolism. Schliemann's book *Ilios* urged readers to go and see this example at South Kensington to look more closely at the detail.[26]

Schliemann's focus on the symbols on the spindle whorls meant that they were redefined as tokens to carry the symbols, rather than useful objects in their own right.[27] For example, the *Illustrated London News* imagined them as a means to control access to religious ceremonies:

> There is great uncertainty about the use that was probably made, in some religious ceremonials of the circular pierced stones or 'whorls,' sometimes moulded of clay and inscribed with mystic characters and figures... It seems generally admitted that some of the forms incised were symbolical of the sacred fire of the altar; and we may conjecture that these portable tokens or badges were held by privileged lay worshippers for their admission to the most solemn religious rites, or as memorials of their past attendance at these, in the temples of the old heathen religion. Some of them are inscribed with Greek or Cypriote letters of the alphabet; others with a rude suggestion of animal figures, the meaning of which is unknown; but all such devices would lead us to ascribe a very high antiquity to the objects in this collection.[28]

Schliemann's careful classification and arrangement of these objects by decoration underlined the centrality of the symbols in his thought. Case 9 was completely filled with classified spindle whorls.[29] The neighbouring cases also contained whorls 'side by side with funnels, crucibles, rings, slate and terra-cotta moulds for casting, idols and other small objects in bone and wood, sling-shots of magnetic iron, bone and flint implements of all sorts'.[30] It is unclear if this jumble of small finds from all levels of Hisarlık continued to follow Schliemann's symbol-driven agenda.

Case 8 contained a small stone object that one reviewer identified as proof of contact with Egypt: 'in case 8 is to be found another clear proof of direct or indirect commerce with the Nile. For there we find, among many other small objects in wood and stone, a veritable little pyramid, about 2in. square at the base, made, too, of Egyptian granite'.[31] Case 7 was a display of tools, with a particular focus on the early levels of the site:

> In another case are some instruments belonging apparently to the age of stone, and found in the lowest stratum. They include knives of obsidian, arrow-heads, stone and flint hatchets, and a few metal instruments. Knives, daggers, bracelets, and nails of copper, silver pins, silver incense pans, and a silver crescent are also shown here. Some very curious instruments are exhibited which serve to illustrate the state of manufacture in this age. They are moulds formed of mica-schist for casting metal.[32]

Putting tools of different materials together was not simply a thematic arrangement, but one with a specific archaeological agenda. Schliemann claimed to have found metal and stone tools side by side and used this to argue against the three-age system as it stood. Not satisfied with being an exception to the rule, Schliemann argued that Troy proved that the whole system was incorrect.[33]

> The significant fact that at Hissarlik the manufacture of neolithic weapons and tools went on contemporaneously with the metallurgic art in all the prehistoric towns, although ever declining even in what Dr. Schliemann calls 'Wooden Troy', the youngest and by far the rudest of the whole has unsettled the faith of many in the received archaeological theory of successive Stone, Bronze and Iron Ages.[34]

Chapter 10 looks in more detail at why one of the founders of Bronze Age archaeology in this region was so sceptical of the three-age system. One of the small finds cases also contained a large number of worked boar tusks: 'Hardly less interesting is a case filled with boars' tusks, many of which have been sharpened at one end to serve as implements of some kind.'[35] Schliemann seems to have resisted the temptation of a Homeric identification for these: the *Iliad* describes a helmet made with tusks on the outside and this has since been recognized as one of the few accurate descriptions of Bronze Age material culture in the text.[36] Instead, the identification of these as tools makes them another refutation of the idea that bronze replaced all other materials when people discovered how to work it.

While the spindle whorls and tools were relatively unprepossessing, they were pivotally important to Schliemann's theories. They were part of his attempt to tie the site into a racial and chronological context and make a case for its importance in studying European origins. It is therefore unsurprising that he made visitors walk past them to get to the treasure.

Cases 4 and 24: large vases

The pot in case 4 was a large storage jar – large enough that (according to *The Times*) two of Schliemann's workmen used to sleep in it:

> [It was] a specimen of the huge jars found at various depths, and used for storage of corn, wine &c. Two of Dr Schliemann's Greek workmen slept night after night in that shown, and the sight of the enormous *amphora* has reminded many of

the oil jars in which the Forty Thieves were hidden. This case further contains handmill stones of trachyte found in the lowest and highest strata.[37]

This little digression (a story which also turned up in other accounts of the exhibition) reflects the enjoyment of orientalist fantasy as an aspect of archaeological excavation.[38] Challis has observed how workers and other locals were used in images of archaeology to provide both local colour and a sense of scale.[39] This example shows how such imagery also crept into the way visitors experienced archaeological exhibitions, framing ancient objects through modern ideas about geography, culture and race.

As in the earlier cases, large storage jars were exhibited with tools for grinding grain.[40] This may have been a convenient way to squeeze in extra objects by using free space around the larger ones. However, it could also be an attempt to combine objects involved in food preparation and storage to link them thematically. An early review that was reprinted in a large number of journals stated that the largest of the jars (probably this one) was labelled 'A substitute for a cellar'.[41]

Case 24 was next to case 4 (the illogical numbering may be an indicator that this case was an afterthought, squeezed in late in the exhibition design). It is not explicitly mentioned in any of the reports on the exhibition, but it may have contained other objects too large to fit in the standard cases, which were mostly placed along the wall.[42]

Cases 11 and 12: *glaukopis* vases

Mirroring the large objects on the opposite side of the gallery was case 11. This contained a large *glaukopis* vase (Fig. 16), deemed particularly important because of its find-spot in the building Schliemann believed to be Priam's Palace. Schliemann displayed it, not with other pottery, but with skulls: 'Here also are three skulls, two found in Priam's City, and the other in that buried beneath it. All three are of marked Aryan type. Two of the crania have plainly been fractured in battle.'[43] Schliemann thought this vase was a royal object of great significance, so the decision to display it alongside human remains is interesting.[44] The clearest effect of associating these disparate kinds of archaeological finds is to associate 'Priam's City' with the battle-wounded crania. This is particularly effective for Schliemann's ends, given the number of head wounds described in the *Iliad*. The third skull was also described in a different *Times* report on the exhibition: 'One skeleton of a woman was found at a depth of 42 ft, with some simple gold

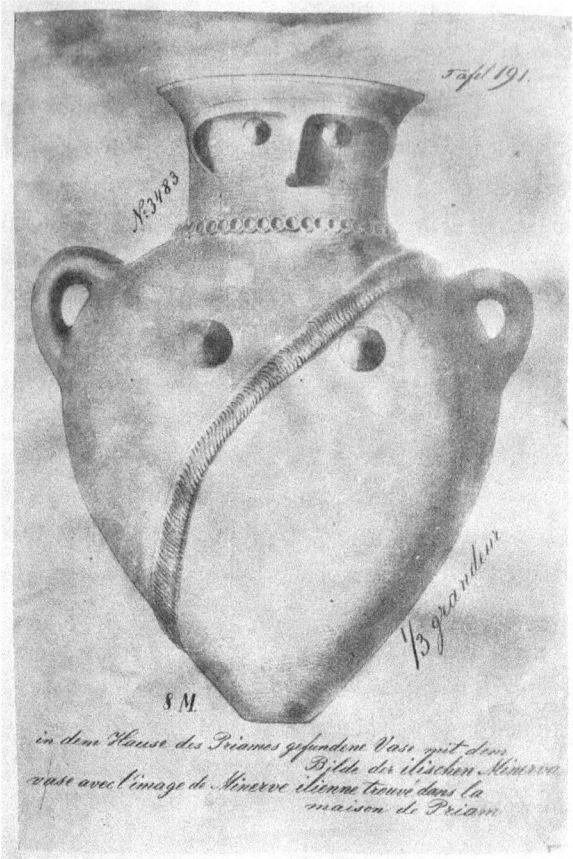

Fig. 16 The *glaukopis* vase Schliemann found in the 'House of Priam'. Heidelberg University Library, Heinrich Schliemann, *Atlas Trojanischer Alterthümer*, Tafel 191 – CC-BY-SA 3.

ornaments, which are shown in one of the cases – a finger ring, three earrings, a dress pin, and some gold beads. The gold is nearly pure. Both the ornaments and the skull (also shown) bear the marks of fire'.[45]

The skeletons from Troy were fragmentary and rather poorly reconstructed (Fig. 17). The reconstruction was probably Schliemann's own work. His diary of finding the female skull reports: 'the skull especially is in a good state of preservation, but has unfortunately been broken in our excavations; however, I can easily put it together again'.[46] Schliemann decided that the skeleton was a woman based on the size of the skull and the fact that it was found with jewellery.[47]

The stress on the simplicity and purity of the jewellery found with this skeleton reflects its association with Schliemann's 'first city' (the phase before

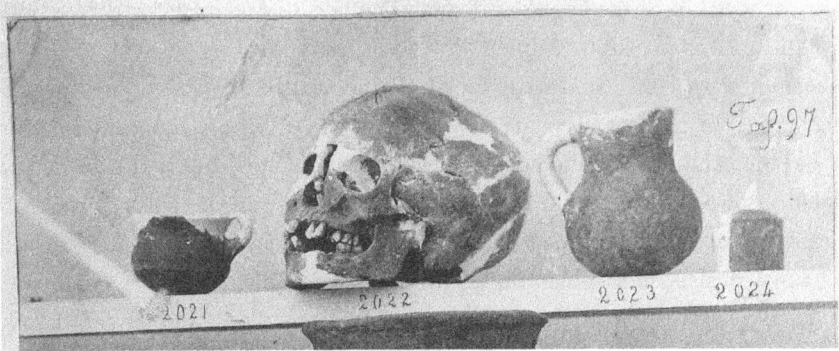

Fig. 17 Skull from Troy, clearly not reconstructed by an expert. Heidelberg University Library, Heinrich Schliemann, *Atlas Trojanischer Alterthümer*, Tafel 97 – CC-BY-SA 3.

'Homeric Troy'). However, the fire damage that Schliemann observed on the skull meant that some reports could not resist reassigning it to Homer's Troy: 'One large, owl-headed vase was found in the King's mansion, 26 1/2 feet deep, and beside it are three human skulls one being that of a woman, who was probably destroyed at the burning of Troy. With her skeleton were discovered gold ear-rings, breast-pin, and finger ring.'[48] The suffering of the Trojan noblewomen at the hands of the invading Greeks was a major topic of classical literature and the idea of an elite woman whose status could not protect her from the burning of her city, proved too tempting to resist.

Schliemann associated the few skulls he had found with two traumatic destructions of the city because he thought these were the only times when people would not have been given a proper funeral. Schliemann had not found many skeletons in the prehistoric layers of Troy.[49] Most of the human remains he found were cremated and buried in pots, but he did not associate the *glaukopis* vases with burials.[50] Instead the display of the *glaukopis* vase with the human remains may have been meant to represent Trojan religion and identity, given the role he assigned these objects as 'idols or sacred vases'.[51]

The three skulls in case 11 represented the bodies of actual Trojans. Schliemann resisted the urge to identify these bodies as individuals from the *Iliad* (as he would famously do in Mycenae), but they still fit into his narrative of the city's destruction, as well as the fallen warriors and cruelly treated noblewomen of literary accounts of the fall of Troy. The fact that only skulls (and not other bones) were displayed reflects the scientific interest in skulls at this time. Skulls were avidly collected and exhibited in the late nineteenth century because they were believed to be the key to understanding personal character and race.[52] By exhibiting Trojan skulls, Schliemann was clearly inviting visitors to South Kensington to consider Trojan racial characteristics. In fact, he specifically encouraged experts to view the collection in one of his early announcements about the exhibition, in the hope of deepening his knowledge and proving the value of the collection to a range of disciplines: 'Scientific authorities will have to determine the ethnological affinities of the human remains found at Troy, and which will also be exhibited at South Kensington.'[53] Schliemann's wish was fulfilled when his friend, the doctor and anthropologist Rudolf Virchow, took these skulls away and reconstructed them again. Virchow then delivered his expert opinion on their racial affinities as one of the contributors to *Ilios*.[54] It is unclear whether the labels reflected this interest in race, but it is worth noting how many responses to the exhibition described them as looking distinctly Aryan.[55] Chapter 11 will explore the role these three skulls came to play in the debate (among both experts and amateurs) about where Troy fitted in nineteenth-century racial hierarchies.

The next case (12) also contained *glaukopis* vases. It displayed a selection of smaller examples from different levels of the site. This demonstrated Schliemann's claim that the type was present throughout the history of Troy. Displaying similar pots from all levels together gave a sense of cultural evolution within a consistent religious framework:

> Thus, case 12, which is filled with vases and their covers representing the owl-faced Athena (Minerva), and with her idols taken from all the pre-Hellenic strata, invites us to such a comparison [i.e. across time periods], besides reminding us of the persistence of this curious type of the goddess among the peoples on whose ashes the Greek settlers were daily trampling although it never penetrated, along with the religio loci, among these Greeks themselves.[56]

The *glaukopis* vases were presented as important evidence of cultural and religious continuity at Troy, in spite of its distinct layers and destruction events. The idea that this type of object spanned the history of Troy allowed people to explore minor stylistic differences as markers of more subtle cultural shifts: Chapters 6 and 11 give examples of how these pots were a focus for evolutionary narratives about the site of Troy.

The proximity of this case to the treasure invited comparison with the *glaukopis* decoration of one of the diadems. Certainly, *The Times* makes this comparison in its review: 'The traces of human form in the idols are more or less conventional. The un-initiated eye has been reminded of a fiddle. But, on comparison with the very numerous examples of Glaukôpis idols and vases in a case filled with them, the owl's heads with the large eyes are unmistakeable.'[57] The repetition of this kind of vase stressed its importance. However, Schliemann had different things to say about them in different cases. In 12, the argument was about cultural continuity across periods, in 11, its specific importance to Homeric Troy (the house of Priam in particular) and its religion. Schliemann implied that these vases were characteristic of Homeric Troy, but that they (along with the religious practice they represented) survived after its fall. Labelling and juxtapositions of objects allowed arguments about Troy to be developed across the exhibition, even with seemingly repetitive material.

Case 26: 'shield'

No reports explicitly list the contents of case 26 – a small square case at the centre of the exhibition, between the pillars and the treasure. However, the special report on the arrangement of the Trojan Treasure notes that the 'shield' (Fig. 18) was given a case to itself, near to the treasure, and no other case fits this description.[58] Visitors who had arrived at the south entrance would almost re-enact Schliemann's experience of discovering the treasure. He described a first glimpse of the bronze 'shield', with gold glittering beyond it. This may not have been a coincidence, given the prominence of this moment in accounts of Schliemann's discoveries.[59] In both written account and exhibition, this order of the shield before the jewellery gives a satisfying narrative tension to the discovery and hints at deliberate concealment in ancient times.[60]

> One shield only was found with the 'Treasure,' but, with its large and stout boss in the middle, it exactly answers to Homer's ἀσπίς ὀμφαλόεσσα. It has a small glass case to itself. It is of the same copper-bronze characteristic of Troy, and may very well have been lined with a number of oxhide folds, like that of Sarpedon in the 'Iliad' (xii, 294-7), even had they been as many as the seven which Tychios, the leather-cutter of Hyla, fastened to the bronze for Ajax (vii, 219-23). The metallic layer is in the shape of an oval salver or waiter, the longer diameter measuring 20in. This was the first object which, with the glittering gold behind it, drew the digger's eye to the find.[61]

This was not the only review that referenced this passage of Homer describing the construction of Ajax's shield.[62] In this case, the *Iliad* references do more than

Fig. 18 'Shield' which Schliemann claimed was used to cover Priam's Treasure. Heidelberg University Library, Heinrich Schliemann, *Atlas Trojanischer Alterthümer*, Tafel 198 – CC-BY-SA 3.

underline Schliemann's claims about Troy, they propose a reconstruction of this object as the metal boss on a larger shield made of layers of leather, and help visitors to imagine beyond the inevitable decay of archaeological material through the apparently authentic means of literature. It was also an opportunity to explain away some of the problems of reading this small piece of metal as a Homeric shield. Not that this satisfied all visitors:

> Among these may be mentioned a navel shield of copper, an example of the *aspis omphaloessa*. The metal is very corroded, especially near the rim and does not seem at any time to have been capable of covering a man's body as the round bossed shield of Homer is supposed to do. It differs from it too, in some details

of construction, but is so altered by decay, and has perhaps so suffered also from fire, that it would be impossible to say what it was originally.[63]

The adoption of *aspis omphaloessa* in multiple accounts of the exhibition (including ones that take issue with the Homeric reading) probably reflects the name given on the label. Even simple names could frame the debate around the exhibition and carry a lot of theoretical and imaginative meaning for visitors who shared Schliemann's enthusiasm for Homer and we will return to the Homeric names in Chapter 9.

A couple of reviewers compared the shield to a dish, or said (correctly) that Schliemann had misidentified it.[64] The most recent catalogue of the Trojan treasure identifies it as a ' "Frying pan" or skillet, without handle.'[65] Schliemann's insistence on reading it as a shield makes sense, given the *Iliad*'s military themes and his own desire to embed the Trojan treasure in the fall of Troy. Schliemann imagined a soldier laying down his shield over the royal treasure to hide it from the Greeks before, presumably, laying down his life for Troy. This story is a lot less poignant with a cooking pot.

This emphasis on the 'shield' as military may also explain Schliemann's decision to exhibit it separately from the rest of the treasure. This was one of the most attractive objects that could be linked to Troy's military history. Most of the other items Schliemann read as arms were heavily corroded pieces of metal and hence much more difficult to imagine as the prestigious and appealing of arms and armour described by Homer. By exhibiting the 'shield' in a separate case, Schliemann could make sure that this reading was not overlooked.

Cases 22–23: Priam's Treasure

Priam's Treasure was literally and conceptually central to the exhibition, occupying two cases right at its heart. It dominated all the reviews and received its own separate guide in *The Times*, with a shelf-by-shelf description of the layout of the contents.[66] As a result, this is the part of the collection that we have most detail on, both in terms of description and evaluation. The reviews unanimously declared the treasure the highlight of the collection, explaining its appeal in terms of workmanship, design, Homeric resonance and the romance of buried treasure.[67] However, the treasure also attracted press attention because of its contested status. Schliemann claimed that these objects were the prized possessions of the Trojan royal family, buried in the chaos of Troy's fall and never reclaimed. This story was far from universally accepted.

The two treasure cases stood out because of the fame and material value of their contents and their prime position within the display. However, they were also separated from their neighbours by a subtly different approach to grouping the objects. Where most cases in the exhibition grouped objects from many layers and areas of the site by the shape of the objects, this was the only pair of cases dedicated to (what Schliemann claimed to be) a single archaeological context. One of the two treasure cases contained only precious metals, the other also included the other items found with the treasure.[68] By grouping together the less glamorous material with the gold and silver, Schliemann asserted their importance as a single find with an important story to tell about the site's heyday, destruction and rediscovery. Reports about the exhibition responded to this by including long digressions that repeated Schliemann's account of finding the treasure, giving a sense that there was something special about this group of material and the conditions of its discovery.[69]

The status of Priam's Treasure as a single archaeological find has been contested and, as we have seen, there were also doubts about the authenticity of the treasure at the time of the exhibition.[70] Schliemann was actually praised by *The Times* for acknowledging these and not putting too much of his own interpretation into the cases:

> The Cynosure of this marvellous collection is, of course, what was from the first made known to the astonished world as 'Priam's,' but now bears, in deference to honest and scholarly scruples, the more neutral name of the 'Trojan Treasure.' Dr. Schliemann having so far waived his right to christen it, everybody is left free to believe or not that the square wooden chest in which it seems to have been packed by the fugitive from the burning city must have been the king's strong-box mentioned in the Twenty-forth Iliad (v. 228).[71]

While Schliemann did not explicitly describe these items as the possessions of Priam and Helen, the exhibition was full of more subtle indications of his Homeric reading. Schliemann's labels for gold diadems (Figs 10 (in Chapter 3) and 19), which were quoted in *The Times* shows how Schliemann presented the treasure: 'Head Dress, 'Plekté Anadesme' gold. Sixty-one chains, with idol-shaped pendants. Found at the depth of 28ft. The Trojan Treasure.'[72] This label seems fairly straightforward and neutral. It starts with a title and description, then gives the depth at which it was found. The act of counting the chains gives a sense of precision to the label and opulence to the object. The 'idol-shapes' at the end might be easily missed since these forms are highly abstract. Pointing these out emphasizes that this is more than just a piece of jewellery, networked

Fig. 19 Gold diadem with decoration that Schliemann saw as owl-headed Athena. Heidelberg University Library, Heinrich Schliemann, *Atlas Trojanischer Alterthümer*, Tafel 206 – CC-BY-SA 3.

into religious and cultural forms that visitors saw repeated throughout the exhibition.

The name given to the object is perhaps the most important piece of information on the label. In this case, we get both neutral, English 'head dress' and the more exotic name: *Plekté Anadesme*. This term is difficult to translate (meaning, roughly, 'coiled binding') and only appears in one passage of Homer.[73] Schliemann's account of his excavations was peppered with such ancient Greek terms, and each item in the treasure was ascribed a Homeric name.[74] This one attracted interest because it marked Schliemann changing his mind about the particular object in Homer to identify it with before the exhibition:

> One is glad to see from this, to which the label on the other side answers, mutatis mutandis, that Dr Schliemann, who at first thought these diadems to be the Homeric kredemna, which seems to have been large veils or mantillas with lappets, such as the sea goddess Ino gives to Ulysses to buoy him up when wrecked (Od. v., 346), has adopted Mr Gladstone's correction.[75]

To those in the know, Schliemann was showing himself to be a thoughtful participant in this debate and crediting the contribution of his influential friend.

For those less informed, this unusual piece of jewellery was given a suitably evocative name, hinting at a deep understanding of the language and customs of the culture that produced it. Schliemann's Homeric names suggested these readings, leaving visitors to make the connection back to Homer for themselves. Several accounts did just that, by citing line references for objects. Reviewers linked the term *Plekté Anadesme* to the emotionally charged moment in book 22 when Andromache throws off her jewellery in mourning of her husband Hector. Hartshorne reproduced those lines of the *Iliad* in his report on the exhibition and observed: 'Either of them may be the very one which she tore from her head in grief at the death of Hector.'[76] Chapter 9 looks in more detail at how visitors to the exhibition used these connections to Homer.

The diadems were not the only objects labelled with an evocative Homeric name. The label of a distinctive gold vessel (Fig. 20) also attracted attention:

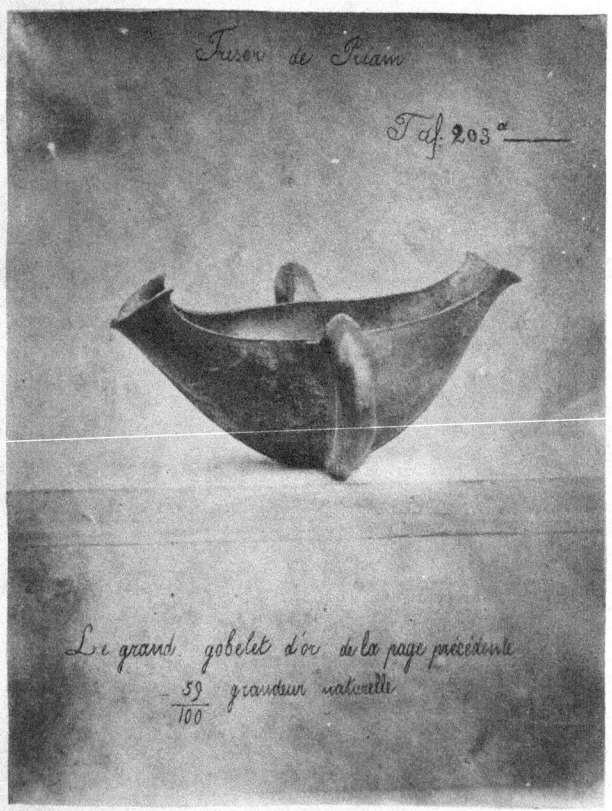

Fig. 20 Gold vessel termed *depas amphikypellon* by Schliemann. Heidelberg University Library, Heinrich Schliemann, *Atlas Trojanischer Alterthümer*, Tafel 203 – CC-BY-SA 3.

'Large solid gold *depas amphikupellon*, weight 601 grammes, two handles, two mouths, marks of fire.'[77] This is a similar formula to that used for the headdresses (name and material, then quantified description) and this pattern may have been used throughout the exhibition. Descriptions of the treasure often give the weight of individual objects, probably from the labels. These may have been a security measure or to show off the quantity of precious metal on display.[78] However, audiences experienced these weights as a demonstration of the wealth of the Trojans and Schliemann's exactitude in documenting his collection.

The technical name of the cup is again drawn from Homer. In this case, a kind of double cup mentioned several times in the *Iliad*, including in the hands of the gods, as a prestigious gift, and used by Achilles to pour a libation in memory of Patroclus.[79] This vessel (Fig. 20) is more commonly named a 'sauce boat' today, because of its shape, not its function. Easton has described being puzzled that Schliemann called it a *depas amphikypellon*, since that is now a technical term for a very different shape of vessel (like the three vessels bottom left in Fig. 21).[80]

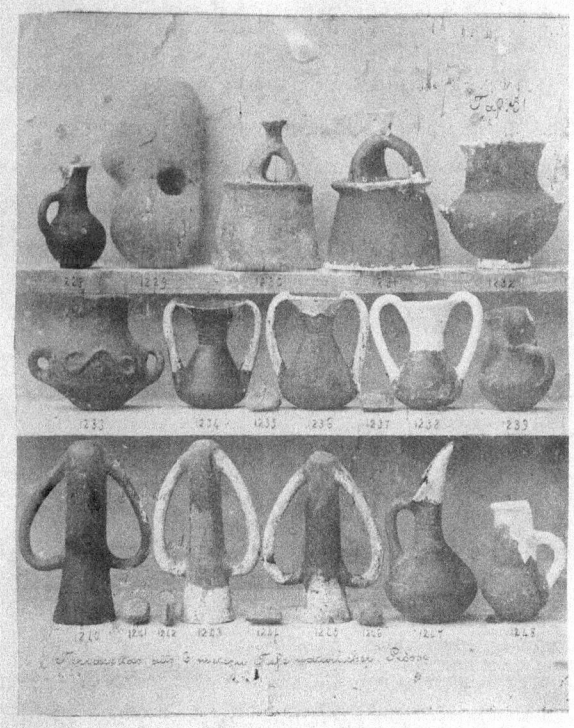

Fig. 21 Assortment of pots from Troy, including the kind called *depas amphikypellon* today (bottom left). Heidelberg University Library, Heinrich Schliemann, *Atlas Trojanischer Alterthümer*, Tafel 51 – CC-BY-SA 3.

Both types fit Schliemann's definition of the term, which he simply used for any cup with two handles. This definition was created against a tradition (starting with Aristotle) of imagining the *depas amphikypellon* as two cups, joined together like cells in a honeycomb.[81] Schliemann's broader definition allowed him to attach it to several of the most striking kinds of vessel from Troy. However, it was the gold cup that has most captured the imagination of poets and artists, as we will see in Chapter 5.

The cup's label mentions 'marks of fire', as another reminder of Troy's violent fall and its role in Schliemann's narrative of the treasure's deposition. It was common for newspaper articles to mention that objects in the treasure cases had been harmed by (or preserved from) the fire that destroyed Troy. This helped to connect damage visible on the objects to the story of Troy's fall.[82] The object that did most work to tell this story was a piece of corroded metal that Schliemann identified as a key. Its label read: 'Key of copper belonging to the wooden box containing the Trojan Treasure, and found at a depth of 28 1–3 feet.'[83] This is another formulaic label. It gives a brief description of the object and its function, mentions the objects it was found with and the depth at which it was found. However, these details transformed people's experience of it. Without this interpretation, this was a nondescript lump of metal (seen hanging from string in Fig. 22 and at the top of Fig. 23) but, as a key, it caught the public imagination. The idea of the Trojans using lock and key mechanisms seemed startlingly advanced, and it was compared with modern locks to make this case.[84] This implied advanced technology and skilled craftsmanship, as well as the presence of valuables that needed locking away.[85] It fits with Schliemann's story that the treasure was usually kept securely locked up, but both chest and key were lost in the heat of some great emergency. This is a lot to read into a simple label, but newspaper reports did just that.[86] It shows how complex theories can be pinned on what seems like a simple object identification. This label was pivotal for Schliemann's theories about the Trojan treasure, and it succeeded in getting a lot of coverage for an otherwise uninspiring object.

The 'key' was displayed with some other pieces that Schliemann identified as part of the box that held the treasure, as well as:

> Some fragments of silver vases, burnt to rottenness by the fierceness of the flames, battle axes, daggers, knives, and a fragment in the form of a double-edged sword, all found with the 'Trojan Treasure'. Like the key, they are of bronze, not of pure copper, as Dr. Schliemann first thought. Still, his former opinion, based on an analysis made by an Athenian chymist, is so far borne out by the results obtained from the more exact analysis.[87]

This additional material, while not 'treasure' by the standard definition was an important way for Schliemann to establish his story of how the treasure came to be hidden in Troy's fall and to dramatize his own discovery of it centuries later. Displaying this material together was a priority, even in Schliemann's early letters planning the exhibition: 'I think the treasure ought needs to be shown together with the copper weapons, shield, casserole and pots with which it was found together.'[88] Schliemann was keen to underline the status of this grouping as a single find with a clear story to tell about the fate of Troy. He had already been accused of including modern forgeries in this treasure, so this was both a defensive gesture and a statement of archaeological significance.[89]

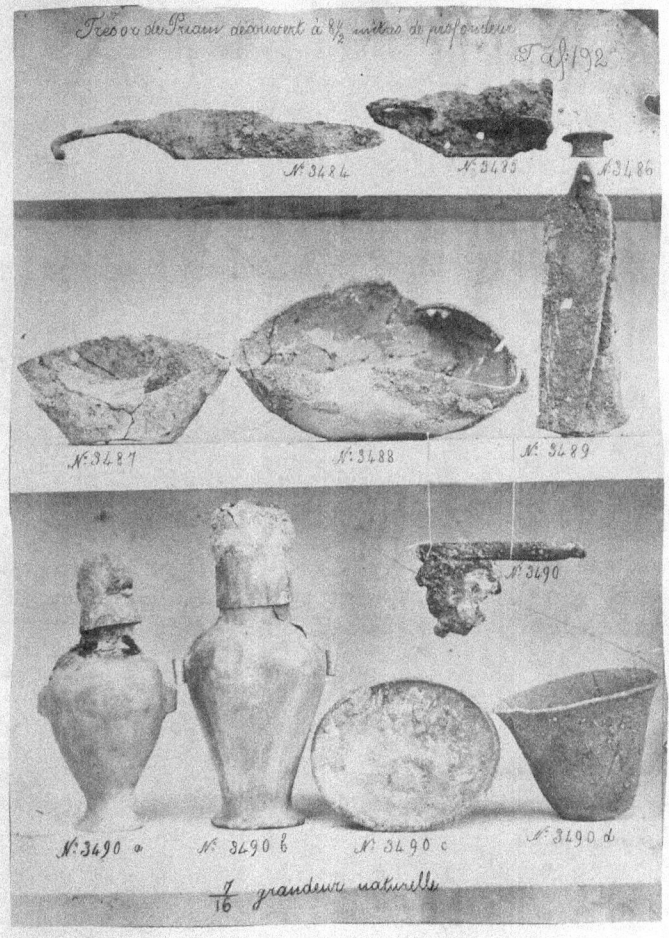

Fig. 22 Objects from 'Priam's Treasure', including the 'key', hanging from strings. Heidelberg University Library, Heinrich Schliemann, *Atlas Trojanischer Alterthümer*, Tafel 192 – CC-BY-SA 3.

Fig. 23 Star objects from the 'Treasure of Priam', including the 'key' (top centre) and 'shield' (bottom right). Heidelberg University Library, Heinrich Schliemann, *Atlas Trojanischer Alterthümer*, Tafel 204 – CC-BY-SA 3.

'Case' 25: metope and stele

There were a couple of items that presented problems for Schliemann and his collaborators while arranging the exhibition, because they were too big: 'Some of these [objects from Hisarlık], however, are too large for the capacity of ordinary cases. Huge amphorae lie supine on the floor or loll against the wall, and fragments of sculptured marble are perched here and there in convenient spots.'[90] One of these was the only piece of classical sculpture Schliemann found at Troy:

Against the West Wall is a fine marble sculpture, of the 4th century, representing Phoebus Apollo Driving the Horses of the Sun, originally forming a Metope of the Doric Temple of Phoebus Apollo at Ilium; beside it is a Stele or Memorial Pillar with Greek Inscription, probably of the 3rd century, found on the site of the temple of the Ilium Minerva.[91]

Sculpture and inscriptions in Greek style would have been much more familiar to London museum visitors but were hardly what they had come to see. The metope was generally appreciated by visitors, described as 'most perfect in expression and effect'[92] and a 'fine specimen of the Doric period of Grecian art, and is remarkable for its vigorous design and execution'.[93] The praise was warm, but discussion did not go much further. Similarly, the inscription did not draw much interest.[94] It did have a label with a translation on it before other object labels were in place, and so features heavily in reports from the previews.[95]

Cases 13–21: pottery

The cases surrounding and beyond the treasure were all dedicated to pottery. Reviewers described these in less detail, whether because they were less

Fig. 24 Apollo Metope from Troy. Heidelberg University Library, Heinrich Schliemann, *Atlas Trojanischer Alterthümer*, Tafel 30 – CC-BY-SA 3.

interesting or perhaps writers were running out of energy and space. The pottery from the Trojan collection was largely undecorated coarse ware, and many items had been stuck back together using bright white plaster. These cases, crammed with similar-looking objects, reduced interest in individual objects to highlight the qualities shared by the group. Schliemann may have failed to engage his audience with his arguments in these cases, or perhaps they were simply less carefully arranged and interpreted.

The Times described Case 13 as containing 'pottery of various kinds from all the elites entombed below the Greek Ilium'.[96] This does not give much clue as to what this case was about. The term 'elites' may indicate that these were finer wares. The object that received the most attention in this case was a double jug (like the one in Fig. 25):

> The most striking crock was found at the depth of 42 ft., and consequently, in the lowest of all, the ruins of which lie from 31 ft. to 52 ft. beneath the surface. It is a bright red vessel in the form of two jugs, with long beak-shaped mouths perfectly upright, the two being jointed together at the bulge, as well as by a handle in common. In short it is a pair of pitchers in one, reminding us of the Siamese twins.[97]

This was accompanied by a number of other double-necked jugs, which were seen as clues to Troy's cultural affiliations and date:

> Great interest attaches to these double-throated jugs, because among the oldest Cyprian pottery both Mr Lang and General Di Cesnola found pitchers of the same characteristic type. In the Lang collection at the British Museum specimens may be seen. Analogous examples have also been found at Rhodes, and under the lava of Santorini, in the Greek Archipelago, as well as in Etruria. The fiery deluge which submerged the Santorini pottery now in the collection of the Ecole Francaise at Athens, is supposed to date as far back as B.C. 2000. The oldest Italian pottery is that found buried under lava at Albano. This, too presents remarkable affinities to the Trojan, as Mr Newton has observed, citing examples under his charge in the British Museum.[98]

These comparisons may have been part of the interpretation or drawn from visitors' own observations. Displays that grouped pottery by shape certainly facilitated such speculation. Objects appeared as types, ready for comparison with other sites. They were also shown in large enough numbers to establish Troy as a major ancient site with an important body of material for such comparisons.

Fig. 25 Pottery from Troy, including a double jug. Heidelberg University Library, Heinrich Schliemann, *Atlas Trojanischer Alterthümer*, Tafel 104 – CC-BY-SA 3.

The double jug also attracted interest from people wondering how it was used. One review speculates it was an oil and vinegar dispenser 'admirably adapted for administering the mixture of oil and vinegar, which is still considered to be the proper dressing for wild asparagus, as to suggest the idea that such was the object of the double flasks of Hissarlik'.[99] Others saw it as a product of Trojan table manners.[100] Schliemann does not seem to have been too concerned with purpose, despite sorting things by type, leaving space for speculation among visitors.

Case 14 was one of the few cases dedicated to a single period of Troy's history, rather than a type of material. Like the cases about Schliemann's 'Homeric Ilium' earlier in the exhibition, this display was also interested in the earliest levels of the city:

> Case 14 is exclusively appropriated to 'Pottery from the First City,' as the Homeric archaeologist prefers to style it. This is all hand-made. It includes fine, highly polished black vases, each with a pair of vertical holes for suspension; large and small bowls with horizontal tubes for the same purpose beautifully polished vessels with incised patterns; lastly what most charms and piques the connoisseurs, a glazed, one-handled goblet, resembling those found at Mycenae, and reminding one of Rhodian ware. Experts think it must have been plunged into a slip and then fired.[101]

The item singled out here is a red clay cup (Fig. 26, left side of middle shelf) which Schliemann described as 'more or less exactly the form of all the goblets of terracotta found by me at Mycenae and Tiryns'.[102] The label may have made this comparison, since both reports that mention this cup point out its similarities with cups found at Mycenae: 'a glazed red goblet with one handle, closely resembling the Mycenaean goblets. All these remains afford evidence of a very early, but not the rudest stage of civilization. They are indeed the relics of the city, which, according to the tradition preserved by Homer, underwent destruction at the hands of Herakles himself'.[103] Schliemann identified the first Troy with a mythic age, with walls built by Poseidon and later destroyed by Herakles.[104] Visitors considered pottery from this period particularly beautiful and it came to be used both as evidence of the visual appeal of so-called 'primitive' material (Chapter 6) and for arguing that the history of Troy was a slow process of aesthetic and cultural decline (Chapter 10).

The next few cases seem to have been roughly arranged by type, with pots from all of the prehistoric layers of the site apart from the first city. Schliemann arranged all of the pots he thought were designed to be hung up in case 15: 'In case 15 have been collected from all strata, save Wooden Troy, vessels for suspension, the Trojan vessels being so often round at the bottom, like soda water bottles or even pointed, as to need hanging up. It comprises other antiques also from the same depths.'[105] Hanging vessels were seen as distinctively Trojan. They were one of several types of object found at Troy which seemed impractical by design. As such, they demanded an explanation, often with reference to the social dimensions of drinking (the need to drain a cup or pass it on, rather than putting it down).[106] The unusual shapes of many of the objects found at Troy, along with Schliemann's groupings by object type seem to have encouraged such reflections on what these objects said about Trojan drinking practice:

Fig. 26 Pottery from Troy, including a one-handled goblet (centre left) like ones found at Mycenae and Tiryns. Heidelberg University Library, Heinrich Schliemann, *Atlas Trojanischer Alterthümer*, Tafel 105 – CC-BY-SA 3.

According to the evidence supplied at South Kensington the ancient Trojans were a convivial race who cared not to drink unless in company, but yet decent – not to say punctilious – in their manners. A double necked as well as double handled vase suggests that a gentleman was expected to keep on his own side of the decanter. That he was expected to keep to his own side of the tankard when liberal compotation was indulged in is proved by the number of upright, almost cylindrical cups, furnished with two or three handles like the 'tygs' and like them furnished with a separate lip or mouthpiece for each person.[107]

The next case also seems to have contained a variety of different types, although with less clear links between them. 'Case 16 contains vases, pitchers, cups, lipped pots, ewers, and tall jugs found at various depths from 6ft to 32ft. below the turf. There are also vessels like small paint pots, others resembling a publican's spirit measure, earthenware bottles, and a good many mugs.'[108]

Case 17 seems to have had some more unusual types in it, including Schliemann's *depas amphikypellon* shape, and the pots shaped like animals.

> No. 17 is filled with pottery generically like, but with specific differences, and reinforced by new types. One variety is a sort of two-headed beakers, which Dr. Schliemann thinks illustrates Homer's δέπας ἀμφικύπελλον. Here, too, are some fine terra-cotta goblets, and some curious vases also of terra-cotta, moulded into animal shapes. Among them is a pig, curiously marked with stars, found at a depth of 13ft., on the boundary line between Wooden Troy, perhaps Cimmerian, and the city next below, which had been thought to be of Lycian origin – an opinion seemingly confirmed by the strange vessel here, which was found at a depth of 22ft., and is in the shape of a hybrid animal, which Dr. Schliemann at once identified with the Homeric Chimaera.[109]

Schliemann's 'chimaera' (Fig. 27, centre of second shelf from top), with its many, heavily reconstructed limbs did not much resemble the *Iliad*'s composite of lion, goat and snake.[110] But Schliemann was keen to link this mythical beast (if that is what it is) to Homer and broader Greek myth, implying that the Trojans shared that cultural knowledge.

The last rank of cases also grouped pottery by type. Case 19 had more miscellaneous items, with little to connect them: 'Case 19 which likewise covers all the Trojan cities but Dardania, presents for comparison in contrast with the oldest stratum plenty more vases, pitchers, plates, saucers &c.'[111] Case 18 included objects from Mycenae alongside pottery from the prehistoric levels of Troy:

> It contains many handsome jars, each with a pair of 'mighty' handles – to cite Dr. Schliemann's own term in describing them – besides pitchers and vases, with single, double, triple, and even quadruple handles, bowls, basins and the like, such as are sure to attract the enthusiastic admiration of ceramic students. Here are also enshrined the few objects, numbering no more than eight, which have found their way from Mycenae to the South Kensington collection. One is a small fragment of painted pottery, and is of some importance in its bearing on the comparative chronology of the Trojan and Mycenaean finds.[112]

Fig. 27 Pottery from Troy, including Schliemann's heavily reconstructed 'chimaera' (centre of second shelf from top). Heidelberg University Library, Heinrich Schliemann, *Atlas Trojanischer Alterthümer*, Tafel 61 – CC-BY-SA 3.

Schliemann's excavation agreement with Greece prevented him from taking most of his finds from Mycenae out of the country. These few objects were transported by special agreement with the Greek government and were probably the most interesting examples Schliemann was trusted to remove.[113] He went to this trouble to demonstrate links between the two sites as proof that they were the ones described by Homer. A review in the *Manchester Courier and Lancashire General Advertiser* gave more details about the Mycenaean material in these cases:

Added to the Trojan collection are a few objects brought by Dr Schliemann from the site of the Heraeon, or Temple of Juno, near Mycenae. They comprise a lentoid porphyry gem, on which two phoenician gods are represented, the one holding thunderbolts in his hand, and the other, apparently lances. There is also a fragment or two of painted pottery, and a finely executed figure of Juno under one of her mythological forms.[114]

This indicates that at least some of the Mycenaean material was not from the site of Mycenae, but the Argive Heraion, which Schliemann briefly excavated in 1874.[115] Schliemann's excavations at this temple of Hera, just outside Mycenae, allowed him to identify a particular form of 'idol' (a type known today as a psi figurine) as Hera.[116] This is the 'mythological form' of Juno mentioned in that *Manchester Courier* piece. Schliemann interpreted one of her epithets as cow-faced to mirror his owl-headed Athena: 'Dr Schliemann, in 1872, anticipated the subsequent discovery of the image of the βοῶπις Ἥρη upon idols, cups or vases at Mycenae ... and a few specimens from that place, exhibiting the cow's head and horns, one being beautifully engraved as a seal on a piece of agate, are added to the Trojan collection at South Kensington.'[117] The idea of religious imagery with animal forms was powerful enough to become a self-fulfilling prophecy. This was an opportunity to present Troy as part of a broader ancient religion and underline the connection Schliemann wanted to make to the language of Homer.

The next case grouped pots that were considered similar to those found in Italy: 'No. 20 gathers within itself all the pottery like the most ancient Etruscan from all strata save the Dardanian, no such analogies having been detected there'.[118] Schliemann was interested in similarities between the pottery from Troy and the distinctive black pottery known as Bucchero, found in the Etruscan cemeteries of Italy.[119] He thought (following Herodotus) that the major Etruscan sites had been founded by Lydians from Asia Minor, who he also identified as occupants of his fifth city at Troy.[120] This body of material may have been meant to represent this later phase of the city. Of course, the idea of a set of colonies in Italy, founded by people from Asia Minor and directly connected with Troy had another resonance. Virgil's *Aeneid* told the story of a group of refugees from the Trojan War, who went on to found Rome. This case (given its central position in the last rank of cases) may also have been meant to imply a role for Schliemann's Troy in the foundation of Rome. If so, the implication was not picked up by Schliemann's peers.

Case 21 contained decorated pottery from a range of levels. Again, the form of the pottery was used to unite material from different phases of the site. This time, the decoration was particularly important:

we find in No. 21 perforated and incised ware from various depths between 9ft. and 45ft. The curious perforated vessels must have been used for burning incense or for carrying fire in general. The Trojan pottery ornamented with incised patterns filled in with white clay has been boldly compared with the costly faience d'Oiron, or Henri Deux ware, and the analogy is undoubtedly strong. The designs must have been damascened before the vessels were fired.[121]

The comparison here with 'Henri Deux ware' refers to a rare and highly-admired kind of pottery made in France in the sixteenth century.[122] This case on the edge of Schliemann's exhibition would have been right next to the more modern pottery, which may have prompted this comparison. Certainly, Schliemann's decision to put some of his more aesthetically pleasing pots on the edge of the exhibition must have been meant to make the whole appear attractive.

Conclusion

The Trojan exhibition at South Kensington made some unusual display decisions. It chose not to order its contents chronologically, instead, mostly grouping objects by type. It (partly out of necessity) strongly featured less charismatic objects, including masses of pottery. It took care to relate the objects back to the site where they were found as well as to Schliemann's other discoveries and theories. In doing so, it built a series of dynamic comparisons that encouraged visitors to think about how the objects on display related to each other, as well as to the landscape and the wider world. The result was an exhibition that made a clear case for Schliemann's theories about Troy. It began with the 'owl-headed' vases that Schliemann linked to his theories of early religion, then guided people past the tools that Schliemann used to argue against the three-age system and carefully sorted spindle whorls that fascinated theorists of symbols. Next, people arrived at the most anticipated material: the treasure, which was displayed as a single, remarkable archaeological find, with Homeric names on the labels. Finally, the exhibition offered an exhaustive exploration of the kinds of pottery found at the site of Troy. On its edges were larger objects and the sort of later material that was much more valued by museums in London at the time (such as the metope) but these were treated more as an afterthought than a climax.

Its approach was not uniform throughout. While the overall guiding idea of the arrangement was to group like with like, individual cases might be read less as a typology and more as representing particular period of the site or (as is the case with the treasure) a single archaeological assemblage. The exhibition may have felt chaotic and overwhelming in places, but its emphasis on Schliemann's theories set the terms for the debate over Troy. While Schliemann had carefully controlled how these objects were seen, he could not control how they would be reimagined.

Part Three

Schliemania?

Caroline Moorehead coined the term 'Schliemania' to capture the moment in the 1870s and 1880s when enthusiasm for Schliemann's discoveries at Troy and Mycenae was at its peak.¹ As well playing on Schliemann's name (and thus centring the excavator, not the sites), the term evokes one of the other great moments of popular engagement with archaeology: Egyptomania. This movement began in the early nineteenth century with Napoleon's conquest of Egypt and the decipherment of hieroglyphics, and had a number of revivals in later decades. The question mark in this part title is not meant to throw any doubt on Schliemann's popularity and influence. We have already seen how eagerly the press covered Schliemann's discoveries and activities and how Londoners visited the first Trojan exhibition in huge numbers. However, Egyptomania was more than just a passing fascination with ancient Egypt; it had a profound impact on visual and popular culture and cemented a clear set of images and ideas that we associate with ancient Egypt to this day. Such movements create a version (or versions) of the past that can be useful in the present.² This chapter explores some examples of visual, imaginative and political engagement with Troy after the Trojan exhibition to consider the cultural impact of enthusiasm for Schliemann's discoveries and ask how Troy was used by the Victorian public.

While the Trojan exhibition aimed to convince people of Schliemann's archaeological claims, the visiting public had their own reasons for taking an interest. Once people had seen the Trojan collection, they were free to make up their own minds about it and use it to their own ends. The novelty of the objects' appearance and the extravagant claims made about their importance raised the possibility that they might transform people's understanding of the past or their attitudes in the present. People were free to play with the motifs and ideas that they encountered.

The Trojan collection arrived at a time when the public was particularly receptive for a number of reasons. Homer occupied a particularly privileged place in elite education, but the story of Troy was also available to a broader public through the popular entertainments and mass media of late nineteenth-century culture.³ Contemporary artists were meticulously reconstructing scenes from the ancient world using the latest archaeological evidence. Meanwhile, the artists that rebelled against this obsession with archaeological accuracy also used classical elements in anachronistic assemblages that pursued art for art's sake.⁴ London had a thriving museum culture and institutions like South Kensington were explicitly intended to influence art and design.⁵ The public was also accustomed to seeing dramatic new archaeological discoveries and affordable publications like the *Illustrated London News* and the *Penny Magazine*.⁶

The Trojan exhibition was a place to meet people and be seen. Visits by royalty and other famous people were eagerly reported by the papers.[7] The illustrator E. Gertrude Thomson described arranging to meet Lewis Carroll for the first time at the Trojan exhibition and worrying that she would not be able to find him, since the room was 'fairly full of all sorts and conditions'.[8] Neither the author nor the artist recorded their opinions on the exhibition, but this shows how it was a social hub: suitable for meeting a person one wanted to impress, but accessible to (and used by) all ages and classes. The impact of the Trojan collection was not limited to the museum space. Press coverage extended its reach far beyond London: detailed reports from the exhibition appeared in British local papers and the international press. The press followed Schliemann as a celebrity and produced coverage of Troy for a range of targeted audiences (from fashionable women to phrenology enthusiasts). Writers of fiction fleshed out a character's interests and personality by mentioning them reading Schliemann or visiting the Trojan exhibition, especially when writing studious young women.[9]

The discovery of Troy revived older debates about whether it was real. Bryant Davies has explored how it extended these debates to an audience beyond the elites that started them in contexts that appealed across class boundaries, like circuses and burlesque.[10] Pearsall has explored how Tennyson's quarrel with Schliemann and Gladstone over these issues shaped his poetry, which tried to show that the literary Troy was more real than its disappointing archaeological counterpart.[11] The idea of a rediscovered, tangible Troy shaped literary modernism's attitude to the past, and Kenner has shown how it is central to the Joyce's earthy engagement with Homeric poetry.[12] Such previous work on the cultural impact of Schliemann's discoveries has focused on literary responses, so I have chosen to focus on visual and material engagements with Troy in the chapters that follow.

Chapter 5 begins by surveying uses of Schliemann's finds across nineteenth-century visual and literary culture, with a particular interest in why direct use of Schliemann's finds was so rare and how artists negotiated the distance between Schliemann's Troy and the classicizing versions that had gone before to make their own comments on the story of Troy. Chapter 6 looks at the aesthetic challenge of the objects from Troy and how it inspired artists and writers to look for value in highly stylized art that many had dismissed as 'primitive'. Chapter 7 explores the impulse to laugh at the strangeness of Schliemann's Troy and asks what jokes can tell us about archaeological reasoning in less formal contexts and how archaeology could be used to critique contemporary mores. Finally, Chapter 8 looks at why bankers and civil servants took an interest in the objects from Troy as an indicator of its systems of measurement and value and how it was used in debates about the gold standard. These case studies are diverse, ranging from cheap replicas, through stage performance and jokes to aesthetic and economic theories. They are unified by the encounter with Troy as something strange and new, which did not easily fit with past visions of the ancient world, but could open up new avenues of exploration.

5

Visualizing Troy

People had been imagining how Troy might have looked for centuries, but Schliemann's Trojan exhibition was the first opportunity (at least according to Schliemann) for the public to see real objects from the city. This had the potential to transform how people imagined Troy, from something broadly modelled on the classical world to a city where the tutelary goddess had an owl's head and stone blades were still in use. The difficulty of reconciling the archaeological and imagined dimensions of the site was never really resolved. Even today, attempts to imagine ancient Troy tend not to limit themselves to material found at the site, and often draw on other ancient imagery to produce a coherent 'look' for Troy that evokes its archaeology without effacing more classical expectations.[1]

To understand what impact Schliemann's collection had on art and design, this chapter surveys some examples of its use from the world of manufacturing, high art and performance. It asks why such uses are relatively uncommon and what they tell us about the place of Trojan archaeology in the public imagination. I begin surveying the visual impact of the finds from Troy with replicas for use in fashion and home décor and reflect on who was using these and how. I then consider whether Troy made much impact on the archaeologically inspired art and poetry of the late nineteenth century, exploring how the two media interact and how they could push back against Schliemann's theories even as they used them. Troy was an incomplete and challenging archaeological site and I end with one of the more heated debates over what counted as accuracy in an artistic reproduction of Troy.

The Trojan exhibition took pride of place in a major institution dedicated to shaping public taste and came with a story that captured the public's imagination. Expectations were high for its cultural impact, but many who came to the exhibition were disappointed or underwhelmed.[2] Reviewers observed that the collection would be interesting to art students, but often left it unclear how these students might use the objects: whether to deepen their understanding of the history of art, as stage dressing in history paintings or as models for emulation in their own right.³ Observations about the exhibition's potential influence were particularly interested in the jewellery, which was widely seen as the highlight of the exhibition. Reviewers observed how modern the jewellery seemed, whether in terms of workmanship or style.⁴ Writers thought that the jewellery would be particularly interesting to female visitors and might even shape modern fashions.⁵ Not all women were impressed:

> At the private view yesterday the golden diadems, earrings, and necklaces were acutely scanned by the fairer portion of the visitors, who failed to perceive in them any models worthy of adoption. In truth, the necklaces of the Andromache period are rather remarkable for monotony than richness of decoration and the bracelets are more like the bangles, just now in favour, than the heavy armlets of other periods.⁶

This interest in the jewellery from Troy reflected a wider fashion for wearing ancient jewellery and replicas. A prominent replica jewellery maker, Carlo Giuliano, closely examined the finds from Troy, but his only 'Trojan' creation was a fantasy necklace that appeared in Sir Edward Poynter's painting *Helen*.⁷ There may have been some influence on fashion. An article in *Harper's Bazaar* (popular enough to be reprinted in *Potter's American Monthly*) showcasing the 'aesthetic' mode of dress included reproductions of the jewellery from Troy.⁸ This featured a 'Neo-Greek costume' (Fig. 28, centre) which attempted to give a more wearable (at least for fashionable nineteenth-century women) version of Greek costume. This appeared alongside a supposedly more authentic 'Ancient Greek' costume (Fig. 28, left):

> The Neo-Greek costume, one of the latest aesthetic ideas, combines the classic characteristics with the requirements of modern fashion. It is composed of pale-blue cashmere, draped over a train of white cashmere, and trimmed with gold embroidery done in Greek key pattern ... Etruscan gold necklace and bracelet, reproductions of the gold ornaments excavated by Professor Schliemann should be worn with this costume.⁹

While Schliemann's finds were described as an important accessory to this outfit, the illustration shows nothing distinctively Trojan. There is nothing as bold as the headdress famously worn by Sophia Schliemann (Fig. 10, in Chapter 3), and only bangle-like bracelets give any hint of connection with Troy.¹⁰

For people who wanted their own little piece of the Trojan treasure, electrotype replicas of vessels from Troy were displayed at the 1887 Royal Jubilee Exhibition in Manchester. These were probably created as expensive curios (some of the items on display were £1,500 each) or as a demonstration of the company's

Fig. 28 Fashion plate recommending wearing replicas of Schliemann's finds ('Neo-Greek costume', centre). 'Aesthetic, Bridal, and Reception Toilettes', *Harper's Bazaar*, 19 November 1881.

ability to reproduce such items, rather than as consumer goods in their own right. Accurately reproducing rare ancient treasures was a way to demonstrate new technologies and produce experiences of the past that were distinctly modern.[11]

Another company that tried to bring versions of objects from Troy to people through modern manufacturing techniques was Hews and Co. of Cambridge, Massachusetts. This pottery manufacturer usually specialized in flower pots. They produced a special range of their 'Albert Ware' (an unglazed biscuit ware) copied from photographs of the pottery from Troy.[12] The illustrated catalogue of this collection boasted twenty designs which were 'exact copies from Dr Schliemann's excavations on the supposed site of ancient Troy ... correct in shape and size'.[13] Among their range of Greek-inspired vases and modern candlesticks and cigar holders appeared some of the most outlandish and distinctive vase types found by Schliemann, including several different owl-faced vases, and versions of cups and jars from the treasure (Fig. 29). Pots were priced between 75 cents and three dollars. It is unclear how much of this range was sold and I have not been able to track down any extant examples, but there is clear evidence of excitement about replicas of the Trojan pots in the nineteenth century. For example, a New Zealand newspaper reported:

> Some months ago, mention was made in these columns of an excellent little collection of Art Pottery which had been obtained from England by Mr Alfred Simpson bookseller, High street. The experimental importation was a decided success. Mr Simpson has to be credited with having materially aided in educating the public taste in this community and also with having introduced a new and refining occupation for ladies that of painting on terra cotta ... One of the groups in the collection consists of reproductions of the celebrated Trojan forms discovered by Professor Schliemann, the decorative details being perfect in their finish.[14]

Although imported by a bookseller, who was presumably selling them, the newspaper describes the display of replicas as if it were a public service. These replicas could offer a sense of the ancient vessels to people who would have no chance to see the originals, but they also (since the Trojan pottery was not painted) offered a perfect canvas for ladies to participate in the fashionable hobby of pottery painting. The idea of applying modern decoration to replicas that boasted of their authenticity does not seem to have troubled people.

While ancient objects were an important source of inspiration for fashion, home décor and amateur craft, there was also no shortage of art on ancient

Fig. 29 Trojan pots (nos 109–114) in the Hews and Co. catalogue [c. 1877]. Courtesy, the Winterthur Library: Printed Book and Periodical Collection.

themes being produced in the late nineteenth century.[15] Trojan War scenes were fairly common, both before and after Schliemann's announcement about discovering the site. The 1860s had been a particularly fruitful time for images of Helen of Troy, with versions by Leighton, Sandys and Rossetti, each with their own version of the character, with different things to say about womanhood and idealized beauty.[16] Artists still largely stuck to classical objects and dress when depicting Troy. For example, Lord Leighton's 1888 painting *Captive Andromache* (Fig. 30) features classical vase types, copied or adapted from ones in the British Museum.[17] In Leighton's case, we can be certain that this was a conscious decision not to use Schliemann's antiquities, since he was working on a mural in the mezzanine of the South Court (overlooking Schliemann's collection) between 1878 and 1880 and he owned books by Schliemann.[18] The only hint of Schliemann's discoveries is in the triangle over the doorway on the left of the picture; characteristic of the architecture of Mycenae.[19]

Artistic and poetic visions of Troy were interested in the idea of the materiality of Homer's world and characters long before Schliemann's discoveries and had to negotiate the new material that Schliemann excavated. In 1869, the year Schliemann published his first book about visiting Troy, Dante Gabriel Rossetti became fascinated with a brief comment by Pliny the Elder about Helen of Troy. Pliny claimed that the Temple of Athena at Lindos owned an electrum cup that had been dedicated by Helen, and was reputed to be the same size as her breasts.[20] Rossetti tried to trace the legend back further and began work on a poem that fleshed it out.[21] *Troy Town* turns the dedication of the cup into a way to

Fig. 30 Frederic Leighton, *Captive Andromache* (1888). Wikimedia: Public domain; original uploader, Ravenous.

foreshadow the Trojan War and give Helen an active role in the desire that caused it. Helen, as the speaker of the poem, offers the cup to Venus (not Athena as in Pliny) in an eroticized prayer for a lover.[22]

After the poem was published, Rossetti began planning a painting to illustrate it (Fig. 31). In this, Helen's dedication is a double cup, perhaps influenced by reports of the finds from Troy. This painting was never completed, possibly in disillusionment with Schliemann's finds after the exhibition. Rossetti's double cup ignored Schliemann's emphasis on the role of these objects in making libations and male social drinking, instead connecting them with a sense of the doomed erotic dimensions of the Troy story which Schliemann's approach largely ignored. The idea of a feminized double cup was picked up by Francis Thompson (a religious poet who was heavily influenced by Rossetti) whose twin poems *sister songs an offering to two sisters* (1895) was written under the title of *Amphicypellon: wrought and upbrimmed for two sisters*.[23] Thompson explained the choice of name, influenced by the Trojan exhibition:

Fig. 31 Dante Gabriel Rossetti, Study for *Troy Town* (*c.* 1870). Photograph © 2019 Museum of Fine Arts, Boston.

It refers to the ἀμφικύπελλον which Hephaestus, in Homer, bears round to the gods when he acts as cup-bearer by way of joke. When Schliemann's things from Troy were first exhibited at South Kensington, I remember seeing among them a drinking-cup labelled 'Perhaps the amphicypellon of Homer.' It was a boat-shaped cup of plain gold, open at the top and with a crescentic aperture at either extremity of the rim, through which the wine could either be poured or drunk. So that you could pour from either end, and (if the cup were brimmed with wine) two people could have drunk from it at the same time, one at either extremity. In a certain sense, therefore, it was a double cup. And it had also two handles, one at either of its boat-shaped sides, so that it was a two-handled cup. You will see at once why I have applied the name to my double poem.[24]

The cup he had in mind must have been the 'sauce boat' from the treasure (Fig. 20, in Chapter 4), but Rossetti's cup also echoes through the poem. While there was good reason not to connect a poem composed as a gift for two young girls and their parents with Rossetti's poem of doomed erotic desire, there are thematic echoes. Thompson's poem kept the theme of offerings for the future of young women, here offering up his poem (named *amphicypellon*) to a 'tender lady' (the Virgin Mary) on behalf of two young girls of a family who supported him. The theme is understandably much more chaste and Christian than Helen's offering, but Thompson deliberately evokes more ancient votive practices through the Homeric reference.

While Rossetti's *Troy Town* sketches came to nothing, there are several paintings that used iconic objects from Schliemann's excavations at Troy. Herbert Gustave Schmalz (a friend of Leighton's who painted in a similar style) included the Apollo metope from Troy in *Queen Zenobia's Last Look upon Palmyra* (1888) (Fig. 32, compare Fig. 24 in Chapter 4). Zenobia leans on a wall that clearly contains it as she looks back over a city already overrun with Roman soldiers. Schmalz was active in London in the 1870s, so this is probably a result of sketches made in the Trojan exhibition.[25] However, this is not a painting of Troy. Those in the know might see the metope as a representation of the far reaches of Zenobia's empire in Anatolia and a reminder of the downfall of another great power, but it was probably used as an interchangeable piece of classical set-dressing. The main focus is on Zenobia as a powerful woman, proud even in defeat, wearing elaborate jewellery and bound in golden manacles.[26]

Of course, Troy had its own impressive jewellery to contribute to nineteenth-century art's fascination with depicting striking female characters. While Schliemann referred to the gold headdresses as 'the *parure* of Helen', and others imagined them on Andromache, the two clearest representations of a headdress

Fig. 32 Herbert Gustave Schmalz, *Queen Zenobia's Last Look upon Palmyra* (1888). Wikimedia: Google Cultural Institute.

from Troy are worn by Clytemnestra.[27] John Collier (a protégée of Lawrence Alma-Tadema) painted two images of Clytemnestra in the moments after killing her husband, Agamemnon.[28] In the first (Fig. 33), she emerges, wild-eyed from behind a curtain with an axe dripping with blood. The headdress is clearly Trojan, including the shapes Schliemann identified as Athena idols (compare Fig. 19 in Chapter 4). This might be meant to imply that she has taken Agamemnon's spoils from Troy. It visually identifies her with Mycenae's dangerous Eastern enemy, making the murder into revenge for the fall of Troy, and perhaps foreshadowing her own murder as another consequence of the city's fall.

The headdress is also part of a broader attempt to imagine the Greek world before the classical period. The chevron and spiral pattern on the column on the left side of the painting are meant to evoke the columns from the Treasury of Atreus, parts of which were in the British Museum at this time.[29] The patterns on the axe are copied from a stone cylinder found at Troy.[30] We can see how slim the pickings were for imagining Mycenaean life by comparing this painting with a second Clytemnestra by Collier, painted about 1914. In this, Clytemnestra's axe has been replaced by a Mycenaean dagger like the one found in shaft grave IV at Mycenae, which was available as an electrotype replica in the early twentieth

Fig. 33 John Collier, *Clytemnestra* (1882). Wikimedia: Stephencdickson – CC-BY-SA 4.0.

century.³¹ Her dress has also been radically changed: she now wears a long skirt and is naked above the waist, in a reference to the Minoan art uncovered by Arthur Evans's excavations on Crete at the start of the twentieth century. In the three decades between the two paintings, understanding of Aegean prehistory vastly expanded because of archaeological discoveries and better access to information about them. The headdress was the one constant, continuing to mark Clytemnestra's connection with Troy.

The use of dramatic golden headdresses to identify a mythological woman as suspiciously Eastern and potentially murderous predates the discovery of the

Fig. 34 Print of John Collier's *Clytemnestra* (c. 1914). Flickr: pixelsniper – CC-BY-2.0.

Trojan treasure. Frederick Sandys's painting of Medea (painted at some time between 1866 and 1868) (Fig. 35) wears a very similar headdress alongside a range of Egyptian and Asian motifs that mark Medea and her magic as foreign.[32] Gold-fringed headdresses were often represented in orientalist paintings, and several people who saw the Trojan treasure compared the headdresses to ones worn in Egypt and India.[33] The difference and opulence of Troy made it perfect for evoking something strange at the edge of classical culture. As such, it may have been easier to depict the Trojan treasure on Clytemnestra than on actual Trojan women, who were more usually seen as doomed than dangerous.

These were highly theatrical images. They represented Greek plays and, like those plays, kept the violence just out of sight. These images are influenced by a fashion for performing Greek plays with accurate props and costume.[34] Two

Fig. 35 Frederick Sandys, *Medea* (painted between 1866 and 1868). Reproduced by kind permission of Birmingham Museum & Art Gallery.

years after the Trojan exhibition closed, and just down the road, Troy was brought back to life for two nights in *The Tale of Troy*. This was a series of scenes from the *Iliad* and the *Odyssey*, performed by a large cast in both ancient Greek and English. It was an amateur production but has attracted a lot of interest because of the fame and expertise of the people involved. Actors included classicists Eugenie Sellers and Jane Harrison (discussed further in Chapter 12) and the production was designed by a number of well-known artists, including Leighton, Edward Poynter and G.F. Watts.[35] Charles Newton (curator of antiquities at the British Museum and lukewarm Schliemann supporter) was in charge of archaeological accuracy, keeping the spectacle in the realm of the plausible. The concern with accuracy was typical of the fashion for archaeologically influenced plays, but it also presented problems.[36] Newton's audience now knew Troy through Schliemann's collection, but those discoveries did not provide enough information to dress the actors and furnish the sets, let alone achieve the ideal of a complete and beautiful past. As in Collier's first Clytemnestra painting, the solution was to turn back to the more familiar classical look:

> Taking first the tableaux, we may at once confess that had we approached them desiring to pick holes, our task would have been difficult, all of them were so well fenced about with care and artistic excellence. Admirable as they were, it must, however, be clearly understood that they did not exhibit any special archaeological endeavour to put before us the people or things Homer describes. Professor Newton tells us that he was careful at the very beginning to impress on every one engaged the desirability of keeping to one style of Greek Art, that, namely, which prevailed in the time of Pericles, B.C. 469–429 of which we possess so much evidence in the marbles and vases of the British Museum. This is the date by which the production must be measured.[37]

Despite Newton's appeal for coherence, the design was not as tightly focused on fifth-century BCE Athens as the above suggests. Poynter gave some of the locations visited by Odysseus in the latter half of the performance a 'semi-Oriental' look, inspired by Phrygian and Etruscan archaeology.[38] Schliemann's discoveries also appeared in places. The gateway of Troy in the first scene was copied from the lion gate at Mycenae and the scenery was specifically modelled on the plain of Troy as seen from Hisarlık. This reflected agreement with Schliemann's argument that this was Troy, and perhaps direct copying of Schliemann's photographs from *Atlas*.[39] Another exception was probably made so that Helen could wear a Trojan headdress. The illustrated book (Fig. 36) that was made of the play text and music was described by R.C. Jebb (who saw the performance) as a 'free reproduction' of the original tableaux. The image of

Aphrodite showing Helen to Paris depicts her in a fringed headdress like the ones found at Troy.[40]

The Tale of Troy was an opportunity to debate how Troy should look in the light of contemporary archaeological knowledge, and many reviewers were keen to share their thoughts. Andrew Lang (a classicist, anthropologist and writer who had recently published a poem on Helen of Troy) thought that more accurate costumes for the Trojans could have been derived from Phoenician and Assyrian art, with only Priam's costume being 'sufficiently unconventional'.[41] The *Saturday Review* article agreed that Priam should look Assyrian, but said that Priam's costume was 'difficult to defend' on the grounds that it did not closely enough resemble the costumes known from Assyrian art.[42]

It was clear that a perfectly period-accurate representation would be impossible, but the *Saturday Review* noted that most people were satisfied and mocked those who nit-picked an amateur production: 'except one austere critic, who objects to "pasteboard pillars" and "property spears." As it was impossible to obtain the actual Pelian spear, and as no one but Achilles, according to Homer could have wielded that weapon, while marble palaces are not easily erected on the private or public stage, most persons were content with the ordinary makeshifts of the theatre'.[43] Despite this, the same review went on to complain about the statue of Athena looking wrong: 'A better xoanon might easily have been contrived for it is improbable that the Trojans worshipped an object like a "dummy" in a milliner's shop. Of course the goddess was presumed to be one of the very ancient wooden images, but on the very important point the stage arrangements were not absolutely adequate.'

Xoana are the simple wooden statues mentioned in ancient Greek texts, which were important in debates about the origins of Greek art at this time, but none of them had been discovered.[44] This critic demanded a more plausible version of a statue type that only existed in texts and the imagination. Despite being couched in archaeological language, this quibble reveals a desire for a beautiful vision of the past. Beauty could easily conflict with archaeological accuracy, especially where ideas of the primitive were at stake. The sense that the two factors were intertwined but not necessarily inseparable runs throughout coverage of *Tale of Troy*: 'each scene in itself was a work of art, and the accessories were not only, as far as might be, archaeologically accurate, but beautiful also'.[45]

There was a wider debate about what archaeological accuracy might mean in a stage production in the 1880s, especially over whether obsessive attention to detail was beside the point in a work of art.[46] Schliemann's discoveries were widely seen as ugly and discordant with the ideals of classical antiquity, and so

Fig. 36 The first tableau from *The Tale of Troy*. George C. Warr and Walter Crane, *Echoes of Hellas: The Tale of Troy and the Story of Orestes from Homer and Aeschylus with Introductory Essay and Sonnets by George C. Warr* (London: Marcus Ward and Co., 1887). Photograph A. Baker, by kind permission of Cambridge University Library.

were particularly difficult to fit into the balance of art and archaeology, which Oscar Wilde thought could 'combine in one exquisite presentation the illusion of actual life with the wonder of the unreal world'.[47] The need to present a beautiful and consistent version of the past made Schliemann's finds doubly challenging. There was not enough in the material culture of Troy as represented in Schliemann's collection to piece together a fully imagined style for Troy that was distinct from ancient Greece. It was not just that the vision of the past was incomplete, but also that it might seem uglier than its classical equivalent. This explains why uses of Troy were either happily anachronistic (like the reproductions of Trojan pottery, painted by Victorian ladies to their own tastes) or use the strangeness of Troy to play up the dangerous and exotic characters they portray. However, there were some attempts by artists and writers to approach the objects from Troy on their own aesthetic terms, which I explore in the next chapter.

6

The Appeal of the Primitive

One of the artists who visited and sketched at the Trojan exhibition was William Bell Scott, a painter and poet who was closely associated with the Pre-Raphaelite Brotherhood.[1] However, he was not working on studies for his next painting. Instead, he said he went looking for what Schliemann had described as 'the great-great grandmother of the art of the Parthenon'.[2] His sketches and notes explore these objects as a potential source of Western art that might explain how art comes to be (Fig. 37).

In a letter to the *Athenaeum* Scott argued against Schliemann's identification of the face pots as owl-headed. In doing so, he replaced Schliemann's idiosyncratic reading of early Greek religion with a more general theory of the development of art:

> Some of them have ears, the later ones mouths and the eyes quite differently represented. It is this difference, showing the progressive steps of imitative art, that drew my attention to them. If we observe a child's earliest attempts at drawing or modelling, the eyes are represented not as a feature but as an organ, the iris and pupil are expressed as a circle. The child and the savage feel alike in this, and art in this follows nature herself, the earliest true eye being bare as in the fish. The second stage of delineation is to express the eye as a feature; the appearance becomes the important thing, the lids are mainly represented, and a long slit is the aspect of the organ. Some of the heads on these vessels have the eyes so modelled. These are the product of a later period, a period of years or centuries.[3]

For Scott, the material from Troy demonstrated a universal process of cultural development. He looked at ancient people in the light of two contemporary groups of people (children and 'savages') who were not seen as fully developed. In doing so, he imagined that individuals and culture could evolve just like physical aspects of biology, hence a representation of an eye might evolve through gradual variation and selection in the same way the organ itself had.

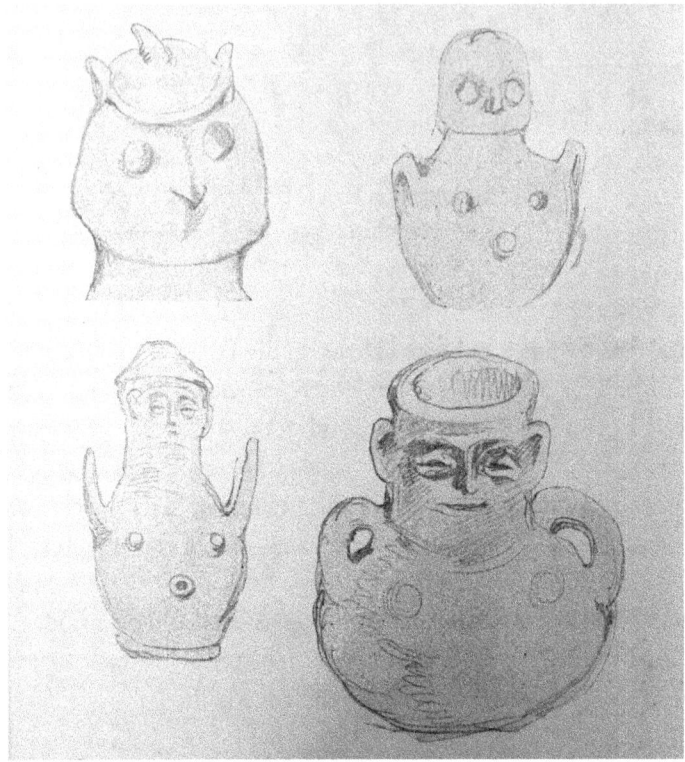

Fig. 37 William Bell Scott's sketches made at the Trojan exhibition, *Autobiographical Notes of the Life of William Bell Scott: and Notices of His Artistic and Poetic Circle of Friends, 1830–1882*, Vol. 2, edited by William Minto (London: James R. Osgood, McIlvaine & Co., 1892), 289. Photograph A. Baker, by kind permission of Newcastle Lit & Phil.

This was the height of the Darwinian controversy: *The Descent of Man* had been published in 1871 and people were still coming to terms with what it might mean that humans had evolved like other creatures. Darwinian theories were being applied to all aspects of human culture. These ideas were used to structure hierarchies of human culture in which some were deemed more advanced than others. Those at the bottom of the hierarchy were described as 'primitive', whether they had lived millennia ago or were modern people.[4]

Scott's sketches show the four phases he identified, in which the human features of the pots became increasingly naturalistic (reading from left to right and top to bottom) in an evolutionary progression. Ideas of progress in art history were nothing new. Johann Joachim Winckelmann's *History of the Art of Antiquity* (1764) was a foundational study of Greek art that traced a development in its style from archaic crudeness through austere simplicity, to beauty and then decline.[5] In the nineteenth century, most accounts of ancient art were still following this pattern and it was widely used to structure museum displays that represented the history of art as a teleological progress towards the Parthenon. The language of evolutionary biology was beginning to be overlaid onto this historical approach, imagining art as changing by gradual process of variation and selection.[6]

Schliemann's collection offered a chance to look for connections between the two ends of this imagined process. In seeing the potters of Troy as ancestors of the art of classical Greece, Scott and his contemporaries made their creations into a missing link between the 'primitive' and the classical and an insight into the early history of European culture.[7] In Scott's sketches, the vases from Troy became more than just examples of art in a particular place and time. They were used as evidence of a universal process of development. Scott thought this process had taken place in the life of every artist, culminating in their mature work. Thinking about and reproducing the pots from Troy was a way to consider his own place in art history. This kind of engagement with very early art also placed contemporary artists on a continuum that included simple craftsmen and also (in however patronizing a manner) children and non-European peoples. The creativity and development Scott saw in Troy could only make sense if these items contained artistic merit. Sketching in the exhibition allowed him to search for this merit by recreating it and placing it within his own understanding of the history of art.

Approaches like this, while superficially dismissive, raised important questions about what to make of Troy. We have seen how the exhibition foregrounded pottery that strongly contrasted with people's expectations for the appearance of Troy (Chapter 4). This prominence was challenging. As one reviewer wrote: 'Were there such a term as the "clay age" in use among archaeologists, one would say that the majority of the things belonged to it.'[8] The strangeness that made these objects difficult to deploy as props in classically influenced art (Chapter 5) made them useful for challenging contemporary taste, inviting artists and theorists to rethink their relationship with aspects of the past that were generally dismissed. The idea of the 'primitive' is a product of colonialism, rather than any inherent property of a work of art or the culture that produced it.[9] As Scott's description makes clear, it is bound up in ideas about evolutionary development in which art evolves towards realism, which disregard the culturally specific motivations for artistic style. While we will look at the ways Troy was assigned to a distant time and associated with racial discourses in Chapters 10 and 11, here I want to get at how the idea of 'primitive' art gave Troy a distinctive appeal as a way of thinking through the relationship between ancient and modern, self and other. I will show how this gave people an alibi for admiring something that contemporary hierarchies of culture thought inherently ugly.

The South Kensington Museum's aim to train artists and improve public taste made it inevitable that the Trojan collection would be evaluated in aesthetic terms.[10] The Trojan collection was displayed next to objects that were held up as examples of good design and craftsmanship.[11] Juxtaposing the plain pottery turned up by archaeological excavation with modern decorative objects allowed for a range of responses that fed on the aesthetic contrast.

> The pottery in particular shows its owlish features unabashed in the presence of the finer clay of Sèvres. It outfaces its highborn rivals, who, after all, cannot deny being its children, although in the hundredth generation the family likeness is not seen at a glance. The spell, however, of a measurably greater age works. The public feels its power, follows the lead of the best judges in such matters, gives the cold shoulder for the nonce to the daintiest faience in the world, and gravitates towards the quaint mugs, jugs, toys, pots, pans, pipkins, pitchers, often coarse-looking enough, but seldom without a certain homely grace, which have been dredged up from the depth of the hill *ubi Troia fuit*.[12]

By stressing the exhibition's appeal to both the public and the 'best judges', this report emphasized the pairing of taste and popularity that was at the heart of South Kensington's work. It also set up a direct contrast with the highly-prized Sèvres porcelain on display nearby. But if the Trojan pottery was not as 'dainty' or 'fine' as the Sèvres, what made it more appealing? As in Scott's approach, the ancestral relationship to other works of art is seen as the root of Troy's appeal. The sense of inheritance seemed to make this strange, ancient pottery more relevant to the present than its later successors.

While the description of a 'measurably greater age' probably refers to the idea of a 'heroic age' it may also have an aesthetic dimension. There was a tradition of valuing simple decoration on pottery as a sign of high quality, which grew out of eighteenth-century taste for porcelain, and these factors fed into both the design of Sèvres and the interest in Greek vases.[13] Excessive decoration and forms that conflict with or disguise function were core 'false principles' that the earliest phases of the South Kensington Museum worked to discourage.[14] In this system, excessively ornate pattern was seen as a symptom of badly designed, mass-produced goods that preyed on the uneducated tastes of the British public. Much contemporary discourse on art believed it could be an antidote to the ugliness of industrial capitalism.¹⁵ The narrative of progress and decline, with roots in Winckelmann's writings, could be used to dismiss modern mass production as decadence. In such a view, objects that were handmade and simple (even if they had a long way to go before they reached the perceived perfection of classical Greece) could be preferable to the excesses of contemporary design.

The pottery from Troy was not delicate or ornate enough to stand as a straightforward decorative model like its neighbours. Visitors could choose to dismiss it or look for other kinds of value in it. Often the word that people settled on for that appeal was 'grace'.¹⁶ According to a reviewer in *The Art Journal*, this was something that could be perceived in the design of the pots, regardless of their execution:

> But in the underlying, or first city, have been found samples of pottery which (although of great rudeness as regards the manipulation of the potter, or the constructive or industrial part of the work,) [sic] display a classic grace in the forms of some of the vessels, and in their bold decoration, which produces a very rich effect by very simple touches, and are truly Greek in taste. There is a direct filiation in Art between these rude pots, many, if not all, of which were made by hand, and the finest type of the purest period of the ceramic art in Greece.¹⁷

The pots from Troy seemed to embody a contradiction between their workmanship and their design. The reviewer goes on to describe them as 'ugly ochreous pots' but sees the potential for beauty within them. To manage this contradiction, this approach distinguishes between skill (which it does not see in these pots) and taste (something internal to the maker that can be perceived despite their failings). The question of how to deal with objects that were examples of good design, but poorly executed (or the reverse) had proved controversial in the early days of the South Kensington Museum, when models of good and poor taste were being acquired as teaching aids.¹⁸ Believing that there is some trace of the Greek culture visible even in its earliest beginnings allowed viewers to justify appreciating very unclassical art while maintaining the distinction between their own ancestors and modern others who were described as 'primitive'.

The review in *The Art Journal* was one of the most detailed analyses of the collection as art objects and described Schliemann's discoveries as a 'canon of primary importance in the history of Art'. The emphasis was on Troy as an example of the early stages of art that could show surprising things about how it had developed: 'the first and most unexpected light which has been thrown on Art history by these objects is to this effect. The art of the potter was in its cradle at a time when the art of the goldsmith had attained an excellence which might put to shame not a few of the workmen of the present day'.[19] This describes an apparent mismatch between the aesthetic quality of pottery and jewellery made at Troy. The pottery is described as 'industrial art' in contrast to the 'fine art' of the goldwork, implying a more functional purpose, and lower-class producers and consumers. This idea that taste might differ between classes reflected anxieties about contemporary British industrial production which drove much of the early public work of the South Kensington Museum.

The best known attempt to tease the beauty from the ugliness at Troy and to find a way to reconcile both with Homer was an essay by Walter Pater (a writer, academic and proponent of the aesthetic movement) on 'The Heroic Age in Greek Art'.[20] Pater argued for the value of early Greek art (anything before 776 BCE), pushing back against the narrative of rise and decline that had dominated histories of Greek art since their origin in Winckelmann.[21] Pater's main source for understanding this period (given the lack of known archaeological evidence) was Homer and the resulting model of early art echoed the epics' emphasis on the quality of materials and craftsmanship. The essay was first published while Schliemann's finds were still on display at South Kensington and it is likely that Pater had seen them. However, his engagement with the Trojan collection remains imaginative – while many of the objects had little appeal to Pater in their own right, he saw them as fragments that attest to the art of a lost time:

> To this view of the heroic age of Greek art as being, so to speak, an age of real gold, an age delighting itself in precious material and exquisite handiwork in all tectonic crafts, the recent extraordinary discoveries at Troy and Mycenae are, on any plausible theory of their date and origin, a witness. The aesthetic critic needs always to be on his guard against the confusion of mere curiosity or antiquity with beauty in art.[22]

With this, Pater dismissed the more challenging objects like the owl-headed vases, and refocused on the objects in the collection which he thought showed broader principles of the earliest Greek art. For Pater, the object most emblematic of this heroic age was the golden cup from Priam's treasure (Fig. 20 in Chapter 4):

> Among the objects discovered at Troy – mere curiosities, some of them, however interesting and instructive – the so-called royal cup of Priam, in solid gold, two-handled and double-lipped, (the smaller lip designed for the host and his libation, the larger for the guest,) [sic] has, in the very simplicity of its design, the grace of the economy with which it exactly fulfils its purpose, a positive beauty, an absolute value for the aesthetic sense, while strange and new enough, if it really settles at last a much-debated expression of Homer.[23]

Pater was not alone in picking out this cup for its combination of design, value and Homeric resonance (as we have seen in Chapter 5). He thought the cup was perfectly designed for its Homeric function and invites his audience to re-evaluate their sense of beauty in Greek art and find it in simple, useable objects. In doing so, he drew on wider movements in Victorian Britain, such as William Morris's valuing of craftsmanship and the Pre-Raphaelite movement to find fresh beauty in early Renaissance art that had been dismissed by past critics.[24] The idea of beauty in simplicity and fitness for purpose also fits with the value placed on the simplicity of Homer's language in the nineteenth century.[25] Just as Homeric heroes express themselves with clarity and without excess, Homeric art fulfils its function without being ornate. Simplicity would become a staple of descriptions of ancient art and of critical language used to evaluate modern art.[26] For Pater, this simplicity was explicitly un-barbaric:

> Use and beauty are still undivided; all that men's hands are set to make has still a fascination alike for workmen and spectators. For such dainty splendour Troy, indeed, is especially conspicuous ... It is no barbaric world that we see, but the sort of world, we may think, that would have charmed also our comparatively jaded sensibilities, with just that quaint simplicity which we too enjoy in its productions.[27]

Pater's essay transforms the 'homely grace' described (but not explained) by other visitors to the exhibition into a harmony of form and function produced by a simpler world. Pater's intervention went further than the reviews that assessed whether the objects were attractive or not. Although the language of simplicity was similar, it formed part of a coherent theory of Greek art and a model of an ancient world as lived in by real people. However, not everyone was convinced by this approach. Although Pater was far from alone in his ability to see both 'curiosity' and 'beauty' in objects from Troy, this idea still attracted scorn from a review in *The Academy*: 'It is all very well to talk about the aesthetic critic and his way of looking at things; but if that individuality can really find beauty in the antiquities from Mycenae he must be surprisingly gifted.'[28] This critic was deeply dismissive of Schliemann's discoveries, implying that Pater has been taken in by the Homeric rhetoric and had not examined the objects for himself. This was an easy way to align Pater and the methods of the aesthetic movement with Schliemann's irrational tendencies. However, there is also some truth in the idea that it took skill to find the value in these objects. Pater had to work to appreciate the objects from Troy, ignoring the 'curiosities' and imagining the best objects as part of a broader world of craftsmanship.

For some visitors to the exhibition, the 'curiosities' were the best part. The *North Otago Times* described the first vase in the exhibition as:

> the most important vase in the large collection of similar vessels. So important, truly, did this wonderful piece of form, triumphing by its bold defiance of ordinary proportion, seem in the sight of Dr Schliemann, that he has had it placed outside his book, under the title on the back of the cover. It is a splendid vessel of terra-cotta, an indescribably brilliant brown in hue, with a throat thrice the circumference of its base, the upward spring from which is noble, and consummately adapted to the poise of a majestic top-weight. Without a single feature directly borrowed from animal life, the tutelar goddess of Troy, with owl-face, a woman's breast, a necklace, and a regal belt or scarf, stands unmistakeable and authentic in poetical force of suggestion. It may be called barbaric and grotesque; but it is withal solemnly calm and beautiful. If the prodigal ingenuity flung upon the fashioning of these many marvellous forms be indeed barbaric, it is barbarism of that pure instinctive excellence which is untainted by the vulgarity of civilisation. There is an inexhaustible study of fictile shape in the curious pottery here assembled.[29]

Where Pater tried to banish 'barbarism' from Troy, this reviewer embraced it as the source of the site's visual appeal. However, for all its glowing praise, this account speaks just as clearly of the difficulties this object presented to its audience. Phrases like 'bold defiance of ordinary proportion' and 'indescribably brilliant brown' reflect an object that is as challenging as it is stimulating.[30] We tend to associate such praise for the creativity of less naturalistic forms with twentieth-century modernism; however, this has roots in the exhibition culture of the nineteenth century and Troy is a useful site for contextualizing such engagement.[31]

While the *North Otago Times* was not the only publication that praised the freshness and creativity of the designs from Troy, it is an outlier in the responses to the Trojan exhibition.[32] Most praise of the Trojan pottery was carefully qualified or restricted to the more familiar styles. One possible explanation for the difference is the New Zealand context for which this review was written. As a settler colony, trying to build a distinctive national identity for itself, New Zealand had a somewhat different relationship to ideas of the 'primitive' in the nineteenth century from the Londoners who comprised most of the exhibition's audience. The forms of Māori art were already being appropriated by designers as national emblems, but these borrowings had more to do with nineteenth-century Romanticism (with its ideas about the 'noble savage') than with the rebellion against older forms that characterized twentieth-century primitivism.

The Trojans were an opportunity to reflect on the early culture of Europe as an analogue to indigenous peoples. The Trojans made a particularly good analogy for the idea of the Māori as a noble, defeated people, with the potential for further development that was prevalent at this time.[33] The ethnologist Edward Tregear went further to theorize that the Māori were Aryan, like the Trojans. Tregear predicted discoveries analogous to Hisarlık somewhere in the South Seas.[34] While little came of this theory, Troy was a useful site for imagining connections between Europe and other parts of the world and we return to these issues in Chapter 11.

While nineteenth-century displays of material deemed 'primitive' tended to be designed to emphasize otherness and naturalize the hierarchies of colonialism, they could also reveal the seductive qualities of the objects on display. The latter type of reading (in which the museum is a place to encounter unusual and exotic objects) tends to dominate in the public imagination, however much the grand narratives of the museum try to control it.[35] London audiences had many opportunities to encounter human variety, including displays of living peoples, and responses were diverse and not constrained by the simple binary of self and other.[36] Troy offered an encounter with a version of the 'primitive' that was strongly identified with European origins and offered a glimpse of a lost heroic past. The idea of finding freshness and authenticity in art 'untainted by the vulgarity of civilisation' was about to become highly influential with modern art's interest in primitivism, which found beauty in the products of non-European culture but still carried the dismissive attitudes of colonialism.[37] In its late nineteenth-century context, the Trojan exhibition was a chance to look for the first seeds of European creativity in some of the earliest art that could be linked to the classical tradition and ponder how European beginnings related to the contemporary cultures that were imagined as somehow belonging to the past. In the case of Troy, its place in classical myth and as a potential progenitor of European culture provided an alibi for enjoying its art – if Homer's Trojans were 'savages' there was no doubt to the nineteenth-century mind that they were noble. Schliemann asked his audience to reimagine the goddess Athena in a form that defied conventional ideas of Greekness and tied her to ideas more commonly associated with the 'primitive'. This remained challenging. While many rejected the idea that there was anything visually appealing about the finds from Troy (and for some this was sufficient grounds to dismiss any connection to Homer), plenty of others were fascinated.

7

Laughing at Schliemann

Schliemann's finds were decidedly odd to nineteenth-century eyes. While there were some serious attempts to stretch the boundaries of aesthetic appreciation to accommodate the pots of Troy, many still found them laughable. One way to manage the strangeness was to imagine that the objects were deliberately humorous creations by the ancient Trojans: 'Comic art seems to have flourished here in this age as many of the articles have received some singularly grotesque forms. Some, for example, are in the form of a pig, others in that of a hippopotamus.'[1] In a nineteenth-century context, with several publications solely dedicated to humour, Troy was able to realize a new comic potential. While many of the jokes published in these were based on bathetic or ridiculous readings of high culture, Troy was already halfway there as a site with grand links to ancient literature but slightly disappointing contents. As a wealthy eccentric, fond of esoteric knowledge and making wild claims, Schliemann also became a figure of fun. Many jokes used specific objects in Schliemann's collection and parodied more serious responses to Troy. In this chapter, I examine how these jokes allowed a broad readership to participate in the debates over Troy, without succumbing to the self-importance of the experts.

Bryant Davies has written an extensive exploration of Troy's place in nineteenth-century popular culture, including comic publications, circuses and burlesque. It is unnecessary to retread all of this material, but I agree that these dimensions of the reception of Troy that have traditionally been ignored have much to tell us about classical reception across social classes.[2] Holtorf has argued that the place of archaeology in modern popular culture 'reveals metaphors we think with, dreams and aspirations we hide inside of ourselves and attitudes that inform how we engage not only with ancient sites and objects, but with our surroundings more generally'.[3] This is also true of nineteenth-century popular engagement with archaeology, especially as many of our expectations about the subject were established at this time. Schliemann was a particularly important figure in establishing the stereotypes about heroic excavators and great discoveries that still shape the public perception of archaeology.[4] Looking closely at the jokes that Schliemann's contemporaries made about him shows an alternative tradition in which people enjoyed puncturing this reputation.

While the point of a joke is usually the punchline, there was often a lot more at stake in jokes about Troy than just a laugh. Many of the humorous responses to Troy use archaeological reasoning, even when reducing it to absurdity. I want to look at how the materiality of Troy offered a particular comic potential because it brought Homer's larger-than-life characters and events into contact with the stuff of everyday life. Jokes about the objects from Troy were useful for thinking about knowledge, authority and the relationship between past and present. I have decided not to confine humour to this chapter, since it has useful things to say about many of the topics covered in this book. Instead, I want to use this chapter to reflect on the specific uses of jokes to manage some of Schliemann's problematic features and the use of objects from Troy (real and imagined) to reinvent the ancient city in new terms.

Of course, jokes about Troy did not have to be complex works of classical reception. Schliemann's excavations at Troy were most often used as a topic for puns.[5] Much fun was had with the coincidence that Schliemann had found a large quantity of gold at Troy and that precious metals were measured by troy weight.[6] However, Troy also offered many appealing subjects for humour that engaged with the site and the debate around it in depth. Humorous publications spoofed the breathless excitement with which Schliemann made announcements to the press, and the uncritical reprinting of those claims by more serious publications:

> A private dispatch from Dr. Schliemann to this journal announces that the following wonderful things have been discovered by him at Mycenae:–
> The chignon of Helen of Troy at the age of 14
> The original Plaster of Paris in case labelled, 'Madame Venus, St. John's Wood House, Champs Elysées'
> Wet Towel supposed to have been worn by Homer round his head while composing the Iliad
> Tenpenny Nail presented by Vulcan to Achilles and worn by the latter as a scarf pin.
> Design by local undertaker for the tomb of Agamemnon. '5 per cent. for prompt cash' in Greek characters at foot.[7]

This article accurately captures the incredulity with which many of Schliemann's announcements of his finds were met. It echoes the style in which

Schliemann's many letters to London's papers were reported. But it is also a comical version of the process of imagining other lost objects from Troy to build up a fuller impression of the past, just like Pater using Homer, alongside his favourite objects from Troy and Mycenae to imagine 'an age of real gold' (Chapter 6).[8] But where Pater had left the corroded metal and simple pots out of his vision of the Homeric age, the stuff of everyday life was perfect for humour. Variations on this joke appear repeatedly, both in specifically humorous publications and in passing in more serious papers. Writers sought out particularly improbable features of classical myth to apply to Schliemann's finds: 'Ancient records – which are invariably strictly correct – inform us that Helen of Troy was hatched from an egg. It is to be hoped that Dr Schliemann may yet discover her shell among the ruins of Troy. This would be an eggstraordinarily eggshellent result of his eggsplorations.'[9] Others traced the process of reading too much into fragmentary evidence: 'We found ... the bones of a horse without a head and of a man without the lower limbs. We had no hesitation in pronouncing this a centaur.'[10]

This is not too far from Schliemann's over-restored pot becoming a chimaera for all to see at South Kensington. Many of the parodies are no more ridiculous than Schliemann writing that Athena herself had handed him a trove of axe heads or that he had found live toads that were 3,000 years old.[11] Schliemann was also often made fun of through personas and nicknames ('Herr Doktor von Ghoulemann', 'Dr Stealmann') that played on his untrustworthy claims and fondness for digging up graves.[12] Many of the criticisms familiar today appear in these jokes. Articles highlighted the destructive nature of Schliemann's excavations: 'Dr Schliemann writes in confidence to deny that he said the relics found at Troy were dis Troyed when he dug them up.'[13] They also pointed out Schliemann's illicit export of his finds: 'In consequence of his successful excavations amongst the tombs of ancient Greece and Troy and his consequent depredations in the name of Science, Dr Schliemann will henceforth be known as Dr Stealmann.'[14]

These jokes involve a scepticism that was being applied in much more serious ways in other places.[15] They rely on their audience feeling confident that their reading of archaeological evidence (real or imagined) was at least as valid as Schliemann's. Some are like opinion pieces with puns:

> As no iron has been found by Dr Schliemann, he boldly asserts that it was unknown in the time of Agamemnon, and that in Homer's time iron was more precious than gold! This is ferruginous perversion. Mention of it occurs ore and

ore, as one may say; and in such a way as to lead incontestably to the conclusion that no banker in Troy or elsewhere was ever asked to give change for a flat-iron in gold or notes. It is flat irony to say so. The Greeks did not shoe their horses with gold, jewelled in so many holes. In fact, whatever value they set on iron, we know that they set the very highest on gold by regarding its possession as equivalent to so much brains. Anticipating modern times in this respect, they spoke of a wealthy man as possessed of so many 'talents'. Dr Schliemann must have a care. He has won renown by finding a good many things; but there are finds which are losses, and it is quite possible for him to lose his prestige by finding – mare's nests.[16]

What seems to be a support system for a series of metal-themed puns is actually a direct response to a talk that Schliemann gave at the Ironmongers' Company just over a week earlier.[17] This had been tailored to suit the interests of the audience, discussing Schliemann's theory that the Trojans had been unable to smelt iron, so the only iron available to them was from meteorites, which were rarer and more precious than gold. The joke rests on Schliemann's claim running counter to common sense – ignoring, whether wilfully or otherwise, the fact that this was a Bronze Age site. Schliemann's tendency to make strange claims in utter seriousness meant that there was plenty to ridicule. But to do so fully, the writer had to engage with Schliemann's arguments and come up with counterarguments. The jokes point out that iron is commonly mentioned in Homer, while gold is only used in prestigious contexts, and so engage directly in a debate about how to relate text to object.

Joking about Schliemann's finds could reveal assumptions present in archaeological discourse that were overlooked elsewhere. For example, one article in *Punch* challenged the assumption that the gold decorations found at Mycenae would only have been worn by the elite:

> There are few things more wonderful, in Dr. Schliemann's wonderful 'find' at Mycenae, than the enormous quantity of buttons he has come upon in these mysterious graves. It has been hitherto supposed that the chieftains of the heroic age had souls above Buttons. But we know that in the earlier obsequies of chiefs slaves were sacrificed to the manes of their owners. The most probable explanation which we can offer of the Mycenian buttons is that they belonged to the garments of the pages who, no doubt, were burned in numbers round the bodies of their buried masters and mistresses.[18]

This makes an analogy between the pierced gold decorations from Mycenae and Troy and the livery buttons worn on the uniforms of Victorian servants. This was not the only joking comparison to the bright and cheap buttons that were mass-produced in Britain at this time.[19] Here, the joke brings together modern fashions with ideas about human sacrifice (something seen as exceptional and horrific in ancient Greece), binding together several layers of anachronism with Schliemann's discoveries. Such anachronisms reflect an awareness that knowledge about the past is constructed in the present and that present concerns can creep in. The joke asks why we should assume the identity of a grave's occupant from something as flimsy as a piece of gold, when the wealthy have always shown off their wealth through their long-suffering servants.

While the *Punch* article playfully reinterprets the archaeological evidence put forward by Schliemann, it also extends this rereading to the world of Homer. The surprising materiality of Mycenae and Troy raised the possibility that the ancient Greek past was not what people had thought. Jokes about Schliemann's discoveries often turn their attention to the less powerful people of the *Iliad* in ways that reflect poorly on the main characters:

> One of the discoveries evoked by Dr. Schliemann's researches is that, according to the shape of the Greeks' heads, they were awful scoundrels – just like their descendants – and generally speaking, a very low lot. This is not so great a discovery as it appears to be, for even Homer, with all his love for his characters, could get no higher theme to start the Iliad with than Achilles' wrath that his housemaid had got a better situation than he could give her.[20]

Identifying Homeric slavery with contemporary service roles was an anachronism that brought larger-than-life heroes down to earth. But it also turns people's attention away from the leaders of the *Iliad* to the ordinary people around them. Archaeology's commonplace details could reinvent the past in ways that seemed very familiar. The tension between past and present in these jokes domesticates the strangeness of excavated objects and the remote world of Homer, but it also imagines a bit of the strangeness of these worlds on the commonplace world of the present. If the disagreement over the fate of a slave girl that forms the central conflict of the *Iliad* or an imagined ritual murder can be compared with the lot of a modern servant, what does that say about the behaviour of Victorian gentlemen to their staff?

In figuring out how people responded to Schliemann's discoveries and made use of them in their own terms, it is crucial to show that not everybody took this exercise seriously. Even silly puns or ridiculous comparisons to the present contain a certain amount of theorizing about the past. Thinking against the grain of archaeological assumptions for comic effect could show up real omissions in the ways that archaeologists see the past, such as holes in their logic or the perspectives of poor people. The human focus of these jokes makes them powerful illustrations of what archaeology could mean to nineteenth-century audiences and what frameworks for thinking about the past that were available to them.

8

Weighing Up Ancient Troy

The treasure of Troy captured the public imagination from the moment Schliemann announced its discovery. These were beautiful and valuable objects that people could imagine in the hands of the Trojan royal family. They represented a wealthy ancient city that conveniently reflected the riches described in the *Iliad*. The gold of Troy is often seen as central to the exhibition's wide popular appeal and Schliemann's public persona as a treasure hunter.[1] It was common to note the intrinsic value of the gold in Schliemann's collection alongside discussion of other kinds of value, doubtless helped by Schliemann's decision to include the weight of gold and silver objects on their labels.[2] However, Troy also became a testing ground for more complex ideas about how metals and other rare commodities were used and valued in the past. This chapter asks why civil servants and bankers published a series of analyses of objects from Troy. As an early site, traditionally seen as the start of the Western tradition, Troy seemed to offer a way of understanding the origins of standardized measures and money. I explore why officials were looking to the past in this way and how this seemed relevant to modern policy issues.

Schliemann himself was the biggest advocate of discussing the value of his collection. The price that Schliemann put on his collection fluctuated from £50,000 when he was trying to sell it to just over £1,000 when he was forced to compensate the Turkish government for its loss.[3] However, he was also interested in the Trojans' systems of value, especially in exploring the composition of some of the rarer materials from the site. Schliemann turned to chemists and other experts to provide more information on these issues, resulting in collaborative scientific analysis of the finds from Troy that was well ahead of its time.[4] He had already sent samples of the metal objects he found at Troy to several scientists to confirm their composition.[5] Metallurgy was central to debates about dating Troy (see Chapter 10), but did not attract much attention from the general public.

A surprising community of experts in London took an interest in Troy as a site that could illuminate the history of their own field or even guide their work in the present. A series of reports by bankers and public servants in the 1870s asked whether there were standards for weights and metal values at Troy and what these might mean for Troy's place in the history of money and its relationships with its neighbours. This interest began with a report to Parliament by the Warden of Standards, H.W. Chisholm, on systems of weights used in various ancient cultures. This appeared as an appendix to the Chisholm's annual report on the business of the Department of Standards, which included constructing standard weights for reference, comparing with other standards held internationally and tackling fraud. Perhaps Chisholm was just a public servant using his office to explore an interest only tangentially relevant to his remit. However, questions of the ancient roots of modern measurements had been an important part of the debates that had led to the creation of his role and the whole Department of Standards. In 1864, a bill was introduced to Parliament to deal with irregularities in the British system of measurements, including the fact that the standard measures had been lost decades earlier. These reforms included optional adoption of the metric system to help with international trade. This measure proved divisive. Some of its opponents argued that measurements of the Great Pyramid at Giza proved that the inch had been handed down by God.[6]

These debates were largely forgotten a decade later, when Chisholm wrote his report, but ancient systems of measurement were still seen as relevant to modern standards. Troy was included in this report, despite its focus on objects in the British Museum, which had nothing from Troy to weigh. Instead, the report cited the weights given in *Troy and Its Remains*.[7] The results were inconclusive:

> The first series is of terra cotta cylinders, balls, pyramids, &c. The second series is of round stones. The greater part of these were found in what is believed to have been the remains of ancient Troy, destroyed about 1200 B.C. The terra cotta specimens there found vary from 26 grammes to 748 grammes, and the stone balls from 100 grammes up to a maximum of 4,260 grammes. But the weights vary so much, that no principal unit of weight can be deduced from them. Nor indeed is there any sufficient evidence of their having been used as weights, or any inscription upon them to warrant such a supposition.[8]

The fact that Troy was included in this report, despite there being no objects to weigh and no clear conclusions to make from reported weights, shows its importance to the Victorian imagination as an early and influential culture.

The question of Troy's system of measurement was picked up again when the Trojan collection was on display in London as part of a new debate over standardization, held at the inaugural meeting of the Institute of Bankers. This organization aimed to share professional knowledge among bankers, but the first paper given (after the inaugural address by MP and prehistorian Sir John Lubbock) was a history of weights and money, which drew on Chisholm's report and included Troy as one of its earliest sites. Barclay Head (a numismatist who worked at the British Museum) reflected on how difficult it was to imagine civilization without money, but that no coins were known for most of the earliest civilizations. He argued, using examples from the Bible, that set weights of precious metal served a similar function before the invention of coins.

The idea that silver, as well as gold, was used as a measure of value was particularly important at this time. A campaign to shift the British economy from one founded on the gold standard, to one based on the value of both gold and silver, in which the two metals would have a fixed value in relation to each other (known as bimetallism) was beginning to attract interest. Proponents of bimetallism believed that the gold standard had caused a reduction in world money supply, leading to recent downturns and recessions. A fall in the value of silver had made it harder for British companies to export to countries which used the silver standard.[9] These anxieties about the relationship between the value of metals and the performance of capitalist economies in a modern market system seem far removed from ancient systems of weight, but Head specifically contextualized his discussions of ancient economies with reference to these contemporary debates. His focus on ancient coins and other measures of precious metals as a way to understand ancient economies seemed a natural approach for a numismatist, but also embedded the idea of underlying value systems as an important economic force that characterized both sides of the bimetallism debate.

Head argued that a bimetallic system had been used throughout Asia in ancient times and that the Hittites had communicated this system to Asia Minor. His main evidence from Troy was a set of six pieces of silver, roughly rectangular with one rounded end, which Schliemann identified as the 'talents' described by Homer (visible on the right side of the top shelf in Fig. 23, in Chapter 4).[10] These were a crucial example for Head of this system in use at an early date:

> Dr Schliemann calls his wedges Homeric talents, but, be this as it may, they are certainly thirds of the Babylonian silver mina of from 8645 to 8656 grains. If my proposed identification of the mina of Carchemish with the mina in use in the Troad about the fourteenth century B.C. be accepted, may it not prove suggestive when considered in connection with the Egyptian text (the poem of Pentaur), in

which the people of Ilion, Pedasos, Dardanos, Mysia, and Lycia are mentioned as allies of the Kheta (Hittites) in their wars with Ramses II. About the same period?[11]

Head believed that these standards linked cultures across Asia through trade. His claims about relevance to modern issues were fairly modest: presenting the question of bimetallism vs monometallism as an enduring one with a number of possible answers. However, most of the debate following Head's talk focused on this issue and its importance in the present:

> It is my unshaken belief that the different Governments of Europe will find it necessary before long to come to a definite arrangement for a Bi-metallic International Currency. The times are not at present propitious for such a change. It would involve the earnest desire of all Governments to maintain peace, whereas every Government in Europe is arming to the teeth.[12]

Looking to past systems was a way to deal with the uncertainties of the present especially with something so messy (and increasingly complicated) as international economic theory.

Head's observations on Troy's talents attracted the attention of the Chemist of the Royal Mint, W. Chandler Roberts, who had already analysed the metal content of Schliemann's collections, but revisited his data in the light of possible relevance to bimetallism. He included his results for the metal content and weight of these objects in his annual report to Parliament:

> But apart from their metallurgical interest these talents are of high numismatic value, and it is interesting to turn to a learned paper by Mr. Barclay V. Head, of the British Museum, who has shown that the weights or minae in use in the ancient Assyrian and Babylonian empires during the long period which elapsed between B.C. 2,000 and B.C. 625 existed in the double form. There was a heavy mina and a light mina, and, towards the end of the eighth century B.C. these minae weighed respectively 1010 and 505 grammes, or were nearly identical with the French kilogramme and half kilogramme. There can be but little doubt that these strips of silver found by Dr. Schliemann are thirds of the Babylonic silver mina, and, although I cannot here follow out the arguments by which Mr. Head leads up from a consideration of these weights to the 'bi-metallism' which in early times was universal in the East, it is interesting to note the connexion which he traces between these discoveries of Dr. Schliemann and a monetary question of much interest in our own day.[13]

Seeing Troy as a site with a proto-metric system and bimetallism offered a possible alternative tradition for those who were interested in challenging current approaches. In the end, not much came of these investigations. Although the debates about weights and measures at Troy hoped to find ways in which it would prove useful in the present, it ended up having very little impact – bimetallism was only ever championed by a minority and did not succeed in shifting the economic system.

As the embodiment of the unreal made real, and a newly discovered starting point for European history, Troy was an appealing place to look for answers in a time of increasing financial abstraction and instability. The golden treasure that was on display in London testified to the wealth of Troy and promised answers about the relationship between metals and more abstract ideas of value. Troy's traditional role was as a defeated and destroyed city, with the potential to warn modern people of their own civilization's end. But this is not the version of Troy we see in the debates over bimetallism. Instead, Head posited a version of Troy surprisingly similar to the one known to archaeologists today: an ally of the Hittites, linked to them by war and trade. This placed Troy in a broader network of ancient economies in which trade was facilitated by shared standards in ways that seemed to foreshadow the global economic system of the nineteenth century. At a time when Britain was reluctant to change its old habits to join the metric system and questioning whether a different basis for its currency might combat financial instability, Troy offered a chance to look for a precedent to proposed changes. The Trojan collection's presence in London made it accessible to a new group of specialists whose detailed investigations of Troy went well beyond Schliemann's priorities. The next part of the book picks up on some more of these debates and how these could present very different versions of Troy from the one imagined by Schliemann.

Part Four

Troy's Place in History

In 1875, *The Times* described the debates that emerged from the discovery of Troy as 'a new War of Troy, destined, probably, to last at least as long as that in which Hector and Achilles strove'.[1] This assessment was correct: the debate over Troy was both fierce and long-lasting.[2] This new Trojan War was not over the land of Troy, but over how to understand it:

> Two principal questions have been raised by the explorations in the Troad, and, as the tendency of the controversy has been at times to confuse the issues, we would ask our readers to bear clearly in mind that these questions are absolutely distinct. The first is – Has Dr. Schliemann found the Homeric Ilium? The second is – To what race and age do the remains which he has found belong?[3]

In this part of the book, I look at some of the answers advanced to these two questions and the ways in which they were tangled up. Most assessments of Schliemann's impact focus on the first question. This makes sense: the connection with Homer was Schliemann's central claim and the main reason that Troy attracted so much attention. However, for many Victorian commentators the second question was an easier one to answer using the material available and (in the words of the review above) 'of an even more direct and vital interest'.[4]

In exploring the debates over the significance of Troy, I have expanded the two questions into three: Was this Homer's Troy? How old was Troy? Who were the Trojans? Chapter 9 begins by exploring how encounters with the objects from Troy were shaped by possible connections to Homer. Despite doubts about Schliemann's claims, the idea of seeing material objects that could flesh out the world of Homer was a tempting one. This chapter looks at a range of strategies and distancing mechanisms that enabled people to try out this new approach to museum objects without seeming gullible. While *The Times* saw Troy's relationship with Homer as a separate question from discussions of date and culture, Homer still came up in these debates. If Hisarlık could be proved to be Homer's Troy, then it could offer independent answers to questions about the world Homer described. Archaeological data might resolve debates about when the events of the *Iliad* took place and whether the Greeks and Trojans were culturally and racially similar, which would shape readers' understanding of the text.

Schliemann firmly believed that he had found the Troy of Homer, but was much more open to debate on questions of date and race. We have seen how he called on the experts of London to examine the metals, skulls and swastikas found at Troy and how he worked closely with Müller to come up with a loose chronology for the site. But there was also a risk in exploring these questions and we will see examples of people whose answers to the date and racial characteristics of Schliemann's Troy were seen as evidence against it being the one described in Homer. The site of Troy was strongly associated with the earliest texts in the Greek tradition, but it had no written histories of its own. Chapter 10 looks at some of the attempts to come up with a system for dating Troy and understanding its history without textual sources. Troy was used on both sides in debates about the early history of humanity and developing ideas about deep time. There were many different ways to make sense of Troy's place in history, but evolution and the three-age system emerged as leading approaches. This chapter argues that Troy's deep stratigraphy and ambiguous material culture made it a particularly useful site for thinking through wider problems of human history.

As a place between Europe and Asia, where representatives of those continents had supposedly clashed for the first time, there was much scope for debate over where Troy's people had come from and what had influenced their culture. Troy occupied a liminal space, both geographically and temporally, that made it especially useful for nineteenth-century debates about race. Attempts to pin down the race of the Trojan people had roots in debates over the *Iliad*, but the objects from Troy opened up new disciplinary approaches from skull-measuring, through linguistics, to speculation about patterns of trade. Chapter 11 shows how Schliemann's focus on proving the Trojans were Aryan was just part of a much wider effort to identify their ethnicity and connect them to bigger narratives of cultural development and spread. These were not simple questions of archaeological fact: they came with extensive baggage about whether Troy should be viewed as primitive or advanced, Eastern or Western, independent or connected – categories that were in extensive use to structure and justify Britain's role in the wider world. Troy was a site that could reaffirm or overthrow these categories depending on how it was used, with real implications for archaeological thought and the wider systems that it upheld.

Troy proved useful in a range of a range of nineteenth-century debates about the nature, toolkit and purpose of history. It was an unusually fruitful site for thinking with, precisely because of its contradictions. Reading poetry as history had its allure but raised questions about which historical sources could be trusted. While material objects seemed easier to subject to scientific analysis, different approaches yielded different results and often reflected the interests of the person doing the analysis. It was hoped that Troy would add new details to grand narratives, whether ancient Greeks' accounts of their own history or more recent stories of Aryan expansion into Europe. Schliemann's failure to pin down Troy's cultural affinities and dating made Troy an ambiguous site in which many possible meanings could be claimed. Given the centrality of the Trojan War to European identity, this was a site that could transform that identity and many different approaches wanted to claim it for themselves.

9

The Other Homeric Question

In spite of not having much to say on the Homeric Question, Schliemann's discoveries were celebrated in the press for overturning the uncertainties Wolf had raised about the authorship and background of the *Iliad*. The week that Schliemann's exhibition at South Kensington opened, the following piece appeared in *The Times*:

> A few years ago the world was startled by the announcement that Troy, the veritable city which Priam ruled and Homer sang had been revealed. The announcement was received with incredulity by most and with ridicule by some, for even the site had been warmly disputed by many generations of scholars. *Etiam periere ruinae* had been the impatient and almost contemptuous exclamation of Mr Lowe when asked for a grant from the Exchequer in aid of explorations in the Troad, and he seemed to imply that the search would be as fruitless as if it had been proposed to look for King Arthur's sword ... if there were many who disbelieved in Homer altogether, there must have been more who disbelieved in the Troy which his poems described and it naturally seemed to them but the pastime of scholars or archaeologists to dispute over the site of a city which might never have existed.[1]

This looks back at the government's refusal to fund British excavations in search of Troy, shortly before Schliemann's treasure announcement.[2] It contrasts this scepticism, founded in a discourse on the *Iliad* that doubted even the author's existence, against the possibility that objects mentioned in Homer were about to go on display in South Kensington. However, this interplay of scepticism and belief was too complex to be resolved by a single museum exhibition. Even enthusiasts like the columnist quoted above realized that the exhibition would not hold all the answers:

> it will be a long time before the wider questions raised by the singular discovery are settled. It is so easy to say that we have here before us the very treasure of Priam, and that Homer was less of a poet and more of a historian than he has

hitherto seemed; but there are more difficulties than we can attempt to enumerate to be got over before that easy and simple solution of the problem can be adopted. We must not think of Troy alone or Homer alone. We have here materials such as we have never had before for the reconstruction of the prehistoric life of the Greeks, and we need a wide induction and a comprehensive survey before we can venture to draw any conclusions at all.[3]

The material from Troy raised more questions than it answered, but (unlike the compositional uncertainties that made up the Homeric Question) these were met with joy by people who wanted to believe in the truth of the Trojan War. These new questions left scope for many different readings and offered the possibility of a new approach to the past that would expand its evidence base and give clearer answers. Controversy fuelled public interest and made more people wish to view and take their own stance on the finds from Troy. It seemed that Schliemann's hopes that the exhibition would pique the British public interest and 'increase their love for the divine Homer' might be fulfilled.[4]

Work on the cultural impact of Schliemann and Troy cannot avoid talking about the question of whether Homer was true. It was crucial to Troy's significance for religious people in the nineteenth century who hoped that archaeology might overturn the scepticism towards biblical narratives and a range of other archaeologies of wishful thinking.[5] The idea that Homeric epic might have been empirically confirmed was central to the public appeal of the Trojan exhibition. However, aligning archaeological finds with the *Iliad* was not easy; even people who believed the *Iliad* was true had to work out its exact relationship with the finds from Hisarlık.[6] Even Schliemann was often evasive about the relationship between the composition of the Homeric epics and his archaeological site of Troy. He believed that Homer was a single individual, who was generally accurate. But Schliemann thought Homer's knowledge of the events at Troy was second-hand, passed on by veterans of the Trojan War or other poets.[7] This, along with a sense of poetic licence, explained why the site and the Homeric description did not match:

> Homer is an epic poet and no historian. He never saw neither the great tower of Ilium, nor the divine wall, nor Priam's Palace, because when he visited Troy, 300 years after its destruction all those monuments were for 300 years covered with a 10 feet thick layer of the red ashes and ruins of Troy and another city stood upon that layer, a city which in its turn must have undergone great convulsions and increased that layer considerably. Homer made no excavations to bring those monuments to light, but he knew them by tradition for Troy's tragical fate had ever since its destruction been in the mouth of the rhapsodes.[8]

By excavating, Schliemann believed he had access to a body of information that Homer did not have. He asserted that his own expertise on Troy and Mycenae (at least in their spatial and material dimensions) was better informed than the poet who made them famous. However, Schliemann's sense of how well Homer knew the site of Troy was flexible. In giving his objects Homeric names, he often insisted that the domestic details of Troy were familiar to Homer.

Schliemann's confidence in his own archaeological judgement meant that he was happy to write off parts of the *Iliad* which did not agree with his discoveries as poetic licence.[9] While we have seen (Chapters 2–4) how carefully Schliemann presented his own version of Homeric Troy, it was not the only possible Homeric reading of these objects. The epics were full of detailed and vivid descriptions of exceptional objects, and Schliemann's collection would inevitably be compared with imaginary objects they could never live up to. Seeing ancient objects through the lens of Homer was not easy and this chapter explores the range of strategies (comparative, evasive and imaginative) that visitors used to negotiate the gap between object and texts. Schliemann's literary claims could not be ignored, and so shaped experiences of the Trojan collection for believers and sceptics alike.

Homeric ekphrasis and real objects

The idea of a relationship between literature and objects is embedded in the Homeric epics. Detailed descriptions of special objects are given an important narrative and poetic role. The most famous example is the shield given to Achilles in book 18, made by a god and with impossibly detailed decoration encompasses all aspects of human life and nature. The shield of Achilles is a foundational instance of ekphrasis: an ancient rhetorical term for a vivid description that evokes a visual experience, used in a more technical sense today for literary descriptions of works of art. As such, it has shaped ancient and modern expectations of the relationship between literature and art and shows the impossibility of text and image ever fully matching up.[10] The shield of Achilles posed a challenge for Schliemann's claims about Troy. It was clearly meant to be an exceptional object: made by a god out of precious materials, with a detailed realism that was more a product of literary imagination than anything that could be achieved in practice. However, it also created a set of expectations for Homeric art with realistic figurative elements that did not easily match anything found at Troy.

Despite the difficult relationship between ekphrasis and real art, the shield of Achilles was seen as a possible way to independently verify the cultural conditions in which the epics were produced (and so provide answers to the Homeric Question). A.S. Murray (an assistant in the British Museum's Department of Greek and Roman Antiquities) argued that the shield might be the key to understanding when the *Iliad* was written: 'If, for instance, it were proved satisfactorily that the condition of art which is implied in the description of the shield of Achilles, really obtained in the time of Homer, a well-known suspicion as to the antiquity of the poems would be removed.'[11] Murray drew complex analogies between the art described in Homer and Assyrian art. He argued that descriptions of art in epic would preserve the stage of development at the time of composition, and that anachronism would creep in if the poems were written down after a long period of oral circulation. This was part of an ongoing debate with Frederick Apthorp Paley and his supporters about how old the text of the *Iliad* and the *Odyssey* was. Paley argued from variations in the Trojan War stories that the epics drew on older oral sources, but were only brought together as a coherent whole in the fifth century BCE.[12] For Murray, the shield of Achilles was an example of the most advanced art in Homer and so could be used to date the poems in relation to early Greek art, proving that there was no sign of fifth-century art in them.[13] This was based on some highly theoretical speculation on the early phases of Greek art, and Murray could point to very few objects that he saw as genuinely Homeric.

When Schliemann's collection came to London, Murray was an obvious choice to review it. Murray found nothing in the Trojan exhibition to live up to the shield of Achilles and described it as 'disappointing to the last degree'.[14] There was nothing to reward the close reading of Homer for themes and style of art that he had applied to Assyrian art three years before, and he tried to discourage others from trying anything similar at the Trojan exhibition:

> the student of Homer, who, should he take with him a text of the poet in the hope of obtaining illustrations of it, will find himself in a worse position than the inexperienced play-goer who takes a common version of a play which he is to see, hoping to be able to follow the actors. There is, in fact, a most signal absence of objects belonging to the stage of art and workmanship with which Homer was acquainted, to judge from the text we now have.[15]

Murray did not abandon his hypothesis about Homer and Assyrian art. Instead, he argued that Schliemann's finds from Troy were not Homeric objects. By Murray's standards, the inhabitants at Hisarlık were in a 'primitive condition', but he argued that this did not necessarily mean that the site was very old. For Murray, the encounter with objects from Troy undermined any connection to Homer and unmoored the site from the expected chronologies, making it part of a timeless world outside of his progressive logic of civilization.

Despite Murray's cautions, there were plenty of people interested in how Schliemann's finds measured up to Homer. *The Times* had published an article only two days before Murray's that quoted the labels and expanded on their line references to the *Iliad*, so the idea of visitors carrying copies of Homer into the exhibition may have been more than empty rhetoric.[16] Responses to the labels use the connection to the text of the *Iliad* as a kind of textual reconstruction of the objects' ancient use. For example, *The Times* quoted the passage Schliemann used to name the diadems in full:

> Far off were flung the adornments of her head,
> The net, the *fillet* (ἄμπυκα), and the *woven band* (πλ. ἀναδ.)
> The Nuptial veil (κρηδ.) by golden Venus given.[17]

This is a highly emotional scene in which Andromache learns that her husband, Hector, has died and throws down her head coverings in grief. However, *The Times* engaged with the passage as a reconstruction of the use of the objects on display at South Kensington, not a moving moment in a larger story. The interest is in the order in which the three layers are worn, and which ancient term corresponds to Schliemann's diadem.

The labels (see Chapter 4) were designed to encourage visitors to imagine the objects into the social and narrative contexts of the *Iliad* in this way. The objects that Schliemann singled out with Homeric names are not examples of detailed ekphrasis, but mentioned in the ongoing action of the epic. This makes sense for practical reasons: meaning fewer awkward details that could contradict Schliemann's reading. Instead of holding his objects up against the detail of the Homeric ekphrases, Schliemann asked viewers of his finds to imagine them in the lives of the characters of Homer, adding a degree of vividness to the objects mentioned in passing in the Homeric texts. As with a textual ekphrasis, the imagination was called in to mediate a relationship between text and object. However, the visitors to South Kensington tended to treat this more as an intellectual exercise and a test of Schliemann's claims, rather than fully giving themselves over to imagination. They could (like Murray) break the interpretive relationship between object and text by denying that the object had anything to do with Homer or (like the *Times* reviewer) maintain a critical distance and analyse Schliemann's claims against object and text.

Walter Pater did exactly what Murray claimed was impossible by looking closely at the craftsmanship of the Trojan treasure and seeing in it a reflection of the objects described in Homer. We have already seen (in Chapter 6) how Pater included Troy in his account of 'The Heroic Age in Greek Art'.[18] This included a description of one of the gold diadems: 'the "diadem," with its twisted chains and flowers of pale gold, shows that those profuse golden fringes, waving so comely as he moved, which Hephaestus wrought for the helmet of Achilles, were really within the compass of early Greek art'. Like the *Times*' description of the diadem, Pater uses the real object to imagine the headwear of a beautiful character from the *Iliad*. This time, in line with Pater's sexuality, the character is a man.[19] However, the shift from conventional interest in female characters reflects more than just personal preference. Pater mirrors the Homeric identification from an object cast off by Andromache in grief to one put on by Achilles in response to his own loss and before his vengeance inflicts Andromache's pain. In switching focus to a different fictional object behind a real one, Pater bound the two into a complex literary interaction that highlighted commonalities in craftsmanship, war and grief. He explored the imaginative potential of the gap between the real object and the object described in Homer.

Where other approaches test (whether seriously or not) Schliemann's claims about this specific object, Pater used it for a much more ambitious purpose. He tests the real diadem against a more central object from the *Iliad*, looking not for an exact match, but for similarities in craftsmanship that might live up to Homeric ekphrasis. The golden plumes on Achilles' helmet are part of the panoply made for Achilles by Hephaestus, which includes the famous shield.[20] For Pater, these items were imaginary, but inspired by real objects seen by the poet. He compared this relationship to the waking world that inspires vivid dreams. For Pater, the magic attributed to Homeric objects could not be imagined without wonder at their real-world counterparts. The fact that these were not precisely the objects described in Homer was no obstacle to seeing them as Homeric. The discoveries of archaeology could never live up to the lost worlds hinted at by ancient texts, and Pater's technique acknowledged this, while using both bodies of evidence to reach towards what had been lost.[21]

Fact and fantasy

While Pater's was probably the most subtle attempt to imagine the diadem as a visual context for Homer's world, he was not alone. Visitors to the Trojan exhibition were reluctant to be seen as credulous, but they could still enjoy imagining the jewellery being worn by a beautiful woman. Where the labels suggested Andromache, Helen of Troy was even more appealing. One way to indulge the desire to imagine the diadems onto the heads of Homer's characters was to do so light-heartedly:

> Besides golden bracelets, fillets, and earrings, of which there are numerous specimens, there are two remarkably fine and perfect examples of the Homeric *ampyx*, or frontlet, with the *plekté anadesme*, or headgear, plaited all of solid gold, one of which may have adorned the brow of the beauteous but naughty Helen, whose misbehaviour brought so much trouble on the world even in those, to us, early days. This article, in its best days, must have been very effective as a feminine ornament.[22]

By keeping it light, this reviewer had an alibi for entertaining Schliemann's ideas, without fully committing to them. The exercise of imagining the diadem onto Helen connected the displayed object to its ancient use, the fantasy was brought back to earth with an assessment of its effectiveness as jewellery. In a broadly sceptical evaluation of the competing claims for the site of Troy, the *Illustrated London News* acknowledged that, when encountering the 'supposed Trojan relics' that some viewers might be happier with the fantasy:

> It can scarcely be doubted that these were worn by royal personages; and Priam and Hecuba may have been accustomed to put them on, when they proceeded to worship at the shrine of the Palladium, while their daughters, Cassandra and others, or Helen, their fatal Greek daughter-in-law, may have been adorned with the multitude of smaller jewels. Let this interesting reflection be cherished in spite of ungenial scepticism, by the lady visitors to the South Kensington Museum, who will do well to read 'the tale of Troy divine', if not in Homer's sonorous Ionic Greek, at least in the graceful English couplets of Alexander Pope, or in the masculine blank verse of the late Earl of Derby. They will like it, we promise them, quite as much as the 'Idylls of the King'.[23]

For this reviewer, different degrees of scepticism were appropriate for different audiences. Homer was often defined as masculine, and this reviewer implies that reading Homer did not come naturally to women, whereas the fantasy of Troy (and the gleam of the jewellery) might make it more appealing. In practice, women experienced deliberate exclusion from the education needed to understand Homer, and some were already overcoming these barriers.[24] This review offered women a gendered mode of reading that is more imaginative, less critical. However, it also hints at the appeal of uneducated, literal readings of the

Iliad (presumably unacceptable for educated male readers) by enjoying them vicariously through the imagined women getting into Homer for the first time.

In practice, women were already reading the *Iliad* and were just as likely to engage with the sceptical discourses around Troy as the men. For example, Elizabeth Barrett Browning's *Aurora Leigh* is a well-known example of a female poet engaging with the implications of Wolf.[25] However, few had access to the publications and learned societies where the debate about Schliemann was happening. Sarah Edith Marshall, an exception who had studied history at Cambridge and was a fellow of the Royal Historical Society,[26] directly challenged Schliemann's claims that Hisarlık was Troy. An interview article written on her later in life described her disagreement with her peers over Schliemann (who was an honorary member of the society): 'When Dr. Schliemann announced that he had discovered ancient Troy, Miss Marshall got down her Iliad in the original and attempted to convince him that he was mistaken. He did not convince "worth a cent," neither did his scientific confreres who went wild over his discoveries.'[27] Marshall (best known today as the mother of the historian Arnold Toynbee and the classicist, Jocelyn Toynbee) used her public disagreement with Schliemann to demonstrate her own skill as a reader of the *Iliad*.[28] She was still priding herself on having been more sceptical of Schliemann than her male peers in 1908. Scepticism was the mark of mature, scholarly engagement with Troy and disbelieving Schliemann was a way to establish academic credentials for people seen as outsiders to the study of the past.

Schliemann's Troy was a site where archaeology was contaminated with literature; disciplined debate was contaminated with emotion; and adult knowledge was contaminated with childlike longing for legends to be true. Where the topography and general engagement with Schliemann's ideas offered the possibility that cities known only through ancient texts might be found, engagement with the objects found at Troy was much more sceptical. People who approached the Trojan collection through Homer usually used some sort of distancing mechanism, whether humour, projecting onto less educated viewers or outright denial. However, even for the most doubtful of Schliemann's audience, encountering objects from Troy forced them to reflect on the truth content of Homer and imagine Troy as a fully realized city, full of tangible objects.

While this distancing is clearest in response to the connections to Homer, it was not limited to his Homeric claims. For some, Schliemann's insistence on Homeric Troy infected all of his work, even the stratigraphy:

In matters of archaeology we can rarely agree with him, even now when he has toned down much that was absurd in his former work on Troy. He has still to learn exactness in the records of his excavations. That would have curbed his imagination and probably have left us with fewer than seven 'cities' one above the other at Hissarlik. If he could but forget the Iliad! But then he would no longer be Dr Schliemann.[29]

This is a call for realism, rather than a call to reality. Troy was a site that was regularly levelled and rebuilt, but this seemed implausible to many.[30] The detailed archaeological attention to the levels of Troy that is called for here ended up producing more levels: there are nine major periods in the chronology of the site used today.[31] Schliemann only identified two of his layers from Troy with iterations of the city described in Homer, so there was little reason to ascribe Schliemann's many levels to his obsession with Homer. In this case, scepticism towards Schliemann's Homeric claims was so strong that it could contaminate issues that had nothing to do with Homer. Schliemann's work often depended more on appearing real than on being rooted in reality, but in this case the reality of the site did not seem real enough.[32] Troy's many phases made it clear that it was not just the city described in Homer and the next section looks at the archaeological approaches used to make sense of this complexity.

10

How Old Was Troy?

While Homer was on everyone's mind when they visited the Trojan exhibition, they also hoped the carefully arranged finds might tell their own story. As one visitor to the previews put it:

> Over the plain of the Troad, where in our time as in Byron's 'the quiet sheep feeds and the tortoise crawls' have successively ruled the men of the stone, copper, and bronze ages, Trojan and Greek, and on the mound of Hissarlik the potter's wheel whirled thousands of years ago. It is no light matter to disentangle the web woven by successive generations: to decipher the often blurred record of byegone civilizations. Yet it was impossible to arrange these evidences of the early life of man without reference to the depths from which they were exhumed, and the character of the art by which they were fashioned. To a certain extent, this work has been facilitated by the memoranda constantly made during the work of excavation by Dr Schliemann of the exact stratum in which each specimen was found. Already the collection has a symmetrical appearance and promises, when Dr Schliemann and Mr Streatfield have concluded their labours, to enable the spectator to turn over at his ease page after page of the history of man, as written in the mound of windy Troy.[1]

If Troy was to be read like a book, it would need substantial editing by Schliemann and his collaborators to make it legible. We have seen Müller's frustration with this process and how, despite efforts to date Troy from close examination of the finds before the exhibition opened, there was no firm date for any of the site's phases (Chapter 3). Troy was clearly rich in history, but exactly what it would mean was not set in stone.

Troy was the first 'tell' site (a kind of man-made mound built up over many generations of occupation) ever excavated, which meant it had an unprecedentedly deep and complex history to disentangle.[2] If the Trojan War was a historical event (something that was far from accepted), it might be possible to link it to the chronology of Mycenae, which had firmer footing. Schliemann used a scarab with a cartouche of Pharaoh Amenophis III, found at Ialysos with similar pottery to date one phase of the site to around 1400 BCE.[3] Schliemann believed firmly in the Trojan War as a historical event but, despite his confident assertions that his second level was Homer's Troy, the presence of stone tools raised doubts.[4] Priam's Treasure is now known to date to the early Bronze Age, too early for most proposed dates for the Trojan War. Schliemann struggled to match up the phases of Troy and Mycenae that he identified with the characters from the Trojan War.[5] He explored several possible solutions to this problem and even suggested that his 'Agamemnon' might have been a contemporary of Homer, while the Trojan War had happened much earlier:

> However, the want of ornamentation on the Trojan jewels, the hand-made, uncoloured pottery, with impressed or engraved ornamentation, and, finally, the want of iron and glass, convince me that the ruins of Troy belong to such a remote antiquity as to precede by ages the ruins of Mycenae, the date of which I thought I could fix by the result of the thirty-four shafts which I sank in the Acropolis in February, 1874. I therefore believed that Homer had only known by an ancient tradition, commemorated by preceding poets, the siege and destruction of Troy, and that, for favours received, he put in his contemporaries as actors in his great tragedy. But I never doubted that a king of Mycenae, by the name of Agamemnon, his charioteer Eurymedon, a Princess Cassandra, and their followers had been treacherously murdered.[6]

Troy had long been framed by textual evidence, both from Homer and from a long tradition of other writers building on these stories. Ancient writers treated the fall of Troy as the dividing line between myth and history, and the date established for it by Hellenistic writers (1184–1183 BCE) was still seen as accurate in the eighteenth century.[7] Schliemann's excavations offered up a new body of evidence that could test this date and also ask what was distinctive about the time at which Troy flourished.

The language and evidence base used to understand a period can make a huge difference to how it is understood.[8] When Pater called Troy's objects products of a 'heroic age', he idealized the period and placed focus firmly on Homeric epic and its cast of elite characters.[9] Charles Newton, the curator of antiquities at the British Museum, preferred to describe Schliemann's finds from Troy as 'pre-Hellenic', which avoided committing to the association with Homer, but still framed the site as a precursor to ancient Greece, rather than a culture in its own right.[10] The categories used to define history (whether the ideas used to create boundaries between periods or the stories used to express change over a succession of periods) are never neutral. Both synchronic periods and diachronic linear histories project stories onto the past which are necessary for making sense of it.[11] However history is broken up and sorted out, the process will simplify the past, prioritizing some aspects and neglecting others. The different ways of analysing and presenting Troy's many phases each carried different implications for what sort of site this was and what lessons it carried for the present. Attempts to make sense of Troy's complexity were used to debate wider questions about the length of human history and what criteria should be used for sorting and ordering human culture.

While the ancients saw Troy as the threshold between myth and history, this role shifted in the light of debates about history in the nineteenth century, to become a threshold between history and prehistory. If Troy was the starting point of the Greek tradition (as Schliemann claimed) it could connect it to the new fields that were deepening human history. It also promised to shift how these fields read their evidence. Schliemann's exhibition emphasized the contemporaneous use of stone and bronze tools at Troy (Chapter 4) and this chapter explores why Schliemann believed this evidence would revolutionize the three-age system. It looks at how Schliemann used Troy's stratigraphy to present the site as key evidence in an ongoing debate among British archaeologists, and how his ideas took on a life of their own for those who wanted to disprove recent archaeological discoveries and argue for a young earth. Schliemann's account of Troy emerges as an attempt to add nuance (and a Copper Age) to the three-age system, but also had important implications for the story the site told. This story was difficult to represent in a museum space, and so the chapter ends by exploring the debates over how the Trojan collection should be arranged. I show how museum arrangements offered a concrete focus for debates about different ways of structuring history by looking at a critique of the Trojan exhibition by one of the foremost proponents of museum arrangement as a form of public education. The large collection of similar objects over a long time-span made Troy particularly appealing for evolutionary approaches to material culture, but some aspects of the site had to be discarded to make it work.

Three ages?

Schliemann is often credited as a pioneering excavator of the Aegean Bronze Age, and he successfully promoted his discovery of Troy as a new window onto a much more distant period of history than people were used to seeing. However, he tried to use the site of Troy to contest the idea that a Stone Age must always be prior to a Bronze Age. To understand this contradiction, we need to explore why Schliemann made these claims and what they meant for nineteenth-century debates about deep time and archaeological periodization.

Even during excavation, Schliemann struggled to make sense of Troy's chronology. His diary-style excavation reports describe peeling away layer after layer of the site, expecting each to reveal Homer's Troy. He then describes his concern at coming down to stone tools and the possibility that he had gone back too far in time, without finding anything suitably Homeric:

> I saw stone implements and weapons brought to light, and none but stone, and was forced to believe that I had penetrated into the stratum of the people belonging to the stone period, I really began to fear that the actual object of my excavations, to find here the Pergamus of Priam, had failed; that I had already reached a period long anterior to the Trojan War.[12]

In keeping with Schliemann's flair for the dramatic, his doubts about these stone implements soon gave way to elation at finding 'ever more and more traces of civilization the deeper I dig'.[13] We have seen how Schliemann's understanding of Troy's stratigraphy was not particularly sophisticated and how objects had a habit of 'tumbling' up and down through the levels (Chapter 3). However, Schliemann's attack on the three-age system was not just a defence of shoddy excavating technique; it was also part of a wider debate about the validity of dating archaeological sites using this system.

In the three-age system, stone tools are replaced by bronze ones, then iron ones as a society progresses, allowing archaeological sites to be dated by the kinds of tools found there. It had been devised within Schliemann's lifetime, but uptake was patchy and shaped by nationalistic concerns.[14] While it was well-known in Britain by the 1870s, many influential archaeologists resisted it.[15] The contemporaneous use of stone and bronze was a particular bone of contention in the debates of the 1860s, used especially in religious arguments against idea of a long human prehistory.[16] In 1858, stone tools had been found among the bones of extinct animals in Brixham Cave, proving that human history was much longer than had previously been assumed. Alongside Darwin's publication of *On the Origin of Species* the following year, this discovery revolutionized understanding of the past. New typological methods from geology, biology and archaeology were used to show long and complex histories in a way that challenged religious faith.[17]

Schliemann's arguments about the use of stone tools were picked up by people who argued against deep time. This included James Cocke Southall, a writer of textbooks on optics who used archaeological evidence from around the world to argue that human history had started about 4,500 years ago.[18] His book *The Recent Origin of Man* built a whole chapter around the idea that the Trojan War had been fought with stone tools. He framed Schliemann's discoveries as a refutation of Sir John Lubbock's idea (drawn from the materials described in Homer) that the Trojan War happened in the transition between Bronze and Iron Ages. Schliemann had not argued this at all, but this ploy allowed Southall to collapse the many layers of Troy into a flatter history that was easier to fit into his Christian world view.[19]

It made sense for Schliemann to present Troy as the key to a big question that was troubling contemporary archaeology, but the stance he took is somewhat surprising. Several major proponents of the three-age theory were also Schliemann's allies in the British archaeological establishment, including Lubbock (whom Schliemann described as 'my honoured friend') and John Evans.[20] Schliemann's approach to the three-age system was somewhat uninformed: proponents of the system accepted that older materials and technologies might continue to be used after the invention of new ones.[21] Schliemann may not have fully understood this, but his interest seems to have been in complicating the system, not abandoning it completely.

Schliemann presented Troy as evidence of a possible Copper Age before the beginning of the Bronze Age. In *Ilios*, Schliemann boasted that he had proved Lubbock's hypothesis that people would have used copper on its own, before discovering that mixing in tin produced the stronger bronze.[22] Schliemann had the metal content of the objects from Troy analysed to prove this and used an early analysis to argue that they were pure copper.[23] Even after other analyses of the objects had established that most were bronze, Schliemann stressed the low tin content.[24] The idea of a Copper Age at Troy caught Gladstone's attention, and he wrote to the Society of Antiquaries to ask for clarification on the metal content of the tools and its significance.[25] Gladstone seems to have preferred a four-age system, including copper, because it explained some features of metal use in Homer, such as the rarity of tin.[26]

While Schliemann's collection was in South Kensington, he asked prominent metallurgist William Chandler Roberts-Austen to perform another analysis. We have already seen how the results piqued the interest of modern bankers (Chapter 8), but Schliemann was most interested in using the results to establish Troy as pre-Bronze Age. He got what he wanted: Roberts-Austen found that there were only trace amounts of tin in objects from the first two levels of Troy, whereas the higher layers used bronze.[27] Put together with Schliemann's ideas about the return of stone tools, this let Schliemann tell a story about Troy as an early city at the cutting edge of ancient metallurgy, which was then destroyed and plundered (perhaps resulting in more use of stone tools) but not held back for long. This narrative of ancient Troy had clear benefits for an excavator who wanted to tie his finds to the Trojan War, but it also put it at the heart of contemporary debates about archaeological chronology.

Chronology or evolution?

While Schliemann's story of an advanced people set back by a destructive war had obvious benefits for fitting Homer with the archaeological evidence, it was difficult to get across in a museum exhibition. Schliemann avoided this difficulty by not presenting the Trojan exhibition in chronological order, but not all visitors to South Kensington were satisfied with this approach. *The Times* spoke highly of the exhibition but complained that it was difficult to make sense of the levels of the site:

> The visitor cannot be struck by the various stages of civilization shown in the diverse objects apparently belonging to one period; delicate gold ornaments and silver goblets, graceful vases of fine terra-cotta and lyres of ivory, side by side with stone, flint and bone implements as rough as any found in the Swiss lacustrine dwellings. It is difficult without very detailed plans of the excavations to account for these incongruities.[28]

The mixture of kinds of objects found at Troy made it difficult to classify and interesting to debate. Troy did not fit easily into a pre-existing narrative of development and visitors struggled to make sense of what they saw. The photographs on display and depths on object labels made clear the depth of Schliemann's trenches and complexity of the site. Schliemann's interpretation did little to offer an overarching narrative to explain changes over time. A later article in *The Times* called for a rearrangement of the collection along chronological lines:

> Many have asked whether the strictly chronological arrangement, of course with proper subdivisions, would not have been far better than that actually adopted. Perhaps it might have been preferable on the whole. It is to be hoped that in the partial rearrangement, which, as we announced the other day, Dr. Schliemann contemplates before long, its merits may be kept in view.[29]

This frames chronology as the logical arrangement for archaeology and a way to make Schliemann's exhibition more intelligible. By the end of the nineteenth century, most museums with archaeological collections were grouping them by the civilization that produced them and arranging those civilizations in a broadly chronological sweep of history.[30] Rearranging the Trojan exhibition to tell a chronological story would make it conform with these expectations and allow visitors to fit it in with broader models of history laid out by them.

However, Schliemann was not alone in displaying functionally related objects from many time periods together. Typological display was a valid alternative, with influential proponents like Augustus Henry Lane Fox Pitt Rivers, who had devised a set of principles for sorting objects by type and then arranging these types to demonstrate the evolution of technology.[31] His approach was guided by his theories of cultural evolution, which placed cultures (ancient and modern) at different stages in a universal progression of technological development.[32] His collection was displayed to the public at the South Kensington Museum's branch at Bethnal Green from 1874 to 1878.[33] It could be compared more closely with Troy when it moved to South Kensington in December 1878.[34] Both dealt with the stuff of everyday life but compared with the Pitt Rivers collection (which included ancient and modern objects from all over the world), the Trojan collection was much more focused in geographical and chronological scope.

Pitt Rivers visited Schliemann's exhibition in 1878 and reviewed it for *Nature*.[35] Although many cases were sorted by type of object, he thought they needed more careful arrangement:

> In short, the history of every form may be traced by connecting links in the specimens exhibited at South Kensington, the whole collection forms a continuous sequence which, by judicious arrangement of connected forms, is capable of demonstration, and it is to be hoped that some such arrangement may be adopted before this interesting collection leaves the place. To apply the expression 'Darwinism' to such a sequence of forms is no mere figure of speech, it expresses the truth as fully in its relation to savage art and ornament as to the forms of nature.[36]

For Pitt Rivers, the Trojan collection offered exciting possibilities. Troy's depth made it particularly fruitful for exploring changes in material in one site through many generations of inhabitants. To achieve this, Pitt Rivers wanted each type of object clearly ordered according to his principles of development.

This criticism may have had an effect. Less than a month after Pitt Rivers's call for rearrangement, Schliemann announced that he had come to London to rearrange his exhibition. He was forced to leave again when his wife became ill, but promised that he would rearrange the collection on his return.[37] It was this announcement that precipitated the hope for a chronological display, quoted from *The Times*, above. No matter how eager Schliemann was to please, he could not please everybody.

These competing demands show a press that took an interest in not only what was on display, but also how it was displayed. They also show a controversy over how the action of time on culture should be modelled in a museum, with opinion split between telling the history of a whole culture and watching individual objects evolve as if they were organisms in a natural history museum.

Pitt Rivers had already tried arranging some of the material from Troy according to his evolutionary principles. In 1875, he sorted pots and other objects from Troy with faces on (Fig. 38) by his evolutionary typology in one of

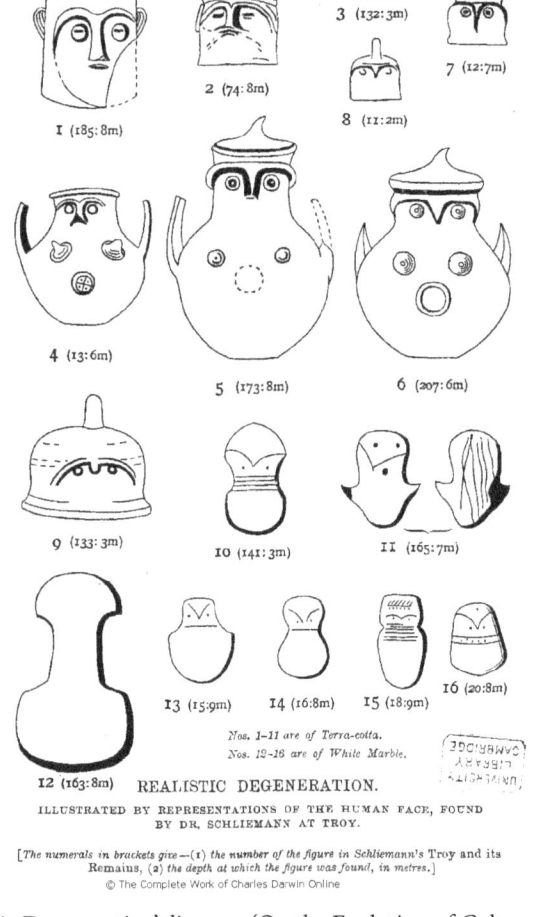

Fig. 38 'Realistic Degeneration' diagram. 'On the Evolution of Culture (1875)', in *The Evolution of Culture and Other Essays by the Late Lt.-Gen. A. Lane-Fox Pitt Rivers*, edited by J.L. Myres (Oxford: Clarendon Press, 1906), 20–44. Reproduced with permission from John van Wyhe, ed. 2002–. *The Complete Work of Charles Darwin Online* (http://darwin-online.org.uk).

the figures for his essay 'On the Evolution of Culture'.[38] He argued that these were not owls but human faces, and that their owl-like appearance was a product of degeneration away from naturalistic human forms to schematic representation. Where some (Scott for one: see Fig. 37 in Chapter 6) saw these figures as examples of art's progressive improvement, Pitt Rivers illustrated them as a process of degeneration away from a realistic human face. This demonstrates a difficulty with such readings when they are unmoored from stratigraphically established dating sequences: multiple contradictory stories can be told with the same body of material. Pitt Rivers's sequence did not use Schliemann's depths as a substitute for dating: for example, number 3 in the series is from 3 m deep, while the supposedly later 15 is from 9 m deep. Pitt Rivers believed his principle of gradual, evolutionary change was so infallible that it proved Schliemann's stratigraphy wrong. Instead, he described a system in which 'every object marks its own place in sequence by means of its form'.[39]

Pitt Rivers's system of visual ordering produced an account of change at Troy that was not driven by natural selection (in which new features are more likely to survive if they provide some advantage). Instead, he imagined it as a process of decay in which the resemblance to the original object deteriorates over time. While Pitt Rivers framed his theories in terms of evolution, Darwin was just one of a number of influences.[40] Here, he was responding to Max Müller's lecture 'The Science of Language: One of the Physical Sciences'. This argued that language was not shaped by the culturally specific processes that shaped other cultural productions and instead was subject to unalterable laws. As a result, Müller argued that the study of language should be counted as a physical science.[41] Pitt Rivers went further to argue that all culture should be studied this way, seeing all creative processes in a culture as products of evolution.[42] He used Troy as an example of decay in material culture as an equivalent to phonetic decay, a result of attempts to reduce the difficulty of saying/creating something. He argued that the face pots had degenerated from something like an Egyptian canopic jar, eventually becoming small, flat idols that merely represent the idea. Troy was a valuable body of material for making this kind of argument, since there was a large quantity of material and clear evidence of long occupation. Troy became one of Pitt Rivers's preferred demonstrations of this process, and he even used this diagram in talks about his own collection.[43]

Attempts to understand Troy depended on a theory of cultural development. Where the three-age system relied on ideas of technological progress for its models of cultural change, the complexity of Troy offered a good case study for refining (or challenging) understanding of this process. Pitt Rivers's system, in which all culture was driven by laws as predictable as the laws of physics but not all cultures were the same, required other variables to explain the differences between cultures. He did not think his argument about Troy's degeneration weakened Schliemann's Homeric claims, but it did tell a story of Troy's art moving further and further from accurate representation and implied that the whole culture might have drifted away from its past glories.[44] Like Schliemann's suggestion that there were stone tools immediately above Homer's Troy, this challenged the use of technological progression alone as a means of dating. However, while Schliemann's model depended on events at that particular site, Pitt Rivers's explanation for why some cultures progressed, while others regressed, was race. Because of the way nineteenth-century models of historical progress worked, the race of Schliemann's Trojans had to be established before their place in history could be understood.

11

Who Were the Trojans?

Schliemann advertised his Trojan exhibition by boasting of his collection's novelty: 'Except two forms of goblets peculiar to the first, and, consequently the most ancient city, built on the virgin soil at Hisarlik, and of which I found similar ones in the Royal tombs at Mycenae, the Trojan antiquities have no resemblance whatever to anything yet found elsewhere: they are, consequently, a new world to archaeology.'[1] Schliemann's characteristic hyperbole makes it sound as if he had discovered a new continent, but he was right that this material looked startlingly new to its London audience. The objects from Troy were unfamiliar in ways that made the site difficult to place in the commonly accepted series of ancient civilizations. Troy had the potential to add a completely new civilization to the history books and perhaps to explain the origins of those already known. However, the novelty of the Trojan material also raised the question of what kind of people these Trojans were and how they might relate to other cultures, ancient or modern. To answer this question, objects found at Troy were compared with ones from different times and places, including ancient Egypt, Central America, Peru, India, Switzerland, Pomerania, Japan and Ohio.[2] Each of these had its own connotations for what life in ancient Troy might have been like and how nineteenth-century audiences should feel about it.

This chapter explores the attempts to assign a racial or cultural identity to Troy's artefacts and human remains. Race has long been recognized as a major issue in responses to Schliemann's Troy, especially the idea that it was Aryan. We have seen how Schliemann highlighted swastikas on the objects from Troy as evidence of connection with other sites in India and Germany. Quinn's history of the swastika as a modern symbol traces its roots to debates over Schliemann's Troy, in which Aryanists (including Schliemann) used the swastika as a marker of a unified Aryan race, present in all of the places where the symbol had been found. Schliemann drew on earlier writing on the topic, especially his collaborator Emile Burnouf, but Troy was critical in shifting Aryanist attention from linguistic connections between Europe and Asia to a malleable symbol. This opened the swastika up to new readings that did not depend on meaning or context and so could project modern identities onto the past. Stripped of nuance, it became the perfect totalitarian symbol.[3] Gere identifies Schliemann's Aryanism as part of a 'wave of archaeologically inspired origin myths' that grew as Christianity receded, becoming particularly influential in modernism.[4] Duesterberg sees responses to the exhibition that saw Trojans as Aryan as a strategy to identify them with contemporary Britain and mark them out as a familiar kind of strangeness compared with other areas of world archaeology.[5]

While the swastika as a marker of a supposed Aryan race at Troy is undoubtedly one of Schliemann's more influential ideas, I want to contextualize this within a broader examination of the role of race in responses to the Trojan collection. Gange has argued that immediate British responses to Troy were dominated by Gladstone's religious approach, and that racial readings of Troy emerged from the intellectual context in Germany and were taken up in Britain after the 1890s.[6] I will show that racial approaches to Troy were already present in Britain in the 1870s and were particularly common among the people who studied the exhibition at South Kensington. We have already seen how Troy offered a controversial opportunity to admire 'primitive' art (Chapter 6) and how Pitt Rivers called for a 'Darwinian' approach to the collection (Chapter 10). This chapter explores Troy as a complex site for establishing identities (past and present) that went well beyond any simple dichotomy between scripture and Darwin.

Trigger has explored a movement in archaeology from the 1860s onwards to see human culture as a unilinear process of development, with living non-European peoples and the archaeological record used as evidence for earlier stages along that development. He saw the racist currents of nineteenth-century archaeology as an abandonment of Enlightenment rationalism.[7] It is certainly true that our conceptions of race have no roots in human biology, despite drawing much of their ideological power from the belief that they do.[8] While the ideas discussed in this chapter are nearly all wrong, I want to explore how they were more deeply entangled with archaeological modes of reasoning. My model owes much more to Horkheimer and Adorno's *Dialectic of Enlightenment* in which the Enlightenment embedded elements of the irrationality that it claimed to overturn.[9] Ideas about human origins were not created from nothing after Darwin, but incorporated earlier ideas of progress from vulnerability towards mastery of nature.[10] Many of Schliemann's contemporaries who doubted his Homeric claims saw racial approaches as a rational, scientific alternative. But Troy owed its potency as an origin myth for European culture to its Homeric associations, and those associations were a useful way to smuggle ancient and modern prejudices into a discipline that claimed to be objective.

Schliemann's finds brought new data and analytical tools to the long-standing question of whether the Trojans were fundamentally Greek or more 'Eastern' in character. This chapter shows how Troy allowed Victorians to integrate Homer and archaeology into contemporary debates about the relationship between Europe and Asia. I explore the search for scientific certainty about the Trojans' ethnicity in the skulls and show how techniques that placed human biology into a hierarchy of intelligence and culture carried anxieties about unheroic ancestors. The most thorough analysis of the skulls from Troy concluded that archaeology was the best place to look for firm answers about the Trojans' race. There was no shortage of attempts to use material evidence from Troy (including language, symbols, material culture and rare stone) to connect it with other cultures. I show how Troy became a useful site for creating broad, universalizing archaeologies that told potent stories about human origins and tied together sites from round the world. The focus on material evidence gave these approaches a veneer of rationality which convinced many that Troy could be understood clearly. However, I show how these approaches generated new mythologies (from the swastika to Atlantis) designed to make European dominance seem inevitable.

Reading race in Homer

Locating Troy culturally carried real implications for how nineteenth-century readers understood the *Iliad*. A different identity for the Trojans could shift the meaning of the Trojan War from a civil war to a war of imperial conquest. In the *Iliad* the Trojans worship the same gods as the opposing army and communicate with them without an apparent language barrier. The 'Greeks' of the *Iliad* were a loosely associated set of local identities, unified by shared goals, but without a shared sense of Greekness.[11] The earliest visual representations of the Trojan War show the two sides as indistinguishable, but around the time of the Persian Wars (early fifth century BCE), Trojans stopped looking like Greeks and began to wear the costume of Persians.[12] As a result, the Trojan War became one of the canonical struggles with Eastern threats used in Greek architectural decoration (most famously the Parthenon) to come to terms with recent history and to project contemporary ethnic identities back onto legendary conflict.[13] The idea of the Trojan War was reinvented as a foundational conflict between Europe and Asia, with lasting influence on Orientalist ideas (both ancient and modern).[14]

While Schliemann's discoveries added a new intensity and a new body of evidence to questions of the ethnic identity of the Trojans, people still drew on the *Iliad* to answer them. For example, Pater saw the Trojans as fundamentally Greek, but more culturally sophisticated than their opponents thanks to Asian influences:

> Homer, as we saw, was right in making Troy essentially a Greek city, with inhabitants superior in all culture to their kinsmen on the Western shore, and perhaps proportionally weaker on the practical or moral side, and with an element of languid Ionian voluptuousness in them, typified by the cedar and gold of the chamber of Paris – an element which the austere, more strictly European influence of the Dorian Apollo will one day correct in all genuine Greeks. The Aegean, with its islands, is, then, a bond of union, not a barrier; and we must think of Greece, as has been rightly said, as its whole continuous shore.[15]

This contrast between European austerity and Asian voluptuousness resulted from reading Homer through a lens of Victorian Orientalism. Said's classic work on the subject identifies the such confident generalities about the East as part of a body of ideas with roots going back at least as far as Homer, but which enjoyed unprecedented institutional support under Victorian colonialism.[16] He describes how these ideas are less about actual understanding of the East than defining the West as its opposite. This is clear in Pater's writing: he does very little to establish why the Trojans have these features, or why that would mean they were under Asian influence. But seeing Troy in this way let him imagine art produced in a place where East and West meet. Pater followed Schliemann in seeing the Trojans as fundamentally Greek, with a material culture influenced by Asia. However, Gladstone used the same set of stereotypes of the Trojans as wealthy, culturally advanced and morally lax to rule out seeing them as Greek:

> Nor have we any right to suppose either that there was an ethnical identity between Greece, or Achaiis, and Troy, or that they had reached, in each and every point, precisely the same point of wealth and social development. More Asiatic in manners, less energetic in character, the Trojans seem to have lived longer together under the forms of civilised society, and to have been less disturbed by wars and revolutions.[17]

Gladstone saw the Trojans as culturally separate from their Greek opponents and from Homer himself, which conveniently explained any differences between the *Iliad*'s description of Troy and Schliemann's discoveries. While Pater imagined culture as something that can be shared and absorbed, Gladstone's

Greeks and Trojans are completely separate and map onto his model of contemporary relations between East and West.

Of course, Gladstone's interest in the relationship between East and West was not purely academic. His political career had been preoccupied with the 'Eastern Question'.[18] Like its Homeric equivalent, this was more a set of interrelated questions concerning how the British government should respond to instability in the Ottoman Empire. Schliemann's discoveries were used to advocate for military intervention against the Ottoman Empire.[19] Gladstone was not immune to such readings of the Trojan War: his identification with the Greeks (something he thought Homer shared) constructed them as proto-democratic antecedents to European culture.[20] The idea of a real Trojan War slotted neatly into a sense of the differences between East and West leading to repeated conflict through the centuries. As Gladstone put it: 'On both sides we find the germ of after-history: the Trojans bearing in many points the more Asiatic, the Greeks the more European stamp.'[21] Gladstone returned to politics in response to Turkish suppression of a Bulgarian uprising shortly after these words were written, so his role in this 'after-history' was an active one.[22] While Schliemann's discoveries were a great excuse to talk about the Eastern Question, ideas about the East were changing rapidly because of newly developed linguistic, biological and archaeological models of difference and hierarchies of cultural development. Schliemann's discovery of Troy came at a perfect time to fit the Trojan War into a racialized model of history in which the effects of the conflict could still be felt. But to do this, the ambiguities over the Trojans' ethnicity (drawn from different readings of Homer) needed to be resolved. The racial sciences of the nineteenth century claimed to offer an objective method for determining race, removed from the ambiguities of cultural influence: the study of human remains.

The skulls from Troy

A couple of weeks after the Trojan exhibition opened, *The Builder* published its review of the collection. The last paragraph described a male skull from Schliemann's Homeric level as 'worth special notice' despite being less appealing to most visitors. It described the skull in detail:

> so extraordinarily *animal* in character, with its narrow receding forehead, projecting jaws, and powerful teeth (the latter almost entirely perfect), that if we are to take this as any typical specimen of the men who were engaged in the conflict about Troy, and who were the authors of much of the work exhibited

here, we must come around to the conclusion that, in spite of the glamour thrown around them by Homer, they were, if physiological character means anything, a set of ruffians very low in the scale of existence.

Certain Homeric critics have already drawn this deduction, mainly from the peculiarly barbaric acts of Achilles and the matter-of-course manner in which they are regarded, besides the general style of the hand-to-hand combat of the Iliad. It is certainly curious to find among these relics a skull so exceedingly calculated to confirm this uncomplimentary estimate of 'the heroic age'.[23]

This highlights the anxieties raised by Schliemann's discoveries. If Schliemann's Trojans were Homer's Trojans, people would need to stop romanticizing the characters of the *Iliad*. Perhaps they had been wrong to do so anyway. The article was broadly positive towards the collection and Schliemann's ideas but could not shake the uncomfortable implications of the material. It also observed that Schliemann was selling his Trojans short by describing the little pieces of carved stone as 'idols' since 'the articles hardly seem designed to represent anything so important as a god'.[24]

While the reviewer thought there would be little interest in this skull, this section of the review took on a life of its own. It was reprinted in a number of publications, including *The Times*.[25] As an excerpt, it almost seemed parodic, and indeed it inspired a more explicitly humorous imitator.[26] This passage seemed to nail some of the discomfort of the debates over Schliemann's collection. Schliemann's Troy brought together two rich sources of nineteenth-century British identity that related past to present: the classics and racial hierarchies. But it did so in ways that made people uneasy, especially because of the hopes pinned on it as a point of origin by both disciplines. *The Builder* managed to reconcile the two by throwing out the unspoken desire for Homeric Troy to be noble and beautiful.

The uncertainty over Troy was compounded by broader uncertainties about human origins raised by the natural sciences. Darwin and other evolutionists had recently troubled assumptions about human origins. The animal features assigned to Trojan skulls in *The Builder* ('receding forehead, projecting jaws, and powerful teeth') evoke the claim that all humans were apes, and particularly evoke strands of racial science that sorted human skulls by perceived development away from ape-like features that were being used at this time to generate a hierarchy of races, with devastating consequences for those deemed inferior.[27] Classical statues often stood for the most developed humans in these hierarchies and skulls of real ancient Greeks were highly sought after for collections of human remains intended to understand human anatomy and racial characteristics.[28] The skulls from Troy promised to extend this system deeper into time and perhaps resolve some of the nagging questions about the site's place in human history raised by its simple objects and uncertain dating. They offered the possibility of insight into the heroes of Europe's legendary past but carried the possibility that people might not like what they found.

These were not remote scientific debates. In fact, public interest in these issues was high. Phrenology had popularized the idea that measuring skulls of individuals could be used to understand aspects of their character. Although it had largely been abandoned by scientists at the time Troy was discovered, it still maintained a popular following.[29] One of the magazines that maintained this interest, the American periodical *The Phrenological Journal of Science and Health* eagerly covered the discovery of Troy:

> The breadth of the forehead indicates comprehensiveness of view and versatility. The fullness of the side-head forward of the ear shows mechanical ingenuity, the desire to acquire money, appreciation of the humorous and artistic, superior ability as a calculator and organizer. The physiognomy does not impress us with the idea of a social nature which is broad, warm, and luxuriant, but rather that its owner is content with few friends, and finds his chief enjoyment in the prosecution of enterprises acceptable to his intellectual and esthetic tastes.[30]

This was not a description of one of the skulls from Troy, but of Schliemann himself. It was published alongside a biography and a portrait. Like the skulls from Troy, Schliemann's head (or at least a two-dimensional picture of it) was seen as a means of reading his personal qualities. These qualities are exactly what we would expect from reading the many other biographical articles about Schliemann, and indeed the rest of the article reproduces these closely. Normally these biographies are fascinated by the idea of Schliemann as a self-made man, navigating though disaster and opportunity with acumen and a fair measure of luck.[31] This version is certainly drawn from accounts like these more than any possible reading of his photograph, but the phrenological angle still carried meaning. It placed the credit for Schliemann's qualities and achievements firmly on his physical make-up, with the racial implications left unspoken, but never fully absent.

Just as Schliemann's head could speak for his character and skills, the skulls from Troy were called upon to represent the character and level of civilization of their society. In both cases, the skulls were not being interpreted in a vacuum, but in the light of the other things known and assumed about their owners. The article in *The Builder* was unusual for imagining the Trojan skulls as violent and uncivilized, most other comments on the shape of the skulls from Troy find a people who fit the qualities their viewers need in Homeric heroes and ancestors of their own race:

> A careful consideration of these relics of ancient humanity leads up to the conclusion that the ancient inhabitants of Hissarlik – whether the Trojans of Homer or not – were undoubtedly of noble race. The brain capacity is large, and the facial angle of the high type of the Aryan. Clearly these are not the skulls of barbarians, or if barbarians, yet of those possessing the capacity for development.[32]

This was one of a number of reports concluded that the skulls looked distinctly Aryan.[33] Duesterberg describes these as phrenological readings, but they do not share phrenology's preoccupation with reading the character traits of individuals out of the shape of their skulls.[34] Instead, these are products of a number of related approaches to skull-measuring that succeeded phrenology and better met the desires of scientists and amateurs to study whole human populations and generalize about their mental capacities. The above reviewer uses Camper's facial angle. This was developed by Petrus Camper to demonstrate similarities between humans of all races, but was commonly used as a proxy for brain size and to generate a racial hierarchy, running from the ideal of Greek statues to the skulls of apes.[35] The distinction between phrenology and the anthropometric disciplines that followed it matters because this was not part of a passing pseudoscientific craze, but a growing set of disciplinary ideas that would go on to shape the disciplines of anthropology and archaeology, embedding racial assumptions under the guise of science.

Most visitors to South Kensington were unable to measure the skulls for themselves, so the repeated designation of the skulls as Aryan may come from Schliemann's labels. Schliemann was deeply interested in proving the race of his Trojans, and in 1878 he took the skulls off of display for closer study.[36] Schliemann's friend, the doctor and anthropologist Rudolf Virchow, examined the skulls and submitted measurements along with detailed 'geometrical' drawings for publication in *Ilios*.[37] For all three skulls, he assigned age and gender (broadly agreeing with Schliemann's guesses from earlier publications). He was also interested in determining whether the skulls were 'brachycephalic' (round) or 'dolichocephalic' (long): two terms for skull shape that came to be used to distinguish racially between different groups.[38] Virchow thought he could see both types at Troy, and believed all of them showed signs of civilization:

> it must not be overlooked that all three skulls present in a striking manner the appearance of the bones of a race in an advanced state of civilization. Nothing of the savage, nothing massive in the formation of the bones, no particularly strong

development of the apophyses of the muscles and tendons can be observed. All the parts have a smooth, fine almost slender appearance ... with savage races the bones acquire earlier a greater thickness and ruggedness, and it is therefore most natural to infer that the ancient owners of these heads belonged to a settled people, who were acquainted with the arts of peace, and who, through intercourse with distant races were more exposed to being mixed in blood.[39]

This preoccupation with levels of civilization as something objectively determinable from the bones of the skull is characteristic of contemporary scientific racism. However, this is much more cautious than the claims in newspapers. Virchow expressed his fear of over-interpreting the evidence, given his data set of three damaged skulls (not to mention the broader controversies about Troy). Where a phrenologist was happy to work from a single individual (whether that was Schliemann or an anonymous ancient person), Virchow was interested in building up racial characterizations of whole peoples from large bodies of evidence. Three broken skulls would not be enough.

> The temptation is very great to make further suppositions regarding the extraction of the individual persons and their social position. This temptation, I believe, I must resist because our real knowledge of the craniology of ancient peoples is still on a very small scale ... But if besides the skull index we take into consideration the entire formation of the head and the face of the dolichocephalic skulls, the idea that those men were members of the Aryan race is highly pleasing. Hence I believe the natural philosopher should stop in the face of these problems, and should abandon further investigation to the archaeologist.[40]

While Virchow was waiting for more information, he was also somewhat sceptical of Aryan theory.[41] Despite his temptation to see the skulls as Aryan (probably in deference to Schliemann's ideas about the site) he passed the responsibility of establishing these facts on to other specialists, studying the site's material culture.

Troy in world archaeology

When Virchow moved away from his specialism to more general issues, he was far less reserved about who the Trojans were. In his preface to *Ilios*, he imagined Troy as a site of conflict between East and West:

> For us Priam and Ilium will remain the designations on which our thoughts fasten, as often as they concern themselves with events of that period. It was here,

where Asia and Europe for the first time encountered in a war of extermination (*in völkerfressendem Kampfe*); it was here that the only decisive victory was won in fight [*sic*], which the West gained over the East on the soil of Asia, during the whole time down to Alexander the Great.[42]

This chilling language sees Troy as the first site of an ongoing struggle between nations in a way that made the Bronze Age appear relevant to contemporary politics and seems to anticipate the genocides of the twentieth century.[43] This idea was made clearer still in the opening lines of Pitt Rivers's review of the Trojan exhibition, which covered the excavations at Troy and Mycenae alongside the exhibition at South Kensington and Cesnola's recent publication on Cyprus.[44] It presented these sites as key to understanding the origins of European culture in a way that could inform contemporary politics:

> Two Eastern questions occupy the attention of Europe at the present time – one relating to the present, and, it is to be feared greatly, to the future; the other has reference to the past, and to the bridging over of that little known protohistoric period which connects the civilisation of the far east, that is, Egypt and Assyria, with the culture of ancient Greece, to which we western Europeans are so much indebted.[45]

For Pitt Rivers, the expanding empires of Europe (particularly British relations with the Ottoman Empire) mirrored the idea that culture had been spread from Asia to Europe millennia earlier. Unlike Gladstone, Pitt Rivers did not see this as a reprisal of an eternal conflict between East and West, but the return of a wave of cultural change. He thought that an expanding Europe would inevitably encounter traces of its own origins in a similar expansion from Asia long ago:

> Different conditions of thought are engaged in the study of these two questions, yet both are connected, for the present crisis in the East represents the returning current of the same stream of culture which was flowing westward towards the dawn of our era. What Egypt and Assyria lent to Greece she passed on to Etruria and Rome, and the Romans carried to the shores of the Atlantic, there developing and fructifying, it has passed back eastward in a return wave, reviving the ancient monarchies in its path. Rome has regained its ancient landmarks. Germany has consolidated. Austria has been pushed, and is still pushing eastward. Greece is proclaiming the revival of its ancient nationality, and this will doubtless be followed in times to come by the resuscitation of Egypt and Palestine. The Turk, representing the last wave of the western flow, has been met and swamped by the returning ebb.[46]

The idea of Troy as a bridge between Europe and Asia had explanatory force not only for the objects found at the site, but also for the contemporary state of the world. There was a long tradition of stories about people from Troy coming to Europe to found cities and inspire cultural development, most famously the role of the Trojan Aeneas in the foundation of Rome. These stories do sometimes appear in explanations of Schliemann's Troy, but they are comparatively rare.[47] A new, equally potent, origin myth for European culture was forming, which was also based on the idea of a migration from the East with Troy playing a major role. However, this model also depended on the other half of Pitt Rivers's equation: contemporary Western empires in the East. These offered access to new archaeological sites and new knowledge but (as Pitt Rivers makes clear) their power relations shaped how that knowledge could be understood, with the logics of the present projected back on the past.

In 1786, Sir William Jones had demonstrated the common roots shared between Sanskrit and several European languages, including Latin and Ancient Greek.[48] He adopted the word Aryan from a Sanskrit word for free man to describe the language group he had identified. A century later, at the height of the controversy over Troy, it was still unclear exactly what these commonalities of language meant, but it was difficult to deny the connection. Discomfort with the idea of common cultural roots with the people of India had given way to an enthusiasm for the idea that Greek culture was Aryan. Bernal's *Black Athena* makes clear how the idea of Aryan roots for Greek civilization offered an appealing alternative to Egyptian origins for disciplines that routinely dismissed African culture.[49] Pitt Rivers does list Egypt as one of the points in civilization's journey to and from Europe, but the main cultural flow he described was between Asia and Europe. The idea of culture being transferred from one place to another is not an automatic fit for his model of objects evolving as if they were organisms. However, it makes perfect sense for the racial logics that underpin Pitt Rivers's theories and explain why he believed one culture might stagnate or move backwards, while others evolved. Pitt Rivers's adoption of models from the study of language reflects a wider phenomenon in nineteenth-century racial theory in which the study of language, biology and culture were being drawn together into a single chronology, often with evolutionary beliefs about gradual change and survival of the fittest at their core.[50] Troy was a particularly promising site for this sort of combined analysis: it was early, deep and complex, and connected to one of the founding myths of contact and conflict between Asian and European peoples.

Schliemann clearly wanted his Troy to demonstrate shared cultural roots between Europe and Asia. It is telling that when arranging his collection at South

Kensington, he asked Max Müller (a prominent theorist of language and Aryan mythology) to help, rather than someone with expertise in ancient pottery. Where Müller explained events in Homer as a solar allegory, Schliemann wanted his Troy to be proof that they were real. Schliemann cited Müller in his reasons for identifying the motifs on the whorls with the Sanskrit term 'swastika' and he often identified it as a solar symbol.[51] Müller warned Schliemann that similar forms did not mean common roots, and that it was inaccurate to use the term 'swastika' outside of India. For Müller, projecting theories from the study of language onto other fields was risky without sufficient evidence. There were no conclusively proven examples of language from the Homeric layer of the site, which meant that ideas about Aryanism got displaced onto symbols in a way that stripped rational analysis and concrete meaning out of the interpretation.[52]

Müller's caveats had little impact on public responses to Troy; indeed the exhibition at South Kensington started a craze for swastika-spotting, as people looked for swastikas around the world and tried to make connections to other similar symbols.[53] Even William Simpson (whose criticism of Schliemann's discoveries we explored in Chapter 1) joined in this exercise and included Troy in his volume of swastikas, crosses and other forms he saw as related.[54] However, one of the reasons for this great exercise of compiling and comparing was that people were not entirely sure what the swastika meant and where it was from. Articles responding to Schliemann's swastika could give it a wide range of meanings and sources and a number of alternatives to the idea of Indian origins were proposed, from imitating the stamps on the back of Greek coins to being a distinctively Hittite motif.[55]

Schliemann was also interested in finding linguistic connections to Asia, and the same whorls that were prized for their swastikas were also searched closely for readable inscriptions.[56] Müller was sceptical about whether the inscriptions (if that is what they were) could be deciphered, given how little there was to work with, but he described being tempted to read one as 'Ilion'. He wrote to the *Academy* with a clear tone of frustration when he discovered that Schliemann and others had been reporting this bit of wishful thinking as a confident assertion.[57] Müller recognized and checked his desire to pull scraps of meaning out of the marks on the objects from Troy, but others were happy to speculate. Both Müller's suggestion and his favourite of the more serious attempts (by the Viennese scholar Theodor Gomperz) used the Cypriot Syllabary.[58] This had been recently deciphered by George Smith, whose discovery of Mesopotamian parallels to the biblical flood story had excited enormous public interest.[59] Smith saw it as a language that was very closely related to Greek, but with influences from Phoenician. If the marks at Troy could be proved to be Cypriot, it would connect Troy to the Greek world, but also imply a role for Troy similar to Cyprus in connecting up the cultures around the Mediterranean to those further East. Meanwhile, Emile Burnouf (a virulently antisemitic theorist of religion who was a major influence on Schliemann's version of Aryanism), suggested a more explicit connection to the East by reading the marks on one of the pots from Troy as Chinese.[60] In practice, the 'inscriptions' from Troy were little better than the swastikas. Readings were more projected on them than drawn out of them, resulting in wildly divergent readings, even of the same objects.

One approach that people hoped might offer a more scientific basis to linking Troy to the East was geological analysis of the most impressive stone tools found at Troy. Thirteen of the axe heads that Schliemann had found at Troy had been identified as jade.[61] The only known sources were in Asia and New Zealand.[62] The presence of this stone at Troy raised the question of how it had got there and what that meant for the site's culture and origins. The two possible explanations were that it had been traded over a long distance and (most promisingly for the Aryanists) that it had been carried with a migrating group of people. The answer to this question seemed to lie in Troy's relationship with the other sites around the world where the stone had been found. These included many important early European sites, but also sites further afield:

> The discovery of jade on the site of Troy by Dr. Schliemann is nothing surprising; the north-western coast of Asia Minor lay, so to speak, on the highroad from Asia to Europe. But of late years jade has been not unfrequently found in Mexico, the West Indies and South America – Particularly in Venezuela and Brazil. Now, Assuming that Jade does not exist in a natural state in this part of the world, where did these pieces come from?[63]

This article goes on to note similar objects found in Troy and Peru, but notes that without the stone this could just be a coincidence. The unwillingness to take the obvious step of suggesting an undiscovered deposit of jade somewhere in the Americas hints that there is more at stake than questions of geology. The fact that no jade had been found in Africa was stated twice in this very short article, underlining jade's special connection with the parts of the word deemed Aryan, and suggesting a further reach for this civilization than previously imagined.

This was not the only example of Troy being connected with parts of the Americas deemed surprisingly civilized. The antiquarian William Borlase pointed out similarities (including objects, symbols and geology) between the Trojan collection on display at South Kensington and the objects associated with the 'mound builders' of Kentucky and Ohio (now known as the Adena and Hopewell cultures).⁶⁴ The presence of impressive earthworks and artefacts in this area stood in opposition to the racial myths that Native Americans were incapable of civilization, which were used as excuses for seizing their lands. Rather than revise these myths, archaeologists speculated that the mounds were the work of another group of people who had been displaced by the Native Americans.⁶⁵ Borlase did not make any claims as to why these 'singular anomalies' existed, but encouraged others to study them further. This sparked some debate in American archaeological circles, who spotted more similarities between the idols from Troy and net sinkers found near them.⁶⁶

The idea of a single originating civilization that provides a simple explanation for all major world cultures will be familiar to anyone who has encountered modern pseudoarchaeologies. Indeed, the idea of owl-headed vases and cyclopean masonry in Peru became one of Ignatius Donnelly's arguments for the existence of an Aryan Atlantis, which in turn went on to influence modern Ancient Aliens discourse.⁶⁷ But many of the people who argued for these connections for Troy thought themselves sceptics and highly rational. Borlase doubted Schliemann's Homeric claims about Troy and condemned others for putting unscientific claims before an 'over-credulous' public.⁶⁸ The idea that material evidence was more rational than the search for ancient myth still held for many, even when patchy and ambiguous material evidence was being used to make extraordinary claims. For some, Troy seemed to suggest that the solution to human origins, cultural similarity and cultural difference was just around the corner in a discourse that brought together approaches as diverse as linguistics, anthropology, geology and close readings of Homer. This joint discourse (which often had Darwinism at its core) could be a direct threat to religious faith and more traditional approaches to the past. However, the idea of a truth behind Homer's Troy and a real ancestry for modern people in the site could also offer common ground in these debates:

> Who were these ancient people who worked in gold and copper, bronze, and stone? We know not anything about Them save what Homer told us and what Dr Henry Schliemann has brought to light of late years; but one thing must strike every student on entering our museum, and that is the resemblance between the objects engraved in Schliemann's book and the decaying relics of a bygone time in our own land which find a place in the cases. These crumbling old pots, these mouldering spear heads, daggers and bracelets in our museum have more to tell us of the universal brotherhood of man than all the preachers in our city can convey by words; and it is surely time to allow the patient students and the men

of science to become preachers of the truth to our toiling people on the one rest day of the week.[69]

This letter to the *Liverpool Mercury* was part of an ongoing debate about the Sunday opening of the local museums, and broader movements to promote 'rational leisure' and better access to public institutions.[70] It posits Troy as a complement to the lessons learned in church, with Schliemann's achievements as a model for working people to emulate. It also offers the Trojans themselves as ancestors for modern audiences that could prove all humans part of a global community – no trite sentiment, given that some still believed that other races were different species. Troy seemed to offer a point where the traditional stories of ancient texts could be reconciled with the new archaeological and anthropological discourses that threatened to undermine these stories, promising a truth that could reconcile the two.

At the time this letter was published, the Trojan collection was long gone from South Kensington, but Troy was still useful to advocate for access to museums as a means to understand humanity and educate ordinary people. Its geographical location and ability to combine ancient literary tradition with the materially based sciences that were transforming perceptions of the ancient world made it particularly valuable as a way to connect past and present into a unified world history. While answers to the question of who the Trojans were (Aryans, Atlanteans, 'savages', Greeks, Orientals etc.) varied dramatically, they always had a bearing on modern identity. The fact that Troy was a material place and could be subjected to scientific analysis made conclusions of European superiority seem rational and inevitable. While there were still large gaps in the evidence, people felt certain that the uncertainties about Troy, as well as its wider global role, would soon be definitively resolved.

Part Five

Troy's Legacy

The sensation over seeing real objects from a legendary city began to die down once Schliemann's collection had moved on to a permanent home. However, it took some time for the full impact of Schliemann's collection to be felt. As the scholar of Greek religion, Jane Ellen Harrison put it:

> Old men began to see visions, young men to dream dreams. I had just left Cambridge when Schliemann began to dig at Troy ... we classical deaf-adders stopped our ears and closed our eyes; but at the mere sound of the magical words 'Golden Bough' the scales fell – we heard and understood. Then Arthur Evans set sail for his new Atlantis and telegraphed news of the Minotaur from his own labyrinth; perforce we saw this was a serious matter, it affected the 'Homeric Question.'[1]

Harrison here tells a story of the development of her discipline, but it is a narrative of progress towards a less rational approach to the past; one with space for dreams. Textual criticism was giving way to new techniques that offered the possibility of making the stories real. While deeper knowledge of ancient myths is, at best, a minor part of the gains made by archaeology at this time, those myths are fundamental to the way the discipline imagined its achievements and the way its story continues to be told. Schliemann's place as an outsider, ignored at first, but able to radically transform the perception of the past, is crucial: both for the actual changes he effected and for the new stories it allowed people to tell about their relationship with the past.

This final part of the book looks at what changed after the discovery of Troy. It examines the work of Harrison, alongside another scholar more conventionally seen as a successor to Schliemann: Arthur Evans. For both, I have chosen to focus on their early public-facing work and how the debates over the discovery of Troy created appetites for novel approaches to the ancient world that drew on archaeology, text and imagination. I consider how the museum had become a place that could offer authentic experiences of the world of Homer and Greek myth and reflect on how the approaches taken at the interface between scholarship and the public adapted to new expectations after the discovery of Troy. Harrison used the popularity of the idea of Homeric archaeology and the new audiences who took an interest during Schliemann's exhibition as a springboard to her own career. Chapter 12 considers the talks on the *Odyssey* and Greek myth that she gave at the British Museum and South Kensington. Although Harrison's model of the relationship between archaeology and Homer was very different Schliemann's, her work reflects a new attitude that came to prominence after the discovery of Troy. By using ancient objects as evidence for lost versions of myths, Harrison offered an appealing new role for archaeological material. She described Schliemann's discoveries at Troy as having transformed attitudes to archaeology by tapping into something valued from literature and inspiring people to ask new questions about familiar texts. She applied this approach in her own work to reach new audiences and experiment with new ways of seeing familiar objects.

The next major discovery of a Bronze Age site, famous from Homer after Schliemann, was Knossos, the reputed site of the Labyrinth. Chapter 13 looks at Evans's first exhibition about Knossos and compares it with the responses to the Trojan exhibition. These show familiar themes from early encounters with the Trojan collection, including a belief that it might transform art and a hope that it might tell another side of the story from the one preserved in literature. Evans's discoveries were much more widely accepted by a public that was now more accustomed to the idea of Greek prehistory. But I argue that Evans also learned from the responses to Schliemann, carefully framing himself as a sceptic, even while making his Homeric claims. In doing so, he left much more space for his audience to imagine beyond the evidence and dramatized the boundaries of archaeological knowledge.

Chapter 14 concludes by asking how the questions raised by Schliemann are still active in museum discourse today. This is clear in the response to *Troia: Traum und Wirklichkeit* (Troy: Dream and Reality), an exhibition showcasing new discoveries from Troy that toured Germany in 2001. This exhibition is best known for bitterly public academic disputes about whether the excavators were over-interpreting the evidence. Much has changed in archaeology since the Trojan exhibition, but the idea of connecting myth and reality remains a potent one for archaeologists and the public, and it often gets used in museum discourse without much comment. However, Troy is a subject that exposes the difficulties of this dichotomy. It raises the question of whether a strictly evidence-based and factual approach is even possible in response to famous sites with diverse cultural meanings.

12

Jane Harrison's Odyssey

After Schliemann's collection moved on in 1881, an appetite remained for exploring the connection between Homer and archaeology. With the world's best-known collection of 'Homeric' antiquities on its way to Berlin, and public attention moving on, one young scholar was experimenting with using the *Odyssey* to re-examine the permanent collections of the British Museum for visitors. This natural sequel to Schliemann's obsession with the *Iliad* proved massively popular, growing from small private groups to packed lecture halls at South Kensington.[1] Jane Ellen Harrison used the vogue for Homer to experiment with new approaches to ancient objects that combined image and text, broached complicated topics in approachable ways and reached out to new audiences.

Harrison arrived in London at the peak of Schliemania in 1879. She had recently finished her Cambridge education, but failed to secure an academic post. By 1880, she was studying archaeology with Charles Newton at the British Museum.[2] She was well integrated with the events of this book in other ways: she performed as Penelope in *The Tale of Troy* and was friends with (and heavily influenced by) Walter Pater.[3] Harrison described how she started lecturing at the British Museum because of a spontaneous suggestion by Newton that she take groups of women round the gallery. While these tours were clearly sanctioned by Newton, she was not employed by the British Museum.[4] The informal guided tours for small groups (sometimes as few as two, or as many as thirty), moved around the galleries, pausing to focus on specific objects.[5] Even the early lectures were novel enough to attract press coverage: in 1881, *The Graphic* illustrated a woman (almost certainly Harrison) leading a group of women and girls around the British Museum (Fig. 39). Demand for this kind of information about ancient art was high. A few years later Harrison began lecturing to larger audiences at the South Kensington Museum.[6] These were accessible lectures that combined Greek art with contemporary aesthetic judgement and a wider sense of the ancient world. They seem to have been a perfect fit for South Kensington's mixture of collections and educational institutions, with a shared focus on

Fig. 39 'At the British Museum – A Peripatetic Art Lecturer', Charles Roberts, *The Graphic*, 5 November 1881. Photograph by A. Baker, by kind permission of Cambridge University Library.

lifelong public education.[7] The lectures had a strong visual focus: looking directly at objects in the galleries of the British Museum or illuminating the dark lecture theatres of South Kensington with beautiful lantern slides.[8] But they also used ancient objects to tell stories from Homer and find a new place for ancient literature in museum experiences.

Harrison is best known for her later work, which used anthropological methods to explore Greek religion as well as for her role as a pioneering woman scholar with an influence on literary Modernism.[9] Her early work used ancient objects to attend to a broader sense of the ancient world, in the mould of Pater's responses to Greek art (discussed in Chapters 6 and 9) and to challenge the dominance of text-based approaches to the ancient world.[10] In this chapter, I explore Harrison's museum lectures as an example of public archaeology that used interest in the relationship between the literary tradition and material culture after Schliemann to promote a new approach to ancient objects. Where Schliemann dug for evidence of the literal truth of the *Iliad*, Harrison used more familiar objects to offer new answers to the Homeric Question. Her vision of how archaeology could reinterpret epics focused on the variants of stories told visually on Greek vases and other objects as clues to the development of the myths retold by Homer. This promised to expand the scope of archaeology, enabling it to contribute to the (more valued) study of literature, but it also made ancient literature accessible to audiences who had not received a classical education. Harrison credited Schliemann as the first to connect the idealized world of classical literature and the realities of ancient life, offering material for new approaches that would revolutionize the study of archaeology.

Contemporary accounts of Harrison's talks describe how she told the stories on objects (hence making the talks accessible without background knowledge of literature) before connecting them to other forms of the myth and explaining social and ritual context.[11] This approach can be seen in greater detail in *Myths of the Odyssey in Greek Art* (1882), a book written by Harrison in her first year at the British Museum and supplemented by objects seen while travelling around Europe.[12] This tells the events of books 9 to 12 of the *Odyssey*, with each chapter covering a self-contained story, quoting at length from Butcher and Lang's translation, and pausing at key moments to introduce and explain relevant works of art. The chapters follow the events in the *Odyssey* from the Cyclops to Scylla and Charybdis, in the order in which Odysseus retells his travels to the Phaeacians.[13] Harrison also explored alternative forms of the myth once the Homeric version had been told. For example, the Cyclops episode is told as in *Odyssey* 9, followed by an exploration of other traditions about the Cyclopes: the talented craftsmen and builders of cyclopean masonry, Polyphemus' love of Galatea and the equivalents of the Cyclopes in other mythologies and contemporary folklore.[14] Harrison described Homer's role as incorporating pre-existing folklore (which she described as 'the common property of both Aryan and non-Aryan peoples') into a coherent whole.[15] The digressions from Homer were presented as possible evidence of the broader mythology that informed the *Odyssey*, with examples drawn from material culture, folklore and literature.

Harrison's emphasis on storytelling is unusual, but makes sense in the context of museum interpretation and public lectures, offering important background information on objects in an engaging way for a non-expert public. It can be difficult to pin down the relationship between the book and the lectures.[16] Not all of Harrison's lectures were on Homer, but most tackled the relationship between myth and art in similar ways, with titles like 'The Myths of Attica as Seen on Greek Vase Paintings' and 'Myths of the Trojan War'.[17] While the book was one step removed from the museum context, it featured many objects from the British Museum and Harrison acknowledged help from the curators in the preface.[18] *Myths of the Odyssey* was written as a stand-alone work, not as a museum guide, but it stressed the importance of museum visiting for a full understanding of its content:

> The pictures I offer are themselves but the shadows, more or less faithful, of other pictures. Where we can look at the original, no copy must suffice us. Some of these originals are in our own Museum. These we are bound to study. Where the original is in a foreign museum beyond our reach, we can at least familiarise ourselves with analogous designs of the same style and period ... Even a few hours will make the dead pictures of the book a living reality.[19]

Myths of the Odyssey aimed to shape the way readers experienced the museum by introducing them to a particular way of looking at the objects. Harrison's tone is didactic, but the emphasis is on learning an approach to ancient art, not just facts. She advised her readers that archaeology was evolving rapidly and that her readers should make up their own minds about her theories.[20] This makes sense in a context in which museum visitor numbers were increasing and anxieties about whether visitors were behaving appropriately and learning the right lessons were commonly expressed.[21] Women's magazines recommended Harrison's museum talks as a way of learning to visit a museum correctly.[22]

The approach to ancient objects through stories from ancient literature may have seemed particularly appropriate for women, who (as we have seen in Chapter 9) were sometimes encouraged to have a more imaginative, less intellectual engagement with the past.[23] However, the central role of Homer in elite education and wider Victorian culture meant that there were also more practical reasons why women might want to become familiar with the stories and culture of ancient Greece. Harrison described how members of her audience wanted to participate in their children's education more fully, help them with their studies and pass on what they had learned at the museum talks.[24] This need to fill in the gaps in women's education provided a practical reason for Harrison to retell the stories on Greek vases.[25] However, Harrison also used these retellings as the basis for a sophisticated examination of how image and story relate to each other.

Unlike Schliemann, Harrison had no investment in proving Homer to be true. Books 9–12 of the *Odyssey* contain many of the epic's most fantastical incidents, and they are framed as a retelling of a retelling. This offers a helpful distancing mechanism that removes questions of truth and fiction from the book. Harrison did touch on Troy, Mycenae and Tiryns when discussing cyclopean masonry, but she did not mention Schliemann's excavations. Instead, she cites Murray (a member of staff at the British Museum and one of

Schliemann's more outspoken critics) on possible connections to Assyrian art.[26] Harrison sought the roots of Homer's stories, not in true events in the Bronze Age but in a complex body of mythology. While the Homeric Question foregrounded literary composition in a way that distanced these texts from any literal truth, Harrison thought archaeology offered the missing versions of myths that would shed light on the process of composition:

> By two voices the tales of Homer have been told to us: to one of these we too often neglect to listen. Because the myths of Homer himself are told in words that are matchless, is it well that the story which art has left us should remain unread? The vase-painter and the gem engraver are indeed sometimes humbler artists than the great epic poet; sometimes they are mere craftsmen, and their work little beyond the rudest symbolic word-painting; but they are Greeks, and they may help us to understand somewhat better the spirit of their mighty kinsman. We who are so far removed, by time, by place, by every condition of modern life, must refuse no aid whereby we may seek to draw the nearer: our eyes must learn to see as well as our ears to harken.[27]

After the Trojan exhibition, the museum-going public of London were more aware than ever of the cultural gap between the world of Homer and their own time. Harrison stressed that ancient objects were not just illustrations, but an 'unread commentary' that might show the work of Homer in a new light.[28] In doing so, she highlighted the fact that none of these artists were working directly from Homer's text and that some may have been working from the oral myths that inspired Homer. This can be seen as part of a wider attempt to theorize the relationship between image and text, and the specific differences in the ways the two media depict stories that began with Lessing's *Laokoon* and continues to be a vital part of any 'reading' of a mythological image.[29] While Harrison was not the first to tackle these questions, it is significant that she was doing this for an audience of non-experts at a time when Homer was particularly controversial.

Harrison's mentor at the British Museum, Charles Newton, advocated a more interdisciplinary model of archaeology to mirror and complement the study of ancient texts. For example, in the talk 'On the Study of Archæology' given to the Archaeological Institute in 1850, he had made a claim for archaeology as a discipline that reached far beyond excavated sites and ancient objects to include all aspects of the ancient world not preserved in historical texts, including oral traditions, customs, inscriptions, buildings, high art and everyday objects.[30] He argued for the importance of museums as a way to gather all the relevant material together and facilitate study. Since the Trojan exhibition had made the relationship between ancient texts and ancient objects the subject of heated public debate, there was an appetite for more accessible versions of this scholarly approach.

Harrison's lectures and writings in the 1880s combined the academic techniques that Newton wanted to include in archaeology with the appeal of visualizing Homer through ancient objects that made Schliemann's ideas so popular. She made a case for exploring a broad cultural context, in which all things produced by ancient Greeks offer a way to understand their culture.[31] However, where Newton described the myths on household objects as a 'dead letter' to modern people, Harrison's focus on stories, looking at texts and images side by side, made them more accessible and gave the impression that objects could be 'read' just like texts.[32] She was able to use humble works of craft to comment on a great work of literature, whereas Newton thought them useful mainly for patching in the parts of literature that had been lost and helping understand more important art.[33] For Newton, objects could not be fully understood without their stories; for Harrison this was true but, additionally, stories could not be fully understood without objects.

Harrison's desire to see both art and literature as part of the same field of study played an important role in her scholarship and teaching throughout her life. It also reflected broader disciplinary changes and would lead to the inclusion of archaeology in the discipline of classics.[34] Research on the ancient world was changing rapidly and nowhere was this clearer than the study of Homer. Harrison was able to use interest in Homer to attract her audience, making a claim for ancient art as a way to answer the Homeric Question. The sense that stories might be read out of objects made them texts in their own right. It responded to the idea that objects might be more directly accessible to people who hadn't studied the classics (using Harrison's own confidence with both) without falling prey to the fallacy that objects spoke for themselves.

Harrison took the enthusiasm for applying Homer to archaeology that had been awakened by the Trojan exhibition and applied it less literally to less problematic material. This tapped into the imaginative engagement that visitors to the South Kensington exhibition enjoyed, while using more familiar material and responding to some of the uncertainties about how the Homeric epics came to exist. For both Harrison and Schliemann, the reality behind Homer was accessible through archaeological material. Where for Schliemann, that meant finding material proof that the stories were true, Harrison's model was messier. She was looking for the conditions from which the literature may have emerged. Both used archaeology to get at a set of real lived experiences, inflected through the touchstone of Homer.

Eventually, Harrison got the academic post she had wanted, and turned from public-facing lectures to more traditional research and teaching. Soon afterwards, she wrote an article reflecting on the discovery of Troy as a turning point for the study of ancient Greece. She credited this to Homer's special appeal to classicists and the public. While other early sites were well known before Schliemann's discoveries, Troy transformed the way they were perceived because of its literary connections:

> We say advisedly 'beginning with Priam's Treasure' – though that as we shall presently show is not strictly true – because with the discoveries of Schliemann began the awakening of public opinion; and the fact is significant. Down to Schliemann's time, scholars, in England at all events, were busy almost exclusively with the interpretation of texts ... To arrest the attention of classical scholars there was needed, not mere facts, but facts that could be related to orthodox tradition, to an accredited department of literary scholarship. Touch the Homeric Question and you gain, at length, the academic ear. This was the true mission of Schliemann. Schliemann sought and fancied he had found the treasury of Priam ... Mr Gladstone believed him; and the world was awake.[35]

For Harrison, earlier studies of archaeological material had been too interested in the classical and the beautiful, treating objects as 'a graceful mode of illustration'. One can almost read this as a critique of her own earlier work, which was certainly more preoccupied with the idea of beauty.[36] However, as we have seen, *Myths of the Odyssey* saw Homeric images as much more than pretty illustrations.

Schliemann claimed a direct role in the stories of Homer for his discoveries, and this required an answer. We have seen Schliemann's success at attracting attention for his ideas and finds throughout this book, but Harrison gives an astute account of why this was effective. It was not just that Schliemann made sensational claims, but that these claims tied archaeology into a previously known body of material. This gave people a frame of reference for examining the objects (whether or not they agreed with it) and offered a starting point for asking new questions about the culture he uncovered: 'The problem came to be not, Can we, by means of antiquities illustrate and elucidate Homer? But rather, What people made the objects called Mycenaean? Whence did they come? Were they one or many, home-born or immigrants? What were their racial affinities? What tongue did they speak? What was the chronology of their civilisation, its rise and development?'[37] We have seen how such questions followed almost immediately from people's first encounters with the Trojan collection, but

Harrison makes clear that they would never have been applied to the idealized world of Ancient Greece, if not for Schliemann's controversial claims. The longing for accurate illustrations of Homer had led to a new kind of attention to the origins of the Greek world, which would in turn provide an understanding of the reality behind the myth.

This was ostensibly a story of Harrison's discipline, but it also describes her own career. *Myths of the Odyssey* used objects to illustrate and elucidate Homer. However, even at this stage of her work, Harrison was using a sophisticated approach that saw objects as versions of the story in their own right, not just illustrations. After Schliemann, the world of objects and the world of texts were clearly related, and Harrison's public work explained how that might work in a way that was more satisfying than Schliemann's arguments of literal truth. We have seen how Schliemann's Homeric claims launched a wide range of new approaches to his Trojan collection. For Harrison's generation, it was the questions about race and culture that inspired the next phase of archaeological work. One of the new archaeological investigations that Harrison saw as the culmination of this approach, was Arthur Evans's work on Crete. These offered a chance to apply the new knowledge of (and interest in) the prehistory of ancient Greece that had grown since the discovery of Troy.

13

Arthur Evans's Labyrinth

In 1900, Arthur Evans began his excavations at the site of Knossos in Crete. Comparisons with Troy and other sites excavated by Schliemann began almost immediately, but much had changed since those discoveries. Newspapers were now able to confidently describe the finds as Mycenaean and associate them with known facts about the Greek Bronze Age.[1] Evans himself spoke with admiration of Schliemann's discoveries and was often asked to comment on his predecessor's work in print.[2] His writings show a self-awareness about their similarities, while also hinting at the ambivalence towards Schliemann's unorthodox methods and ideas that we have seen throughout this book. This ambivalence extends to the discoveries of mythic landscapes for which both are well known: 'Archaeology has perhaps little call to concern itself with the fitting on of poetical topography to altered physical conditions.'[3] This difficult relationship is particularly clear in Evans's museum work, which picked up on precedents set by Schliemann, but did so selectively in ways that suited a much-changed context. Evans's handling of myth shows an awareness of its power in capturing the public imagination, and care to distance himself from Schliemann's claims of the literal truth of ancient stories. This chapter looks at the public response to the first exhibition that Evans organized to show off his work at Knossos. I show how this reflects many of the responses to the Trojan exhibition, from hopes that it would influence artists to the desire to relate finds back to their archaeological context. However, echoing the sceptical responses to Schliemann, Evans was careful to distance himself from the idea that he had proved the myth. Paradoxically, this performative doubt left more room for the press to speculate about the myths.

Evans was a pioneer of Aegean prehistory with a dramatic personality that attracts fascination and criticism.[4] While many of his theories about Knossos have been superseded or challenged, his version of Minoan society played an important role in constructing a prehistory for modernity.[5] Museums and their interpretation techniques were a particularly important tool for his work to make archaeology meaningful in the present.[6] In 1903, Evans held a temporary exhibition at Burlington House in London to show off his discoveries from Knossos. He had made several dramatic finds and was keen to publicize them and fundraise for the next season.[7] Because of limitations on export, Evans had little to display and so this first Knossos exhibition was dominated by replicas, photographs and diagrams.[8] Evans liked to include mounted pages from his published work in his exhibitions. Even later, when he had access to more original material, his writings were as important a part of exhibiting Knossos as its material remains and the Ashmolean Museum Archive holds many pages of Evans's published work, still framed for display in exhibitions. This willingness to make such heavy use of diagrams and photographs may owe something to Schliemann's use of material from *Atlas* in his Troy exhibition, which Evans had travelled to London to see years before.[9]

The Knossos exhibition occupied a single room of a larger exhibition organized by the Royal Academy, otherwise dedicated to old masters. This juxtaposition made a dramatic claim for Minoan art as the root of Western art and placed it on a par with celebrated easel paintings by artists such as Gainsborough, Constable, Rembrandt and Tintoretto.[10] The catalogue directly compared Minoan art with later works, including Gothic and Renaissance art.[11] The exhibition was also seen as potential inspiration for contemporary art:

> Four thousand years old! To think of it makes a poor present-day painter's brain grow giddy. We noticed last week how many of our Royal Academicians came to pore over these vestiges of what may verily be called 'old masters'. Mr MacWhirter for one, with a look almost as of awe on his leonine Scottish face, returned again and again to study an art so unique.[12]

The influence of the images from Knossos on twentieth-century art is well documented, but John MacWhirter was no modernist revolutionary.[13] He specialized in traditional landscape paintings with an emphasis on natural detail.[14] The idea that artists could find the roots of their discipline and figure out their own place in history from very ancient material that looked nothing like their main output was well established after Schliemann, to the extent that replicas of the frescoes from Knossos were now being exhibited together with old master paintings in a way that made them seem wonderful, not deficient.

This is all the more remarkable given that Evans had no original objects to display and depended on reproductions. None of the paintings were 'four thousand years old', as the above review suggested.[15] This does not seem to have troubled the audience, and some reports describe reproductions as though they were originals. Responses to Evans's discoveries stressed how modern Knossos seemed.¹⁶ Given the small amount of original material and large amount of creative input from those doing the reconstructions, the exhibition had as much claim to be a display of modern art as of very ancient art.

Whether seen in comparison with old masters or modern avant-garde, there was no question that the exhibition was staking a claim for the Minoans as great artists. The exhibition put its most dramatic visual material straight ahead of visitors as they entered the room, including casts of the painted reliefs and of the gypsum throne. Illustrations of the western part of the palace were shown on the left side of the room, and those from the east on the right. This arrangement reflects a desire to root the exhibition in the layout of the site, similar to Schliemann's determination to place objects within their respective strata. But this spatial ordering is also strikingly immersive, considering that this was a single room that could not hope to fully reconstruct the experience of the site and depended mostly on photographs and plans.¹⁷ Even the driest of plans (Fig. 40) could have a surprisingly vivid effect on visitors:

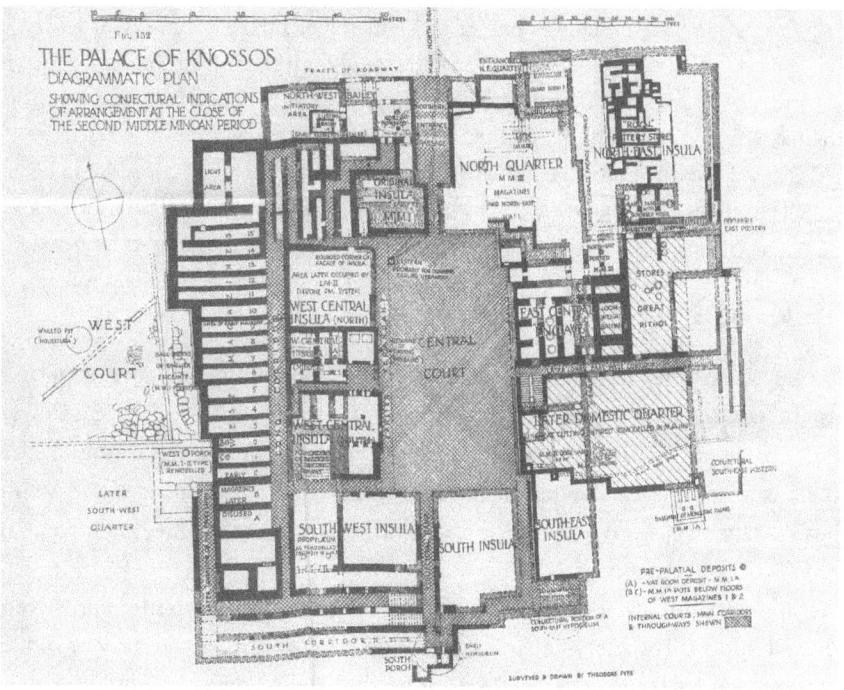

Fig. 40 Map of the palace at Knossos (1921). Heidelberg University Library, Arthur Evans, *The Palace of Minos: The Neolithic and Early and Middle Minoan Ages* (London, Macmillan, 1921), 202b – CC-BY-SA 3.0.

Nothing, however, in the collection is so pregnant with romance as the curiously unromantic map that hangs on the wall by the door. It is like a fairy tale, to be shown the ground plan of the famous labyrinth of Minos, where the Minotaur devoured his yearly tribute of seven youths and seven virgins, and whence Theseus escaped by the clue given him by Ariadne. Yet here it is, with its network of corridors.[18]

Where Schliemann's maps and plans had largely not drawn any comment, beyond their availability as sources of information, the ground plan of Knossos was seen as a marvellous window on the myths attached to the site. The complexity of the ground plan, with its many rooms and corridors was a perfect fit for the pre-existing idea of the Labyrinth. More than one news source indulged in speculation about the relationship between myth and reality, based on the plan: 'The plan which the excavations of Mr. Evans have made it possible to prepare exhibits a building which though not professedly a maze, presents in the intricacy of its corridors and chambers so complicated a series of passable and impassable compartments that a stranger wandering in its recesses might well need the help of some Ariadne's clue.'[19] The *Academy* even used the plan to speculate about Minos' character:

> [The palace plan] resembles one of those mazes or puzzle pictures which are devised for the amusement of children. It would have been an advantage for the ordinary visitor if the corridors, halls and approaches had been coloured, for in that way the difficulty of reaching certain chambers would be manifest at a glance. Minos had the reputation of a tyrant and it would be safer for him to be able to change his apartment whenever he pleased. There may have been degrees of inaccessibility among the rooms... Few can believe that the many-chambered dwelling was arranged for the Minotaur... but the subtle ambages might well be taken as a confirmation of the terrible legend.[20]

The layout of the site of Knossos was fuel for imagining what sort of person might have lived there. The question is: how far into imagination should a viewer go? *The Academy* hints that the convoluted maze might cause viewers to lose their way and start believing in the Minotaur. The 'subtle ambages' can stand both for the twists and turns of the Labyrinth and the complexities and potential pitfalls of the evidence.

Myth was not just a temptation for the press; and it was also used directly in the exhibition. The first words of the introduction to the Knossos room in the catalogue managed to cover all the famous mythical names:

> Knossos, according to the legendary account, was the abode of King Minôs and the scene of the magnificent artistic achievements of his craftsman Dædalos,

who moreover here built for him the mysterious Labyrinth. In its mazy depths dwelt the Minotaur – the Bull of Minôs, half bovine and half human in form – fed with the tender flesh of Athenian captives, till such time as the hero Theseus, with the aid of the clue of thread supplied by the King's daughter, Ariadnê, was able to slay the monster and lead forth the tribute children. Such, at least, was the Athenian tale.[21]

This is characteristic of Evans's use of myth: it tells the story, uses its full evocative power then problematizes it. The introduction goes on to say that the myths probably contain truths about sea power, laws and artistic achievement, but this is a much more cautious approach than Schliemann's. By framing traditional narratives about Knossos as the Athenians' side of the story, the guide stresses that the textual record is partial and fragmentary, while offering the hope that archaeology might give a truer picture of Minoan life. The catalogue recognized Schliemann's importance in this context: 'The underlying truth in early tradition had been vindicated by Schliemann at Troy and Mycenae; at Knossos, too, the spade alone could supply the real solution of these interesting problems.'[22] Evans embraced the scope for comparison with the famous and successful discoverer of prehistoric sites, and this was picked up on by the press.[23] Evans cleverly publicized his finds by tapping into excitement about Schliemann's famous discoveries and hinting (but, unlike Schliemann, only hinting) at truths behind the myths.[24] Scepticism about Schliemann's claims was dying down as evidence accumulated for the idea of a Greek Bronze Age and broader anxieties over deep time subsided. The Royal Academy exhibition made conscious use of people's expectations of and hopes for archaeology to get their attention and donations. By being less forceful with his claims about the myths, Evans gave his audience a little more freedom to imagine alternative possibilities, and the news coverage reflects this. Writers were free to find their own version of Knossos. Some chose to concentrate on the fearsome Minotaur, others on Daedalus' creativity.[25] Minos could either be a cruel tyrant or the first democrat.[26] By not claiming that the ancient world reflected the ancient texts precisely, Evans left more space both for scepticism and for imaginative engagement with the ancient material.

Evans's policy of more gentle suggestions does not seem to have limited press imagination at all, but it allowed them to cast him in the role of spoilsport rationalist:

Dismiss at once the obsession of the Minotaur from your fancy. He is a literary terror, a rhetorical figure. Mr Evans has unearthed the fresco that explains him.

In all probability he was simply a bull of a large and shapely breed, which plunged and capered in some prehistoric arena for the pleasure of the Minoan Court...

Mr Evans has copied for us dumb examples of Cretan script. But he forbids us to see in them the prehistoric poems or obscure revelations. They are the catalogues of some rich treasure houses.[27]

The alternatives to Minotaur and lost epic suggested here are hardly disappointing rationalizations. Dramatic public games and undecipherable lists of lost treasure are exactly the kind of exciting material that draws public attention to archaeology. The possibilities of an undeciphered language were particularly exciting for many writers, indeed this was the interest that drew Arthur Evans to Knossos in the first place.[28] The gap between Greek literature and the ancient site, along with the frustrating illegibility of Knossos' tablets meant that literature (and its limitations) was an inevitable theme of the exhibition. Its relationship with archaeology was complicated by the awareness of how much had been lost:

If there was some Cretan Harmodius who wreathed his tyrannicide sword 'in myrtle boughs,' the song that told of his deed is silent. If there was some preacher of the wilderness who called this comfortable world to repentance, his protest built no churches. One turns again from Knossus to Piccadilly, doubting after all whether it be not the material half of life that is permanent. Who knows but some Cretan Horace may have raised to himself monuments 'more lasting than brass.' And yet it is the brass which lives.[29]

This shows how much of the hopes and expectations for a new archaeological discovery depended upon questions and priorities laid down by classical texts. A great society is assumed to have had its own historical figures, religious dissenters and great poets, and the loss of these is felt all the more keenly for what has been found. The fact that political and religious revolutionaries have left no trace stresses that, contrary to Evans's suggestions in the guide book, the material record may be no more balanced than the Athenians' old stories. The long-standing dichotomy in which texts preserve the life of the mind while objects preserve baser sensuous or practical aspects is also active here. As always, reflecting on the legacy of past societies is partially a reflection on the present. It is suggested that the Piccadilly that displays silent objects today will one day become a ruin itself – without the redeeming capacity of spiritual, political or poetic discourse. Where Evans was keen to emphasize how much could be learned about Knossos from the material record, and how it should not be seen exclusively in the mould of classical literature, not all reviewers followed this agenda. Evans had managed to sell his subject as a field in which archaeology triumphs over the study of literature but already anxieties were creeping in.

Press coverage was usually more positive about the achievements of archaeology and Evans was even thought by some to have surpassed the myth:

> Who shall say that the explorer in laying bare the home of Minos, or in digging out the very birthplace of Zeus is destroying the romance of mythology? He has shown us that the beauty of life in those days, its power, its refinement, were greater than we had ever dreamt; that the age of Theseus and Ariadne was an age very like our own; that Minos was a greater man than we knew-perhaps more rather than less likely to be the son of Zeus! And as for Daedalus, may it not be that he has achieved increase of fame, being found to be not only sculptor and inventor, but (greatest of all) architect?[30]

Newspaper coverage of both Evans's and Schliemann's exhibitions was much more interested in this 'romance of mythology' than in discovering any truth behind it. Evans's approach, with its glamorous replicas and loose links to known stories seems to have been accepted much more readily than Schliemann's use of genuine (if less beautiful) ancient objects to claim that stories were literally true. Evans benefited from being able to use the pre-existing fame of Schliemann and having more visually appealing material, but his success also demonstrates a greater awareness of why the mythic narratives had captured the public imagination. Evans negotiated a relationship between myth and archaeology in which archaeology was not just about finding relics of myth, but also offered new insights into the past. This was a rhetorical coup that allowed archaeology to use the fame of ancient stories, without being constrained by their contents.

14

Dream and Reality

In 2001, a blockbuster exhibition opened in Stuttgart, kicking off an unusually heated (and unusually public) debate among academics. *Troia: Traum und Wirklichkeit* (Troy: Dream and Reality) has become a textbook example of public controversy over disciplinary knowledge and how public debate can shape academic discourse, rather than just reproduce it in accessible form.[1] While much had changed in archaeology, the debates over this exhibition echo those over the first Trojan exhibition more than a century before. At both moments, Troy was a useful site for debating how we generate knowledge about the past and what kinds of claims archaeology should make. The nineteenth-century public interest in a site known from ancient literature had persisted, resulting in a very public debate, despite archaeology having become much less open to amateurs than it was in Schliemann's time. These debates reveal an unresolved discomfort with the idea of a Homeric archaeology, made all the more complicated by Schliemann's influence on public ideas about archaeology. Because of Schliemann's role in transforming the study of the past and his untrustworthy reputation, this exhibition offered an opportunity to air anxieties over the direction archaeology was taking. By looking at this controversy over a museum exhibition in the light of what we know about similar debates immediately after the discovery of Troy, we can explore why Troy remains such a difficult topic. Given the enduring uncertainties over Troy, it is important to ask why museums still market their exhibitions with the idea of exploring myths and gaining truths.

Troia: Traum und Wirklichkeit was the product of new excavations in the Troad. These had been conducted since the 1980s by a multidisciplinary international team, led by Manfred Korfmann from Tübingen University. The exhibition included objects from these excavations, on loan from the Turkish government. Some were very similar to the ones exhibited by Schliemann in 1877, including gold jewellery and *depas amphikypellon*.[2] However, it was also a much more eclectic and all-encompassing vision of Troy than Schliemann's: it traced the history of the Trojan War story from the ancient world to the present, through objects as varied as vases, sculpture, manuscripts, oil paintings, plans, contemporary mixed-media artwork, beer packaging and a hairdryer. It included Schliemann's excavations as part of its discussion of the history of the site, but its main aim was to complicate and update Schliemann's vision with the results of recent research. In the title's framing, the longevity of the story of Troy was the 'dream' which could now be tied to a known 'reality' by the process of modern, scientific excavation.[3]

Where Schliemann's exhibition aimed to prove that the dream of Troy was true, *Troia: Traum und Wirklichkeit* made a much clearer distinction between the dream and reality elements. This distinction was clearly dramatized by the separation between the two institutions that were hosting it in Braunschweig: the 'myth and its reception' sections of the exhibition were in the Herzog Anton Ulrich-Museum, and the 'reality' (consisting of past and present excavations, as well as the section on Troy today) in the nearby Braunschweigisches Landesmuseum.[4] The inclusion and acknowledgement of the Troy we know from Homer and Hollywood helped manage and explore the expectations that caused so much trouble for Schliemann in his first exhibition. Yet, despite the desire to contain and clarify the relationship between the things we know and the things we imagine about the site (or perhaps because of it) the controversy over the exhibition focused on whether the 'reality' presented was really true.

As with the debate over Schliemann's levels, and the raptures over Evans's site plan of Knossos, it was an attempt to represent the layout of the site that was the core of the controversy. In this case, the focal point was a wooden model showing how Troy included both the mound that Schliemann excavated and a lower city on the plain around it.[5] The discovery of a Bronze Age settlement on the plain of Troy, surrounded by a second wall, overcame a long-standing objection to the idea of Hisarlık as Homer's Troy: that it seemed too small.[6] This expanded footprint for Bronze Age Troy was represented in the exhibition by a wooden scale model, showing a settlement with dense buildings between its two sets of defensive walls. However, as with all archaeological reconstructions, this involved some subjective interpretation, building on what was known from surveying the surface and extrapolating from the areas that had been excavated.[7] Such reconstructions are standard practice in communicating archaeology, allowing people to visualize the interpretations made by the excavators. However, this one provoked controversy by projecting the archaeologists' interpretations onto the landscape itself, and letting people see the whole as an apparently conclusive overview of the site.

The first objections were raised by Frank Kolb, a colleague of Korfmann's at Tübingen University, who spoke against the idea of a dense settlement on the plain in a newspaper interview.[8] Kolb objected to the model's interpretation of the evidence, believing it a deliberate attempt to mislead the public. While the disagreement started in newspapers, it was followed up by academic symposia and papers as supporters on both sides sought to clarify their positions.[9] The debate was haunted by the idea that Korfmann might be over-interpreting the evidence to line up better with Homer's account of the city of Troy, following in the footsteps of Schliemann. While the new excavations had paid attention to all layers of the site, it never would have been explored in such depth if not for the idea that it was Homer's Troy, and Kolb and his supporters argued that this inflated the site's importance relative to others in the region. A group of Korfmann's supporters summarized why Troy was so controversial: 'The site of Troy has the misfortune to stand on not one but two academic fault-lines, one on either side of the Aegean: the Homeric problem concerned with the historicity (or otherwise) of the *Iliad*; and the problem of Anatolian historical geography of the Arzawa lands as reconstructible (or not) from Hittite texts.'[10] This echoes the two great nineteenth-century questions about Troy's relationship with Homer and its relationship with Asia. The evocative metaphor of fault-lines imagines these problems as integral to the landscape itself, causing problems at unpredictable intervals. But, of course, these disputes are not accidental products of nature and are tied to the site's long history and deep cultural significance.

Just like the nineteenth-century debates, the anxieties over Troy in the first years of the twenty-first century were about more than just archaeological epistemology. Where Schliemann's Troy became implicated in the Eastern Question and debates over the gold standard, Korfmann's Troy had its own political implications. Professional identities in German academia were shifting after reunification and scholars were moving from aspiring to perfect neutrality (something stressed by Kolb) to a model that acknowledged that academia could not be separated from public interest and political realities.[11] Korfmann spoke of his hopes that Turkey would be allowed to join the European Union and subsequent exhibitions of the material from Troy have reflected changing relationships between ancient Troy and the people of Europe, depending on contemporary international relations.[12] The idea of an archaeological reality that fulfils long-held dreams was used to imagine an ideal of peace and shape new national identities and respond to contemporary political realities.[13]

This is far from the only museum exhibition to contrast the idea of an imagined and a real ancient world. Exhibitions often promise to get to the bottom of a myth, with titles such as: *Babylon: Myth and Reality*; *Founding Myths: From Hercules to Darth Vader*; *The Siren: Only a Myth? New Ideas for a History of Medicine Between Myth, Religion and Science*; and *Gods, Myths and Mortals: Greek Treasures Across the Millennia*.[14] Such exhibitions offer the possibility of encountering myth in an institution we usually associate with real objects and professional authority. Academics tend to think of themselves as representing an accurate, evidence-based approach to reality and dispelling myths. However, titles like these offer a kernel of truth to narratives that are compelling enough to survive for centuries, and indeed to tempt visitors into the museum today. The museum's role as a site where research and real objects meet the public makes the promise to ground evocative stories in fact particularly compelling.

The idea that archaeology might be able to combine romance and rigor in this way owes much to Schliemann's public persona. But the reason it is compelling today (just as it was in 1877) is that myth is not somehow cut off from reality. These are stories we still tell, both to learn about the past and for our own entertainment. *Troia: Traum und Wirklichkeit* acknowledged the role that these stories play in our own culture through the inclusion of objects (e.g. beer, hairdryer, movie poster) that are familiar parts of contemporary experience and not usually considered museum-worthy. The diversity of objects on display demonstrated the broad cultural reach of Troy, and the importance of understanding the actual site. But it also shows Troy as a contested ground, with many different possible readings and raised the question of what counts as dream, and what counts as reality. Every representation of Troy is linked to a reality in which the story is told. We have seen, for example, how Harrison's approach tried to link the pots in the British Museum back to a context in which potters retell popular stories, with their own quirks. Today, we might look at the 'Helen of Troy' hairdryer and reflect on its mixture of a millennia-old fantasy of feminine beauty and a peculiarly modern desire to give a consumer product an edge with branding.

The idea that an object can have an imaginative dimension that taps into broader cultural ideas is nothing new. Barthes described these sorts of meaning as *Mythologies* – a kind of modern myth that might be attached to objects as diverse as soap, Garbo's face, the Romans (as represented in film) and steak and chips. He saw these as containing two levels of meaning: the one directly signified and a second order meaning tied into the culture's prevailing ideologies.[15] The exhibition was clearly exploring Troy's mythology in this sense, but reading complexity into the everyday (such as asking what broken pottery tells us about a whole society) is also the lifeblood of archaeology. This kind of deeper cultural meaning not only serves as the intellectual grounding that gets things like hairdryers into museum exhibitions but also demonstrates how it is impossible to separate the reality from the dream. Things that seem 'real' cannot be separated from the literary baggage of Troy, things that seem thoroughly inauthentic turn out to be tied to their own realities that explain why the dream was evoked in the first place. We have seen how Pater described the world of Homeric epic, with its seamless mixture of plausible and implausible and its vividly realized objects, as a dream generated from a waking world that contained Schliemann's treasures. But that dream is also an inseparable part of our lived reality.

Troy's meaning in our culture depends on anxieties about the relationship between history and fiction. White has explored how our desire to keep history separate from fiction (despite the imaginative work involved in retelling the past and the use of historical events in fiction) is rooted in two conflicting models of history. He defined the historical past of professional historians (working to create a perfectly accurate representation of a past that cannot be directly observed) against the practical past, which is a working model that can be useful for understanding the present.[16] A museum exhibition is a meeting point between a precise, professional understanding of the past and an interested public who want a history that is both authentic and tells them something about modern interests and identities. As such, it is a place where the historical and practical pasts can clash. Kolb's historical approach was uncomfortable with extrapolating beyond the excavated areas to help the public visualize Troy as a complete settlement, while Korfmann's practical past was available for reflecting on Turkey's relationship with the European Union.

Troy has been the focus of repeated conflicts between historical and practical past because of its role in a literary work that has offered useful stories about the past for millennia. The desire to use Troy to think about identity, violence, love, wealth and a host of other concerns did not disappear when Schliemann discovered a material Troy, even though it was now easier to subject to the kind of evidence-based approach associated with the historical past. People continued to find stories that helped them make sense of their relationship with the past (even in apparently empirical exercises such as measuring skulls or weighing strips of silver) because that was the reason they were interested in the first place. The divide between the two kinds of past explains the sense of distance between academics and the public. It is why Evans took care to distance himself from speculation about Knossos that seemed too fantastical, and why Harrison distanced herself from her early work at the British Museum once she got a job at Cambridge. It also explains why Schliemann's contemporaries were so horrified at his mixing of Homer and archaeology, and why it is so upsetting for us today to see how nineteenth-century racism tried to present itself as an objective science. Throughout this book, we have seen how difficult the practical and historical past are difficult to keep separate. While Kolb wanted to stick to a strict, disciplinary model of history for understanding Troy, even when presenting the past to the public, he intuited that he could shape the academic discourse best by telling the public they were being lied to and that this was not the useful past they had been promised.

This book began by exploring some of the ways in which Troy's relationship with the truth has been troublesome. Troy has been a city best known from an epic poem since ancient times. Its excavator, Heinrich Schliemann, is a difficult figure, even by the standards of nineteenth-century archaeologists and the site he excavated has been subject to a number of controversies over the years. These included questions over the origin of Homeric epic and the topography of the Troad that meant that Troy was controversial even before Schliemann's announcement. Where past debates were conducted entirely in words, the arrival of Schliemann's collection in London enabled people to explore and debate the materiality of Troy. The timing was perfect for the nineteenth-century fascination with object-oriented approaches to the past and the thriving museum culture that emerged from it. But it also let people explore the relationship between imagination and strict documentation of facts in archaeology and ask where the line between the two should be drawn. This role for Troy continues to this day.

The Trojan exhibition was not a neutral encounter with objects from Troy. It was carefully framed by Schliemann to make the case for his theories. We have seen how he used the technology of photography, the science of materials analysis and the idea of archaeological stratigraphy to highlight the scientific dimensions of his work. The resulting exhibition was a strange experience, with vast quantities of similar-looking material arranged together, giving a sense of the scale of the site and turning individual objects into 'types' for archaeological analysis. The exhibition gave pride of place to stone tools, spindle whorls and pots with odd stylized faces, in a way that challenged contemporary values and foregrounded Schliemann's own theories. The objects were given names from the *Iliad* and details such as fire damage were used to tie them to the story of the fall of Troy.

Despite the heavily structured experience, responses to the exhibition were diverse. Initial enthusiasm for a new wave of Trojan-inspired jewellery, homewares and painting never bore much fruit. However, Schliemann's Troy became a useful shorthand for the dramatically alien in the ancient world. The idea of 'primitive' origins for Greek art, as represented in objects from Troy became a compelling one for artists and writers, who began to find ways to appreciate the beauty in such objects. However, the oddities of Troy also offered rich material for jokes, and particularly for thinking about the commonplace world that might lie behind the ideal of Homer. Meanwhile, the idea of Troy as an early culture with great riches attracted the attention of numismatists, bankers and public servants, considering how value could be standardized and what the relationships between different ancient cultures might teach them about the problems facing modern economies.

After people had seen the Trojan collection, the terms of the debate shifted away from Schliemann's preoccupations. People were still eager to reflect on the relationship between Hisarlık and Homer's Troy, but many who approached Schliemann's collection through Homer did so with an attitude of irony, or scepticism, and people began to develop their own theories to understand these objects. In particular, Troy was now available to the active debates over human history and how objects and people might change over time. Troy became useful for people on both sides of debates over the three-age system and cultural evolution. The biggest question was about Troy's origin and cultural affinities, something that could transform how the *Iliad* was understood and explain European origins. While these debates were framed as neutral readings of material evidence, modern identities (including disciplinary, national and racial) were as important for their conclusions as any reading of anatomy, geology or symbols.

After Schliemann, there were further experiments in understanding the relationship between archaeology and Homer. Jane Harrison made both the stories and her own answer to the Homeric Question available to a broad public who sensed that Schliemann's idea of the literal truth of Troy was too good to be true but wanted to understand how archaeology related to literature. Arthur Evans stepped into Schliemann's niche as an excavator whose dramatic finds could prove substance behind ancient myths, but he also learned from the responses to Troy and was careful to negotiate a different relationship with the press and the public in which more was left to the public's imaginations. Such approaches cemented a role for the museum as a public place where myth and reality might meet to create a past that is useful to people today.

Myth and reality tend to be seen as fundamentally opposed, but many museum exhibitions offer to guide their visitors through the relationship between the two. They offer to find a kernel of truth in the myth or explain the force of the myth in our world. This rarely attracts the sort of controversy that has come up repeatedly in exhibitions of material from Troy. There are many reasons why Troy is seen as more problematic, from the unresolved question of how much we can trust Schliemann to the centuries of retellings that contradict each other and could never perfectly fit reality. Even the idea of Troy as a site of enduring conflict (always ready for 'new' Trojan Wars) gives debate a sense of inevitability. We tend to think of the public-facing bits of archaeology as less rigorous, and so less real, but often the complexities of how knowledge is made are pared out, resulting in a version of the past that appears more real and solid than the evidence on which it is based. Troy makes this problem of communicating archaeology starkly clear. Archaeologists at the site will always be called upon to explain how foundations and pots can be related back to a work of literature. Troy's difficulties make public conversations about epistemology and the difficulties of reading archaeological evidence inevitable. They are a rare opportunity for honesty about the difficulties of understanding the past from scraps of evidence that were never meant to be 'read'. The choice for archaeologists is not between a neutral, dispassionate approach and an imaginative, engaging one, but over whether or not to acknowledge that our understanding of the past comes from fallible human beings, working to make sense of patchy evidence in ways that serve present needs and interests.

Notes

Part One: Introduction

1. Richard Jenkyns, *The Victorians and Ancient Greece* (Oxford: Blackwell, 1980), 193–210.
2. Robert Fowler, 'The Homeric Question', in *The Cambridge Companion to Homer*, ed. R. Fowler (Cambridge: Cambridge University Press, 2004), 220–32.
3. Jenkyns, *The Victorians and Ancient Greece*, 193–210.
4. Peter Jablonka, 'Troy', in *The Oxford Handbook of the Bronze Age Aegean*, ed. E.H. Cline (Oxford: Oxford University Press, 2012), 849–61.
5. Suzanne L. Marchand, *Down from Olympus: Archaeology and Philhellenism in Germany, 1750–1970* (Princeton, NJ: Princeton University Press, 1996), 116–24.
6. Cathy Gere, *The Tomb of Agamemnon* (Cambridge, MA: Harvard University Press, 2006).
7. Naoíse Mac Sweeney, *Troy: Myth, City, Icon* (London: Bloomsbury Academic, 2018).
8. Rachel Bryant Davies, *Troy, Carthage and the Victorians: The Drama of Classical Ruins in the Nineteenth-Century Imagination* (Cambridge: Cambridge University Press, 2018).
9. Lesley Fitton, *Heinrich Schliemann and the British Museum* (London: British Museum, 1991). Geraldine Saherwala, Klaus Goldmann and Gustav Mahr, *Heinrich Schliemanns 'Sammlung Trojanischer Altertümer': Beitrage Zur Chronik Einer Grossen Erwerbung Der Berliner Museen* (Berlin: Spiess, 1993).
10. Kate Nichols, *Greece and Rome at the Crystal Palace: Classical Sculpture and Modern Britain, 1854–1936* (Oxford: Oxford University Press, 2015). Can Bilsel, *Antiquity on Display: Regimes of the Authentic in Berlin's Pergamon Museum* (Oxford: Oxford University Press, 2012). Johannes Siapkas and Lena Sjögren, *Displaying the Ideals of Antiquity: The Petrified Gaze* (New York: Routledge, 2013).
11. For example, the work of the Archive of Performances of Greek and Roman Drama. Available online: http://www.apgrd.ox.ac.uk (accessed 28 August 2018).
12. Recent contributions include: James Delbourgo, *Collecting the World: The Life and Curiosity of Hans Sloane* (London: Allen Lane, 2017). Simon Knell, *National Galleries The Art of Making Nations* (Abingdon: Routledge, 2016). Lucilla Burn, *The Fitzwilliam Museum: A History* (London: Philip Wilson Publishers Ltd, 2016).
13. For example, Tony Bennett, *The Birth of the Museum: History, Theory, Politics* (London: Routledge, 1995). Eilean Hooper-Greenhill, *Museums and the Shaping of Knowledge* (London: Routledge, 1992).

14 Andrea Witcomb, *Re-Imagining the Museum: Beyond the Mausoleum* (London: Routledge, 2003), 1–18.
15 Francis Haskell, *The Ephemeral Museum: Old Master Paintings and the Rise of the Art Exhibition* (New Haven, CT: Yale University Press, 2000).
16 Susan Pearce, 'William Bullock: Collections and Exhibitions at the Egyptian Hall, London 1816–25', *Journal of the History of Collections* 20, no. 1 (2008): 17–35.
17 Donald F. Easton, 'Priam's Gold: The Full Story', *Anatolian Studies* 44 (1994): 221–43.
18 Dariusz Maliszewski, 'Trojan Schematic Idols at Munich', *Anatolian Studies* 43 (1993): 111–15.
19 Eilean Hooper-Greenhill, 'Education, Communication and Interpretation: Towards a Critical Pedagogy in Museums', in *The Educational Role of the Museum*, ed. Eilean Hooper-Greenhill (Abingdon: Routledge, 1999), 3–27.
20 Indeed this was a major subject of concern and debate in the nineteenth century; see Bennett, *Birth of the Museum*, 59–88.
21 'Dr. Schliemann', *Daily Evening Bulletin*, 6 September 1877.
22 Hans Robert Jauss, *Toward an Aesthetic of Reception*, trans. Paul de Man (Minneapolis, MN: University of Minnesota Press, 1982).
23 Charles Martindale, 'Introduction: Thinking Through Reception', in *Classics and the Uses of Reception*, ed. Charles Martindale and Richard F. Thomas (Oxford: Blackwell, 2006), 1–13.
24 Anthony Burton, 'The Uses of the South Kensington Art Collections', *Journal of the History of Collections* 14, no. 1 (2002): 79–95.
25 Martindale, 'Introduction: Thinking Through Reception', 10.
26 Fitton, *Heinrich Schliemann and the British Museum*, 39. 'Excavations at Troy', *The Times*, 27 November 1878, 4.
27 Cornelia D. Pearsall, *Tennyson's Rapture: Transformation in the Victorian Dramatic Monologue* (Oxford: Oxford University Press, 2008).
28 Andreas W. Vetter, *Troia: Traum und Wirklichkeit Ausstellungsführer* (Braunschweigisches Landesmuseum und Herzog Anton Ulrich-Museum Braunschweig, 2001).

Chapter 1: Troy and truth

1 'Troy', *The Times*, 16 August 1877.
2 Delia Millar, 'Simpson, William (1823–1899), Watercolour Painter and Journalist', *Oxford Dictionary of National Biography* (Oxford: Oxford University Press, 2014), https://doi.org/10.1093/ref:odnb/25597, accessed 26 May 2018.
3 William Simpson, 'Mycenæ, Troy and Ephesus', in *The Autobiography of William Simpson*, ed. G. Eyre-Todd (London: T Fisher Unwin, 1903), 273–5.

4 William Simpson, 'The Schliemannic Ilium', *Fraser's Magazine*, July 1877.
5 Ibid.
6 Susan Heuck Allen, *Finding the Walls of Troy: Frank Calvert and Heinrich Schliemann at Hisarlık* (Berkeley: University of California Press, 1999), 175.
7 William M. Calder III and Justus Cobet (eds) *Heinrich Schliemann Nach Hundert Jahren* (Frankfurt am Main: Vittorio Klostermann, 1990).
8 E. Meyer, 'Schliemann's Letters to Max Müller in Oxford', *Journal of Hellenic Studies* 82 (1962): 75–105.
9 'Troy – Mr. Bertram F. Hartshorne Writes to Us', *The Times*, 21 August 1877. For Schliemann's description of Hartshorne as a friend see: 'Troy', *The Times*, 16 August 1877.
10 'Troy' *The Times*, 16 August 1877.
11 'Dr. Schliemann', *Daily Evening Bulletin*, 6 September 1877. 'Schliemann and His Enemies', *Daily Arkansas Gazette* no. 242, 5 September 1877. 'Treasures from Troy', *Royal Cornwall Gazette* 24 August 1877, 2.
12 'Troy', *The Times*, 16 August 1877.
13 Lesley Fitton, *Heinrich Schliemann and the British Museum* (London: British Museum, 1991), 39–40.
14 'Troy', *The Times*, 16 August 1877.
15 Simpson, 'The Schliemannic Ilium'.
16 'Letters from Abroad' *Independent Statesman*, 29 May 1879.
17 Tony Bennett, *The Birth of the Museum: History, Theory, Politics* (London: Routledge, 1995), 39–44.
18 Suzanne L. Marchand, *Down from Olympus: Archaeology and Philhellenism in Germany, 1750–1970* (Princeton, NJ: Princeton University Press, 1996), xx, 116–17.
19 Simpson, 'The Schliemannic Ilium'.
20 Kathrin Maurer, 'Archeology as Spectacle: Heinrich Schliemann's Media of Excavation', *German Studies Review* 32, no. 2 (2009): 303–17.
21 Cathy Gere, *The Tomb of Agamemnon* (Cambridge, MA: Harvard University Press, 2006), 6.
22 Fitton, *Heinrich Schliemann and the British Museum*, 48.
23 James I. Porter, 'Homer: The History of an Idea', in *The Cambridge Companion to Homer*, ed. R. Fowler (Cambridge: Cambridge University Press, 2004), 324–43.
24 Lucan, *Pharsalia*, 9.965–1000.
25 Untitled article ['Troy and the New Archaeology'], *The Times*, 20 December 1877, 9.
26 Allen, *Finding the Walls of Troy*, 37–8.
27 C.R. Cockerell, *Travels in Southern Europe and the Levant, 1810–1817*, ed. Samuel Pepys Cockerell (London, 1903), 40. Allen, *Finding the Walls of Troy*, 38. Plutarch, *Vitae Parallelae: Alexander*, 15.4.

28 Lesley Fitton, *The Discovery of the Greek Bronze Age* (Cambridge MA: Harvard University Press, 1996), 50.
29 Ibid., 51.
30 Because of inconsistent spellings in nineteenth-century sources, these will sometimes appear as Hissarlik and Bunarbashi in quotations. Allen, *Finding the Walls of Troy*, 41–2.
31 Rachel Bryant Davies, *Troy, Carthage and the Victorians: The Drama of Classical Ruins in the Nineteenth-Century Imagination* (Cambridge: Cambridge University Press, 2018), 47–67.
32 Allen, *Finding the Walls of Troy*, 115–27.
33 Charles Brian Rose, *The Archaeology of Greek and Roman Troy* (Cambridge: Cambridge University Press, 2013), 40–3.
34 Joachim Latacz, *Troy and Homer: Towards a Solution of an Old Mystery* (Oxford: Oxford University Press, 2004).
35 Naoíse Mac Sweeney, *Troy: Myth, City, Icon* (London: Bloomsbury Academic, 2018), 34–5.
36 George Grote, *A History of Greece: Volume 1* (1846; Cambridge: Cambridge University Press, 2009), xii–xiii.
37 Pliny, *Historias Naturalis*, 35.60–7.
38 Peter Rowley-Conwy, *From Genesis to Prehistory: The Archaeological Three Age System and Its Contested Reception in Denmark, Britain, and Ireland* (Oxford: Oxford University Press, 2007), 7.
39 Thomas Burgon, 'XVI An Attempt to Point out the Vases of Greece Proper Which Belong to the Heroic and Homeric Ages', *Transactions of the Royal Society of Literature of the United Kingdom*, 2 (2nd series) (1847): 258–96.
40 Susan Sherratt and John Bennet, 'Introduction', in *Archaeology and Homeric Epic*, ed. S. Sherratt and J. Bennet (Oxford: Oxbow Books, 2017), vii–xvi.
41 Anthony Snodgrass, 'Homer, the Moving Target', in *Archaeology and Homeric Epic*, ed. Susan Sherratt and John Bennet (Oxford: Oxbow Books, 2017), 1–9.
42 Katherine Harloe, *Winckelmann and the Invention of Antiquity: History and Aesthetics in the Age of Altertumswissenschaft* (Oxford: Oxford University Press, 2013), 137–92.
43 Richard Jenkyns, *The Victorians and Ancient Greece* (Oxford: Blackwell, 1980), 197–210.
44 Eric Csapo, 'Max Müller and Solar Mythology', in *Theories of Mythology* (Oxford: Blackwell, 2005), 18–30.
45 Friedrich Max Müller, *Comparative Mythology: An Essay* (London: George Routledge and Sons, 1909), 99.
46 Amanda Hodgson, 'The Troy Connection: Myth and History in Sigurd the Volsung', in *William Morris: Centenary Essays; Papers from the Morris Centenary Conference*

Organized by the William Morris Society at Exeter College Oxford, 30 June–3 July 1996, ed. Peter Faulkner and Peter Preston (Exeter: University of Exeter Press, 1999), 71–9.

47 David Gange and Rachel Bryant Davies, 'Troy', in *Cities of God: The Bible and Archaeology in Nineteenth-Century Britain*, ed. David Gange and Rachel Bryan Davies (Cambridge: Cambridge University Press, 2013), 39–70.

48 David Bebbington, 'The Study of Homer' in *The Mind of Gladstone: Religion, Homer, and Politics* (Oxford: Oxford University Press, 2004), 142–77.

49 Cornelia Pearsall, 'Locating Troy', in *Tennyson's Rapture: Transformation in the Victorian Dramatic Monologue* (Oxford: Oxford University Press, 2008), 1–42.

50 Heinrich Schliemann, *Troy and Its Remains; a Narrative of Researches and Discoveries Made on the Site of Ilium, and in the Trojan Plain* (London: John Murray, 1875), 1–8. Heinrich Schliemann, *Ilios: The City and Country of the Trojans* (London: John Murray, 1880), 1–66.

51 David A. Traill, *Schliemann of Troy: Treasure and Deceit* (London: John Murray, 1995). Lynn Poole and Gray Poole, *One Passion, Two Loves: The Story of Heinrich and Sophia Schliemann, Discoverers of Troy* (New York: Thomas Y. Crowell Company, 1966).

52 Schliemann, *Troy and its Remains*, 1–4.

53 Traill, *Schliemann of Troy*, 19–22.

54 Jan Haywood and Naoíse Mac Sweeney, *Homer's* Iliad *and the Trojan War: Dialogues on Tradition* (London: Bloomsbury Academic, 2018), 134.

55 Fitton, *The Discovery of the Greek Bronze Age*, 60.

56 Ibid., 60–7.

57 Debbie Challis, *From the Harpy Tomb to the Wonders of Ephesus: British Archaeologists in the Ottoman Empire 1840–1880* (London: Duckworth, 2008), 153–4.

58 'The Trojan Treasure', *The Times*, 20 December 1877. 'The Gold Masks of Mycenae', *The Times*, 20 December 1877.

59 Fitton, *Heinrich Schliemann and the British Museum*, 24.

60 Donald F. Easton, 'Priam's Gold: The Full Story', *Anatolian Studies* 44 (1994): 221–43.

61 'Dr Schliemann's Excavations', *The Lichfield Mercury*, 15 March 1878.

62 Susanne Duesterberg, *Popular Receptions of Archaeology: Fictional and Factual Texts in 19th and Early 20th Century Britain* (Bielefeld: Transcript, 2015), 209–304.

63 'Workmen and Museums', *The Liverpool Mercury*, 14 February 1887. 'Dr Henry Schliemann', *Peter Parley's Annual for 1880* (n.p.: Ben. George, 1880), 82–101.

64 Traill, *Schliemann of Troy*, 6.

65 Ibid., 4–5.

66 Ibid., 8–13. Fitton, *Heinrich Schliemann and the British Museum*, 1.

67 David A. Traill, '"Priam's Treasure": Clearly a Composite', *Anatolian Studies* 50 (2000): 17–35.
68 Donald F. Easton, 'The First Excavations at Troy: Brunton, Calvert and Schliemann', in *Studia Troica Monographien 5*, ed. Ernst Pernicka, Charles Brian Rose, and Peter Jablonka (Bonn: Dr. Rudolf Habelt GmbH, 2014), 32–103.
69 Wout Arentzen 'Frank Calvert, Henry Austen Layard and Heinrich Schliemann', *Anatolian Studies* 51 (2001): 169–85.
70 Manfred Korfmann, 'Introduction – Troia and the Natural Sciences', in *Troia and the Troad: Scientific Approaches*, ed. Günther A. Wagner, Ernst Pernicka and Hans-Peter Uerpmann (Berlin: Springer, 2003), 5–6.
71 Cornelius Holtorf, *From Stonehenge to Las Vegas: Archaeology as Popular Culture* (Walnut Creek, CA: Altamira Press, 2005), 56–7.
72 Norman Levitt 'The Colonisation of the Past and the Pedagogy of the Future', in *Archaeological Fantasies: How Pseudoarchaeology Misrepresents the Past and Misleads the Public*, ed. Garrett G. Fagan (Abingdon: Routledge, 2006), 270–2.
73 Caroline Moorehead, *The Lost Treasures of Troy* (London: Quality Paperbacks Direct, 1994), 44. Traill, *Schliemann of Troy*, 31.
74 Simpson, 'The Schliemannic Ilium'.
75 Jorje Luis Borges, 'Pierre Menard, Author of the Quixote', in *Labyrinths: Selected Stories and Other Writings*, trans. JEI (New York: New Directions Publishing Corporation, 1964).
76 Charles Martindale, 'Introduction: Thinking Through Reception', in *Classics and the Uses of Reception*, ed. Charles Martindale and Richard F. Thomas (Oxford: Blackwell, 2006), 12.
77 Shane Butler, ed., *Deep Classics: Rethinking Classical Reception* (London: Bloomsbury Academic, 2016).
78 Simpson, 'The Schliemannic Ilium'.
79 Michael Shanks and Christopher Y. Tilley, *Re-Constructing Archaeology: Theory and Practice* (London: Routledge, 1992), 17–22.
80 See for example, Pearsall, *Tennyson's Rapture*, 133. Malcolm Quinn, *The Swastika: Constructing the Symbol* (London: Routledge, 1994), 34–5.

Part Two: Putting Troy on show

1 'Agricultural Hall', *The Times*, 27 December 1877, 9.
2 'South Kensington Museum', *The Times*, 27 December 1877, 9.
3 Ibid.
4 Tony Bennett, *The Birth of the Museum: History, Theory, Politics* (London: Routledge, 1995).

5. Helen Rees Leahy, *Museum Bodies: The Politics and Practices of Visiting and Viewing* (Abingdon: Routledge, 2016).
6. Caspar Meyer, 'Ancient Vases in Modern Vitrines: The Sensory Dynamics and Social Implications of Museum Display', *Bulletin of the Institute of Classical Studies*, forthcoming.
7. Fiona Candlin, *Art, Museums and Touch* (Manchester: Manchester University Press, 2010).
8. Can Bilsel, *Antiquity on Display: Regimes of the Authentic in Berlin's Pergamon Museum* (Oxford: Oxford University Press, 2012).
9. Kate Nichols, 'Reproducing Greece and Rome', in *Greece and Rome at the Crystal Palace: Classical Sculpture and Modern Britain, 1854–1936* (Oxford: Oxford University Press, 2015), 87–124.
10. Ibid.
11. Donald F. Easton, 'Priam's Gold: The Full Story', *Anatolian Studies* 44 (1994): 221–43.
12. Lesley Fitton, *Heinrich Schliemann and the British Museum* (London: British Museum, 1991).
13. Geraldine Saherwala, Klaus Goldmann and Gustav Mahr, *Heinrich Schliemanns 'Sammlung Trojanischer Altertümer': Beitrage Zur Chronik Einer Grossen Erwerbung Der Berliner Museen* (Berlin: Spiess, 1993).
14. Beth Lord, 'Representing Enlightenment Space', in *Reshaping Museum Space: Architecture, Design, Exhibitions*, ed. S. Macleod (Abingdon: Routledge, 2005), 146–57.
15. V&A Archive, MA/4/37-8: Abstracts of Correspondence, 1864 to 1914.

Chapter 2: Bringing Troy to London

1. Donald F. Easton, 'Priam's Gold: The Full Story', *Anatolian Studies* 44 (1994): 221–43. Lesley Fitton, *Heinrich Schliemann and the British Museum* (London: British Museum, 1991), 5. E. Meyer, 'Schliemann's Letters to Max Müller in Oxford', *Journal of Hellenic Studies* 82 (1962): 77.
2. William C. Borlase, 'A Visit to Dr. Schliemann's Troy' *Fraser's Magazine*, February 1878.
3. Ibid.
   William Simpson, 'The Schliemannic Ilium', *Fraser's Magazine*, July 1877. 'Troy – Mr. Bertram F. Hartshorne Writes to Us', *The Times*, 21 August 1877.
4. Fitton, *Heinrich Schliemann and the British Museum*, 11.
5. British Museum Collections Online, 'Prof Athanasios Rhousopoulos (Biographical Details)', http://www.britishmuseum.org/research/search_the_collection_database/term_details.aspx?bioId=61758, accessed 28 August 2018.
6. Fitton, *Heinrich Schliemann and the British Museum*, 28.

7　Images from *Atlas* are used throughout this book to show specific objects, for example: Figs 16–25. Easton, 'Priam's Gold', 226–7. Heinrich Schliemann, *Atlas Trojanischer Alterthümer* (Leipzig, 1874), http://digi.ub.uni-heidelberg.de/diglit/schliemann1874/0001, accessed 28 August 2018.
8　'Our Illustrations', *The Graphic*, 16 June 1877.
9　Fitton, *Heinrich Schliemann and the British Museum*, 43.
10　'The Discoveries at Mycenae', *Illustrated London News*, 24 February 1877.
11　Fitton, *Heinrich Schliemann and the British Museum*, 11. Geraldine Saherwala, Klaus Goldmann and Gustav Mahr, *Heinrich Schliemanns Sammlung Trojanischer Altertümer: Beitrage Zur Chronik Einer Grossen Erwerbung Der Berliner Museen* (Berlin: Spiess, 1993), 11–18.
12　Fitton, *Heinrich Schliemann and the British Museum*, 39–40.
13　Ibid., 11; Saherwala, Goldmann and Mahr, *Heinrich Schliemanns Sammlung Trojanischer Altertümer*, 11.
14　Fitton, *Heinrich Schliemann and the British Museum*, 39. 'Excavations at Troy', *The Times*, 27 November 1878, 4.
15　Anthony Burton, 'The Uses of the South Kensington Art Collections', *Journal of the History of Collections* 14, no. 1 (2002): 79–95. Christopher Frayling, *Henry Cole and the Chamber of Horrors: The Curious Origins of the Victoria and Albert Museum* (London: V&A Publishing, 2010).
16　Tony Bennett, *The Birth of the Museum: History, Theory, Politics* (London: Routledge, 1995), 70.
17　'Relics of Troy', *The Derby Mercury*, 26 December 1877.
18　V&A, 'Architectural History of the V&A 1862–1863: The North and South Courts – A Double-Sided Showpiece', http://www.vam.ac.uk/content/articles/a/architectural-history-of-the-v-and-a-1862-1863-the-north-and-south-courts-a-double-sided-showpiece, accessed 21 March 2019.
19　Bennett, *The Birth of the Museum*, 84.
20　'Architectural History of the V&A 1862–1863'.
21　Science and Art Department of the Committee of Council on Education, South Kensington Museum, *Drawings of Glass Cases in the South Kensington Museum, with Suggestions for the Arrangement of Specimens* (London: Vincent Brooks, Day & Son, 1876).
22　South Kensington Museum, *A Guide to the Art Collections of the South Kensington Museum: Illustrated with Plans and Wood Engravings* (London: Spottiswoode & Co., n.d.), 20–3. Examples can be seen on the V&A website, e.g.: http://collections.vam.ac.uk/item/O1137978/titian-mosaic-watts-george-frederick/.
23　Ann Eatwell, 'Borrowing from Collectors: The Role of the Loan in the Formation of the Victoria and Albert Museum and Its Collection (1852–1932)', *Journal of the Decorative Arts Society 1850 to the Present* 24 (2000): 20–9.

24 *Guide to the Art Collections*, 24-6.
25 Ibid.
26 'The Collection of Art Objects from the Site of Troy', *The Art Journal*, London, April 1878.
27 *Guide to the Art Collections*, 41, 4.
28 Edward Walford, 'West Brompton, South Kensington Museum, &c.', in *Old and New London: Volume 5* (London: Cassell, Petter & Galpin, 1878), http://www.british-history.ac.uk/old-new-london/vol5/pp100-117, accessed 28 August 2018.
29 Christopher Whitehead, *Museums and the Construction of Disciplines: Art and Archaeology in Nineteenth Century Britain* (London: Duckworth, 2009), 52-3.
30 Lindsay Allen, 'From Silence: A Persepolis Relief in the Victoria and Albert Museum' *V&A Online Journal*, 5 (2013), http://www.vam.ac.uk/content/journals/research-journal/issue-no.-5-2013/from-silence-a-persepolis-relief-in-the-victoria-and-albert-museum, accessed 15 March 2017.
31 'Rethinking Pitt Rivers: Museum Displays at South Kensington Museum', http://web.prm.ox.ac.uk/rpr/index.php/article-index/12-articles/282-museum-displays-at-south-kensington-museum, accessed 15 March 2013.
32 Science and Art Department of the Committee of Council on Education, South Kensington Museum, *Twenty Fifth Report of the Science and Art Department of the Committee of Council on Education, with Appendices* (London: Parliamentary Papers, 1878), 460.
33 *Twenty Fifth Report of the Science and Art Department*, 433.
34 V&A archive, MA/31/7: Register of Loans In, 1878-1937, 5.
35 *Twenty Fifth Report of the Science and Art Department*, 433.
36 *Guide to the Art Collections*, 24.
37 'The Trojan Treasure', *The Times*, 20 December 1877, 6.
38 'Troy', *The Times*, 6 December 1877, 6.
39 Ibid.

Chapter 3: Making sense of the Trojan collection

1 'The Trojan Treasure', *The Times*, 20 December 1877, 6. 'Troy', *The Times*, 6 December 1877, 6.
2 Christopher Frayling, *Henry Cole and the Chamber of Horrors: The Curious Origins of the Victoria and Albert Museum* (London: V&A Publishing, 2010), 76.
3 Malcolm Baker, 'Bode and Museum Display: The Arrangement of the Kaiser-Friedrich-Museum and the South Kensington Response', *Jahrbuch Der Berliner Museen* 38 (1996): 143-53.

4 Andrew McClellan, *Inventing the Louvre: Art, Politics, and the Origins of the Modern Museum in Eighteenth-Century Paris* (Berkeley: University of California Press, 1994), 108–14.
5 Ian Jenkins, *Archaeologists and Aesthetes in the Sculpture Galleries of the British Museum, 1800–1939* (London: British Museum Press, 1992).
6 Tony Bennett, *Pasts Beyond Memory: Evolution, Museums, Colonialism* (London: Routledge, 2004).
7 'The Trojan Treasure', *The Times*, 20 December 1877, 6.
8 'Relics of Troy', *Daily News*, 10 December 1877.
9 Susanne Duesterberg, *Popular Receptions of Archaeology: Fictional and Factual Texts in 19th and Early 20th Century Britain* (Bielefeld: Transcript, 2015), 295–302.
10 Laurel Brake, ' "Time's Turbulence": Mapping Journalism Networks', *Victorian Periodicals Review* 44, no. 2 (2011): 115–27. Anne Dewitt, 'Advances in the Visualization of Data: The Network of Genre in the Victorian Periodical Press', *Victorian Periodicals Review* 48, no. 2 (2018): 161–82.
11 E. Meyer, 'Schliemann's Letters to Max Müller in Oxford', *The Journal of Hellenic Studies* 82 (1962): 75–105.
12 Geraldine Saherwala, Klaus Goldmann and Gustav Mahr, *Heinrich Schliemanns 'Sammlung Trojanischer Altertümer': Beitrage Zur Chronik Einer Grossen Erwerbung Der Berliner Museen* (Berlin: Spiess, 1993), 17–18.
13 Georgina Adelaide Müller, ed., *The Life and Letters of the Right Honourable Friedrich Max Müller*, Vol. 1 (London: Longman Green and Co., 1902), 449.
14 Ibid.
15 David A. Traill, 'Schliemann and His Academic Employees', in *Heinrich Schliemann Nach Hundert Jahren*, ed. William M. Calder III and Justus Cobet (Frankfurt am Main: Vittorio Klostermann, 1990), 237–55.
16 Lesley Fitton, *The Discovery of the Greek Bronze Age* (Cambridge, MA: Harvard University Press, 1996), 158–61.
17 'Relics of Troy', *The Derby Mercury*, 26 December 1877. 'Troy', *The Times*, 18 April 1878.
18 V&A, '1858 Exhibition of the Photographic Society of London', http://www.vam.ac.uk/content/articles/0-9/1858-exhibition-of-the-photographic-society-of-london/, accessed 28 August 2018.
19 It is the earliest example that I have found of photography used for this purpose, although (like other claims to have found the first example of anything ever) this is nearly impossible to prove.
20 Frederick N. Bohrer, *Photography and Archaeology* (London: Reaktion, 2011), 27.
21 Sinclair Hood, 'Schliemann's Mycenae Albums', in *Archaeology and Heinrich Schliemann: A Century After His Death. Assessments and Prospects. Myth – History –*

Science, ed. George S. Korres, Nektarios Karadimas and Georgia Flouda (Athens: Aegeus Society, 2012), 70–8.
22 Donald F. Easton, 'The First Excavations at Troy: Brunton, Calvert and Schliemann', in *Studia Troica Monographien 5*, ed. Ernst Pernicka, Charles Brian Rose and Peter Jablonka (Bonn: Dr. Rudolf Habelt GmbH, 2014), 32–103.
23 Bohrer, *Photography and Archaeology*, 27–68.
24 J.A. Baird, 'Photographing Dura-Europos, 1928–1937: An Archaeology of the Archive', *American Journal of Archaeology* 115, no. 3 (2011): 427–46.
25 Heinrich Schliemann, *Atlas Trojanischer Alterthümer* (Leipzig, 1874). http://digi.ub.uni-heidelberg.de/diglit/schliemann1874/0239, accessed 28 August 2018. Homer, *Iliad*, 2.811–14.
26 Debbie Challis, *From the Harpy Tomb to the Wonders of Ephesus: British Archaeologists in the Ottoman Empire 1840–1880* (London: Duckworth, 2008), 7–9.
27 Susan Heuck Allen, *Finding the Walls of Troy: Frank Calvert and Heinrich Schliemann at Hisarlık* (Berkeley: University of California Press, 1999).
28 Hood, 'Schliemann's Mycenae Albums', 71.
29 Lesley Fitton, *Heinrich Schliemann and the British Museum* (London: British Museum, 1991), 5.
30 'Dr Schliemann's Researches at Mycenae', *Illustrated London News*, 31 March 1877.
31 'Dr. and Madame Schliemann', *The Graphic*, 20 January 1877. 'Dr. Schliemann's Discoveries at Mycenae', *The Graphic*, 20 January 1877.
32 'The Trojan Treasure', *The Times*, 20 December 1877, 6.
33 'Troy', *The Times*, 17 December 1877.
34 'Troy', *The Times*, 18 April 1878, 7. V&A Archive, MA/31/7: Register of Loans In, 1878–1937, 5.
35 'Dr Schliemann's Collection of Trojan Antiquities', *The Manchester Courier and Lancashire General Advertiser*, 21 December 1877.
36 Schliemann, *Atlas Trojanischer Alterthümer*.
37 Science and Art Department of the Committee of Council on Education, South Kensington Museum, *Twenty Fifth Report of the Science and Art Department of the Committee of Council on Education, with Appendices* (London: Parliamentary Papers, 1878), 431.
38 Hedley Swain, *An Introduction to Museum Archaeology* (Cambridge: Cambridge University Press, 2007), 9–10. Johannes Siapkas and Lena Sjögren, *Displaying the Ideals of Antiquity: The Petrified Gaze* (New York: Routledge, 2013).
39 Margaret M. Miles, *Art as Plunder: The Ancient Origins of the Debate About Cultural Property* (Cambridge: Cambridge University Press, 2008), 326.
40 Ian Jenkins, *Archaeologists and Aesthetes*, 91–101.

Chapter 4: How Schliemann displayed his treasures

1 Donald F. Easton, 'Priam's Gold: The Full Story', *Anatolian Studies* 44 (1994): 221-43.
2 Geraldine Saherwala, Klaus Goldmann and Gustav Mahr, *Heinrich Schliemanns 'Sammlung Trojanischer Altertümer': Beitrage Zur Chronik Einer Grossen Erwerbung Der Berliner Museen* (Berlin: Spiess, 1993), 19-30.
3 Easton, 'Priam's Gold'.
4 Saherwala, Goldman and Mahr, *Heinrich Schliemanns 'Sammlung Trojanischer Altertümer'*, 31-5.
5 Ibid., 28, 66. H. Glenn Penny, *Objects of Culture: Ethnology and Ethnographic Museums in Imperial Germany* (Chapel Hill, NC: University of North Carolina Press, 2002), 136.
6 Penny, *Objects of Culture*, 136.
7 'Relics of Troy', *Daily News*, 10 December 1877.
8 V&A archive, MA/31/7: Register of Loans In, 1878-1937, 5. Saherwala, Goldman and Mahr, *Heinrich Schliemanns 'Sammlung Trojanischer Altertümer'*, 17, Abb.5, 66.
9 Saherwala, Goldman and Mahr, *Heinrich Schliemanns 'Sammlung Trojanischer Altertümer'*, 17, Abb.5.
10 'Dr Schliemann's Relics of Troy', *North Otago Times*, 30 March 1878.
11 Used throughout the *Iliad*. See for example, Homer, *Iliad*, 1.206.
12 E. Meyer, 'Schliemann's Letters to Max Müller in Oxford', *Journal of Hellenic Studies* 82 (1962): 75-105.
13 Schliemann, quoted in Lesley Fitton, *Heinrich Schliemann and the British Museum* (London: British Museum, 1991), 8.
14 For an example of the debate, see: 'Dr. Schliemann's Discoveries at Troy', *The Times*, 2 May 1874.
15 Homer, *Iliad*, 6.297.
16 'Dr. Schliemann's Collection', *The Manchester Weekly Times*, 29 December 1877.
17 'Troy', *The Times*, 18 April 1878, 7.
18 'Troy', *The Times*, 17 December 1877.
19 'Dr. Schliemann's Collection', *The Manchester Weekly Times*, 29 December 1877.
20 Heinrich Schliemann, *Troy and Its Remains: A Narrative of Researches and Discoveries Made on the Site of Ilium, and in the Trojan Plain* (London: John Murray, 1875), 84-5.
21 'Troy', *The Times*, 17 December 1877.
22 'Troy', *The Times*, 18 April 1878, 7.
23 Schliemann, *Troy and Its Remains*, 118-21. Cathy Gere, *Knossos and the Prophets of Modernism* (Chicago: University of Chicago Press, 2009), 38-44.
24 'Troy', *The Times*, 17 December 1877.

25 Bertram Fulke Hartshorne, 'Dr. Schliemann's Trojan Collection', *The Archaeological Journal* 34 (1877): 291–6.
26 Heinrich Schliemann, *Ilios: The City and Country of the Trojans* (London: John Murray, 1880), plate no. 1997, 344.
27 Malcolm Quinn, *The Swastika: Constructing the Symbol* (London: Routledge, 1994), 35–6.
28 'Dr. Schliemann's Excavations in the Troad', *Illustrated London News*, 5 January 1878, 11.
29 'Troy', *The Times*, 17 December 1877.
30 'Troy', *The Times*, 18 April 1878, 7.
31 Ibid.
32 'Dr Schliemann's Collection of Trojan Antiquities', *The Manchester Courier and Lancashire General Advertiser*, 21 December 1877.
33 Fitton, *Heinrich Schliemann and the British Museum*, 34–5.
34 'Troy', *The Times*, 18 April 1878, 7.
35 'Relics of Troy', *Daily News*, 10 December 1877.
36 Susan Sherratt and John Bennet, 'Introduction', in *Archaeology and Homeric Epic*, ed. S. Sherratt and J. Bennet (Oxford: Oxbow Books, 2017), vii–xvi. Homer, *Iliad*, 10.260–5.
37 'Troy', *The Times*, 18 April 1878, 7.
38 'Dr Schliemann's Collection of Trojan Antiquities', *The Manchester Courier and Lancashire General Advertiser*, 21 December 1877.
39 Debbie Challis, *From the Harpy Tomb to the Wonders of Ephesus: British Archaeologists in the Ottoman Empire 1840–1880* (London: Duckworth, 2008), 8–9.
40 'Troy', *The Times*, 18 April 1878, 7.
41 'Dr Schliemann's Collection', *The Citizen*, 26 December 1877. 'Dr. Schliemann's Collection', *Birmingham Daily Post*, 20 December 1877. 'Dr Schliemann's Collection of Trojan Antiquities', *The Manchester Courier and Lancashire General Advertiser*, 21 December 1877.
42 'Relics of Troy', *Daily News*, 10 December 1877.
43 'Troy', *The Times*, 18 April 1878, 7. For another brief description of the contents of this case, see: Hartshorne, 'Dr. Schliemann's Trojan Collection', 294.
44 Also noted by Hartshorne, 'Dr. Schliemann's Trojan Collection'.
45 'Troy' *The Times*, 17 December 1877.
46 Schliemann, *Troy and Its Remains*, 209.
47 Schliemann, *Ilios*, 270–1.
48 'Dr Schliemann's Collection', *The Citizen*, 26 December 1877.
49 Schliemann, *Ilios*, 38–9.
50 Schliemann, *Ilios*, 214, 292.
51 Ibid., 292.

52 Małgosia Nowak-Kemp and Yannis Galanakis, 'Ancient Greek Skulls in the Oxford University Museum, Part I: George Rolleston, Oxford and the Formation of the Human Skulls Collection', *Journal of the History of Collections* 24, no. 1 (2011): 89–104.
53 'Troy', *The Times*, 6 December 1877.
54 Schliemann, *Ilios*, 271–2, 507–12.
55 'Relics of Troy', *The Derby Mercury*, 26 December 1877. 'Troy', *The Times*, 18 April 1878. Emile Burnouf, 'Cyprus and Mycenae', *The Athenaeum*, 22 March 1879.
56 'Troy', *The Times*, 18 April 1878.
57 'The Trojan Treasure', *The Times*, 20 December 1877, 6.
58 Ibid.
59 Ibid. Schliemann, *Troy and Its Remains*, 324.
60 Jan Haywood and Naoíse Mac Sweeney, *Homer's* Iliad *and the Trojan War: Dialogues on Tradition* (London: Bloomsbury Academic, 2018), 137–8.
61 'The Trojan Treasure', *The Times*, 20 December 1877, 6.
62 'Dr Schliemann's Collection of Trojan Antiquities', *The Manchester Courier and Lancashire General Advertiser*, 21 December 1877. 'Relics of Troy', *The Derby Mercury*, 26 December 1877.
63 'Dr Schliemann's Collection of Trojan Antiquities', *The Manchester Courier and Lancashire General Advertiser*, 21 December 1877.
64 'The Trojan Treasure', *The Times*, 20 December 1877, 6. Alexander Stuart Murray, 'Dr. Schliemann's Trojan Antiquities', *The Academy*, 22 December 1877.
65 Vladimir Tolstikov and Mikhail Treister, *The Gold of Troy: Searching for Homer's Fabled City – Catalogue of an Exhibition 'Priam's Treasure' Held in April 1996 at the Pushkin State Museum of Fine Arts in Moscow* (New York: Harry N. Abrams Inc., 1996), 28.
66 'The Trojan Treasure', *The Times*, 20 December 1877. 'Dr Schliemann's Excavations in the Troad', *Illustrated London News*, 5 January 1878.
67 'Special Correspondence (by Private Telegraph)', *The Leeds Mercury*, 21 December 1877. 'Relics of Troy', *The Derby Mercury*, 26 December 1877. 'The Trojan Treasure', *The Times*, 20 December 1877.
68 'The Trojan Treasure', *The Times*, 20 December 1877.
69 For example: 'The Trojan Treasure', *The Times*, 20 December 1877. 'Troy', *The Times*, 17 December 1877. 'Dr Schliemann's Excavations in the Troad', *Illustrated London News*, 5 January 1878.
70 David A. Traill, ' "Priam's Treasure": Clearly a Composite', *Anatolian Studies* 50 (2000): 17–35.
71 'The Trojan Treasure', *The Times*, 20 December 1877.
72 Ibid.
73 Lloyd Llewellyn-Jones, *Aphrodite's Tortoise: The Veiled Woman of Ancient Greece* (Swansea: The Classical Press of Wales, 2003), 31.

74 Haywood and Mac Sweeney, *Homer's Iliad and the Trojan War*, 136–7.
75 Ibid.
76 Hartshorne, 'Dr. Schliemann's Trojan Collection', 292.
77 'The Trojan Treasure', *The Times*, 20 December 1877.
78 Ibid.
79 Homer, *Iliad*, 1.584, 6.220, 23.220.
80 Easton, 'Priam's Gold'. Alix Hänsel, *Schliemann Und Troja: Die Sammlungen Des Museums Für Vor- Und Frühgeschichte Band 1* (Regensburg: Schnell Steiner, 2009), 62.
81 Schliemann, *Ilios*, 300–2; *Troy and Its Remains*, 313. Fitton, *Heinrich Schliemann and the British Museum*, 10.
82 'Dr. Schliemann's Collection', *The Manchester Weekly Times*, 29 December 1877. 'Dr. Schliemann's Excavations in the Troad', *Illustrated London News*, 5 January 1878, 11.
83 'The Trojan Treasure', *The Times*, 20 December 1877.
84 T.W. Greene, 'Old Keys', *The Magazine of Art*, January 1879. 'The Trojan Treasure', *The Times*, 20 December 1877.
85 'Dr Schliemann's Relics of Troy', *North Otago Times*, 30 March 1878. 'The Trojan Treasure', *The Times*, 20 December 1877. Greene, 'Old Keys'.
86 'The Trojan Treasure', *The Times*, 20 December 1877. 'Dr Schliemann's Excavations in the Troad', *Illustrated London News*, 5 January 1878. 'Dr Schliemann's Collection', *Illustrated London News*, 29 December 1877.
87 'The Trojan Treasure', *The Times*, 20 December 1877.
88 Fitton, *Heinrich Schliemann and the British Museum*, 40.
89 Ibid., 28.
90 'Relics of Troy', *Daily News*, 10 December 1877.
91 South Kensington Museum, *A Guide to the Art Collections of the South Kensington Museum: Illustrated with Plans and Wood Engravings* (London: Spottiswoode & Co., n.d.), 23.
92 'Dr Schliemann's Collection of Trojan Antiquities', *The Manchester Courier and Lancashire General Advertiser*, 21 December 1877.
93 'Relics of Troy', *The Derby Mercury*, 26 December 1877.
94 Ibid.
95 'Dr. Schliemann's Collection', *The Manchester Weekly Times*, 29 December 1877.
96 'Troy', *The Times*, 18 April 1878, 7.
97 Ibid.
98 Ibid.
99 'The Collection of Art Objects from the Site of Troy', *The Art Journal*, April 1878.
100 'Relics of Troy', *Daily News*, 10 December 1877.
101 'Troy', *The Times*, 18 April 1878, 7.

102 Schliemann, *Ilios*, 224.
103 Hartshorne, 'Dr. Schliemann's Trojan Collection'.
104 Schliemann, *Ilios*, 156.
105 'Troy', *The Times*, 18 April 1878, 7.
106 'Relics of Troy', *Daily News*, 10 December 1877.
107 Ibid.
108 'Troy', *The Times*, 18 April 1878, 7.
109 Ibid.
110 Homer, *Iliad*, 6.179–82.
111 'Troy', *The Times*, 18 April 1878, 7.
112 Ibid.
113 Lynn Poole and Gray Poole, *One Passion, Two Loves: The Story of Heinrich and Sophia Schliemann, Discoverers of Troy* (New York: Thomas Y. Crowell Company, 1966), 203.
114 'Dr Schliemann's Collection of Trojan Antiquities', *The Manchester Courier and Lancashire General Advertiser*, 21 December 1877.
115 David A. Traill, *Schliemann of Troy: Treasure and Deceit* (London: John Murray, 1995), 128–9.
116 Schliemann, *Ilios*, 290.
117 Hartshorne, 'Dr. Schliemann's Trojan Collection', 294.
118 'Troy', *The Times*, 18 April 1878.
119 Schliemann, *Ilios*, 588–607.
120 Herodotus, *Histories* 1.94. Schliemann, *Ilios*, 587.
121 'Troy', *The Times*, 18 April 1878, 7.
122 V&A Collections Online, 'Candlestick: Palissy, Bernard, born 1510 – died 1590', http://collections.vam.ac.uk/item/O86254/candlestick-palissy-bernard/, accessed 15 January 2019.

Part Three: Schliemania?

1 Caroline Moorehead, *The Lost Treasures of Troy* (London: Quality Paperbacks Direct, 1994), 172–5. See also Debbie Challis, *From the Harpy Tomb to the Wonders of Ephesus: British Archaeologists in the Ottoman Empire 1840–1880* (London: Duckworth, 2008), 153.
2 Michael Rice and Sally MacDonald, 'Introduction – Tea with a Mummy: The Consumer's View of Egypt's Immemorial Appeal', in *Consuming Ancient Egypt*, ed. Sally MacDonald and Michael Rice (Walnut Creek, CA: Left Coast Press, 2010), 1–22. David Gange, *Dialogues with the Dead: Egyptology in British Culture and Religion, 1822–1922* (Oxford: Oxford University Press, 2013).

3   Richard Jenkyns, *The Victorians and Ancient Greece* (Oxford: Blackwell, 1980), 192–226. Rachel Bryant Davies, *Troy, Carthage and the Victorians: The Drama of Classical Ruins in the Nineteenth-Century Imagination* (Cambridge: Cambridge University Press, 2018).
4   Elizabeth Prettejohn, 'Victorian England: Ruskin, Swinburne, Pater', in *Beauty and Art, 1750–2000* (Oxford: Oxford University Press, 2005), 111–55. Richard Jenkyns, *Dignity and Decadence: Victorian Art and the Classical Inheritance* (London: Harper Collins, 1991), 192–290.
5   Tony Bennett, *The Birth of the Museum: History, Theory, Politics* (London: Routledge, 1995), 69–75.
6   Challis, *From the Harpy Tomb to the Wonders of Ephesus*, 40–54.
7   'Summary of This Morning's News', *The Pall Mall Gazette*, 7 December 1877. 'The Court', *The Graphic*, 15 December 1877.
8   Stuart Dodgson Collingwood, *The Life and Letters of Lewis Carroll* (London: T. Fisher Unwin, 1898), 196.
9   George Gissing, 'Chapter X', *Isabel Clarendon* (London: Chapman and Hall, 1886). Frances Awdry, 'Lucy's Romance', *The Monthly Packet of Evening Readings for Members of the English Church*, 1 December 1881.
10 Bryant Davies, *Troy, Carthage and the Victorians*.
11 Cornelia D. Pearsall, 'Locating Troy', in *Tennyson's Rapture: Transformation in the Victorian Dramatic Monologue* (Oxford: Oxford University Press, 2008), 1–42.
12 Hugh Kenner, 'Renaissance II', in *The Pound Era* (Berkeley: University of California Press, 1971), 41–53.

Chapter 5: Visualizing Troy

1   Eric Shanower, 'Twenty-First-Century Troy', in *Classics and Comics*, ed. George Kovacs and C.W. Marshall (Oxford: Oxford University Press, 2014), 200–1. Daniel Petersen 'Live from Troy: Embedded in the Trojan War', in *Return to Troy: New Essays on the Hollywood Epic*, ed. Martin M. Winkler (Leiden: Brill, 2015), 27–48.
2   See for example: Alexander Stuart Murray, 'Dr. Schliemann's Trojan Antiquities', *The Academy*, 22 December 1877. M. Betham-Edwards, 'Social Aspects of the Paris Exhibition', *The Eclectic Magazine of Foreign Literature*, October 1878.
3   'The Schliemann Treasures', *The Western Daily Press*, 21 December 1877. 'Dr. Schliemann's Collection', *The Citizen*, 26 December 1877. 'Dr. Schliemann's Collection', *Illustrated London News*, 29 December 1877.
4   'Relics of Troy', *Daily News*, 10 December 1877. 'Dr Schliemann's Relics of Troy', *North Otago Times*, 30 March 1878.

5 'Dr Schliemann's Excavations in the Troad', *Illustrated London News*, 5 January 1878, 11.
6 'Relics of Troy', *The Derby Mercury*, 26 December 1877.
7 Geoffrey C. Munn, 'The Archaeologist, the Collector and the Jeweller 1820–1900', in *Heinrich Schliemann Nach Hundert Jahren*, ed. William M. Calder III and Justus Cobet (Frankfurt am Main: Vittorio Klostermann, 1990), 326–34.
8 'Aesthetic, Bridal, and Reception Toilettes', *Harper's Bazaar*, 19 November 1881, 749. 'The Art World', *Potter's American Monthly*, March 1882.
9 Ibid.
10 Debbie Challis, *From the Harpy Tomb to the Wonders of Ephesus: British Archaeologists in the Ottoman Empire 1840–1880* (London: Duckworth, 2008), 153.
11 'Industries at the Manchester Exhibition', *The Times*, 27 May 1887. Kate Nichols, *Greece and Rome at the Crystal Palace: Classical Sculpture and Modern Britain, 1854–1936* (Oxford: Oxford University Press, 2015), 93–4.
12 Edwin Atlee Barber, 'The Rise of the Pottery Industry', *Popular Science Monthly*, 40 (December 1891).
13 A.H. Hews and Company, *Price-List and Illustrated Catalogue of Antique Pottery: Known as the Albert Ware Manufactured by A.H. Hews and Company, Inc. North Cambridge Mass.*, https://archive.org/details/pricelistillustr00ahhe, accessed 11 July 2018.
14 'Artistic Pottery', *Lyttelton Times*, 26 May 1882, https://paperspast.natlib.govt.nz/newspapers/LT18820526.2.35, accessed 11 July 2018.
15 Richard Jenkyns, *Dignity and Decadence: Victorian Art and the Classical Inheritance* (London: Harper Collins, 1991), 192–290.
16 Jan Haywood and Naoíse Mac Sweeney, *Homer's* Iliad *and the Trojan War: Dialogues on Tradition* (London: Bloomsbury Academic, 2018), 68–9.
17 Ian Jenkins, 'Frederic Lord Leighton and Greek Vases', *Burlington Magazine*, October (1983): 597–605, http://burlington.org.uk/media/_file/article-11722.pdf, accessed 29 March 2019.
18 V&A, 'Colour Sketch for Spirit Fresco "The Arts of Industry as Applied to War"', V&A Search the Collections: http://collections.vam.ac.uk/item/O133138/colour-sketch-for-spirit-fresco-oil-painting-leighton-frederic-lord/, accessed 28 August 2018. Keren Rosa Hammerschlag, ' "Nature Straight from God" or "Galvanised Mummy"? Resurrecting Classicism in Frederic Leighton's *And the Sea Gave Up the Dead Which Were In It*', *Nineteenth-Century Art Worldwide* 9, no. 2 (2010), http://www.19thc-artworldwide.org/autumn10/frederic-leightons-and-the-sea-gave-up-the-dead-which-were-in-it#_ftn51, accessed 11 July 2018.
19 Jenkyns, *Dignity and Decadence*, 210–12.
20 Pliny, *Historias Naturalis*, 33.81.
21 Rosalie Glynn Grylls, 'Rossetti and Browning', *The Princeton University Library Chronicle* 33, no. 3 (1972): 232–50.

22 Dante Gabriel Rossetti, 'Troy Town', *Poems* (1870; Cambridge: Cambridge University Press, 2013), 16–20.
23 Francis Thompson, 'Sister Songs (1895)', in *The Poems of Francis Thompson*, ed. Brigid M. Boardman (London: Continuum in association with Boston College, 2001), 59–94. See also Brigid M. Boardman, 'Introduction', in *The Poems of Francis Thompson* (London: Continuum in association with Boston College, 2001), xxv–xxxiv.
24 Everard Meynell, *The Life of Francis Thompson* (New York: Charles Scribner's Sons, 1913), 105–6.
25 Caroline Dakers, *The Holland Park Circle: Artists and Victorian Society* (New Haven and London: Yale University Press, 1999), 214–16.
26 Rex Winsbury, *Zenobia of Palmyra: History, Myth and the Neo-Classical Imagination* (London: Duckworth, 2010), 13–35.
27 'Dr and Madame Schliemann', *The Graphic*, 20 January 1877.
28 Jill Springall, 'Collier, John (1850–1934)', in *Oxford Dictionary of National Biography* (Oxford: Oxford University Press, 2006), https://doi.org/10.1093/ref:odnb/32499, accessed 11 July 2018.
29 British Museum Collection Online, 'The Treasury of Atreus, column. 1905, 1105.1–3', http://www.britishmuseum.org/research/collection_online/collection_object_details.aspx?objectId=457905&partId=1, accessed 28 August 2018.
30 Heinrich Schliemann, *Ilios: The City and Country of the Trojans* (London: John Murray, 1880), plate no. 1522, 693. My thanks to Andrew Shapland for pointing this out.
31 British Museum Collection Online, 'Electrotype/dagger, 1908, 1230.17', http://www.britishmuseum.org/research/collection_online/collection_object_details.aspx?objectId=447686&partId=1, accessed 11 July 2018.
32 Elizabeth Prettejohn, *Rossetti and His Circle* (London: Tate Gallery Publishing, 1997), 32.
33 George C.M. Birdwood, 'Handbook to the Indian Court, Paris Universal Exhibition 1878'. In *Report of Her Majesty's Commissioners for the Paris Universal Exhibition of 1878* (London: George E. Eyre and William Spottiswoode, 1880). 'Troy', *The Times*, 18 April 1878.
34 Edith Hall and Fiona Macintosh, *Greek Tragedy and the British Theatre 1660–1914* (Oxford: Oxford University Press, 2005), 453–4. T.D. Olverson, *Women Writers and the Dark Side of Late Victorian Hellenism* (Basingstoke: Palgrave Macmillan, 2010), 90–1.
35 Mary Beard, 'Myths of the Odyssey in Art and Literature', in *The Invention of Jane Harrison* (Cambridge, MA: Harvard University Press, 2002), 37–53. Ian Jenkins, 'Frederic Lord Leighton and Greek Vases'.
36 Iain Ross, 'Archaiologia', in *Oscar Wilde and Ancient Greece* (Cambridge: Cambridge University Press, 2012), 97–126.
37 'The Tale of Troy', *Art Journal*, July 1883.

38 'Dramatic Gossip', *The Athenaeum*, 26 May 1883.
39 Andrew Lang, 'The Tale of Troy', *The Academy*, 9 June 1883.
40 R.C. Jebb, ' "Echoes of Hellas" by Prof. George C. Warr, with Illustrations by Walter Crane', *The Classical Review* 2, no. 8 (1888): 248–9. George C. Warr and Walter Crane, *Echoes of Hellas: The Tale of Troy and the Story of Orestes from Homer and Aeschylus with introductory essay and sonnets by George C. Warr* (London: Marcus Ward and Co., 1887).
41 Lang, 'The Tale of Troy'.
42 'The Tale of Troy', *The Saturday Review*, 9 June 1883.
43 Ibid.
44 A.A. Donohue, *Greek Sculpture and the Problem of Description* (Cambridge: Cambridge University Press, 2005), 47–50.
45 'The Tale of Troy', *The Athenaeum*, 2 June 1883.
46 Ross, 'Archaiologia', 111–18.
47 Oscar Wilde, 'The Truth of Masks', in *Intentions* (London: Osgood McIlvaine & Co., 1894), 235.

Chapter 6: The appeal of the primitive

1 John Batchelor, 'Scott, William Bell (1811–1890), Poet and Painter', in *Oxford Dictionary of National Biography* (Oxford: Oxford University Press, 2004), https://doi.org/10.1093/ref:odnb/24938, accessed 11 July 2018.
2 William Bell Scott, 'The Hissarlik Antiquities at the South Kensington Museum', *The Academy*, 16 February 1878.
3 Ibid.
4 Tony Bennett, *Pasts Beyond Memory: Evolution, Museums, Colonialism* (London: Routledge, 2004), 61–3.
5 Alex Potts, 'Introduction', in *History of the Art of Antiquity*, ed. J.J. Winckelmann and A. Potts (Los Angeles: Getty Publications, 2006), 1–37.
6 Ian Jenkins, *Archaeologists and Aesthetes in the Sculpture Galleries of the British Museum, 1800–1939* (London: British Museum Press, 1992), 56–74.
7 Scott, 'The Hissarlik Antiquities at the South Kensington Museum'.
8 A.S. Murray, 'Dr. Schliemann's Trojan Antiquities', *The Academy*, 22 December 1877, 581.
9 David Richards, 'At Other Times: Modernism and the "Primitive" ', in *The Cambridge History of Modernism*, ed. Vincent Sherry (Cambridge: Cambridge University Press, 2017), 64–82.
10 Christopher Frayling, *Henry Cole and the Chamber of Horrors: The Curious Origins of the Victoria and Albert Museum* (London: V&A Publishing, 2010), 23.

11 South Kensington Museum, *A Guide to the Art Collections of the South Kensington Museum: Illustrated with Plans and Wood Engravings* (London: Spottiswoode & Co., n.d.), 24–6.
12 'Troy', *The Times*, 18 April 1878, 7.
13 Michael Vickers, 'Value and Simplicity: Eighteenth-Century Taste and the Study of Greek Vases', *Past & Present* 116, no. 1 (1987): 98–137.
14 Frayling, *Henry Cole and the Chamber of Horrors*, 33–55.
15 Amy Woodson-Boulton, *Transformative Beauty: Art Museums in Industrial Britain* (Redwood City, CA: Stanford University Press, 2012).
16 Ibid. Bertram Fulke Hartshorne, 'Dr. Schliemann's Trojan Collection', *The Archaeological Journal* 34 (1877): 291–6.
17 'The Collection of Art Objects from the Site of Troy', *The Art Journal*, April 1878.
18 Frayling, *Henry Cole and the Chamber of Horrors*, 29.
19 'The Collection of Art Objects from the Site of Troy', *The Art Journal*, April 1878.
20 First published in the *Fortnightly Review*, February 1880. Walter Pater, 'The Heroic Age of Greek Art', in *Greek Studies* (London: Macmillan, 1895), 194–233.
21 Elizabeth Prettejohn, 'Pater on Sculpture', in *Pater the Classicist: Classical Scholarship, Reception, and Aestheticism*, ed. Charles Martindale, Stefano Evangelista, and Elizabeth Prettejohn (Oxford: Oxford University Press, 2017), 220–38.
22 Pater, 'The Heroic Age of Greek Art', 219.
23 Ibid.
24 Prettejohn, 'Pater on Sculpture', 220–38.
25 Richard Jenkyns, *The Victorians and Ancient Greece* (Oxford: Blackwell, 1980), 196–7.
26 Elizabeth Prettejohn, *The Modernity of Ancient Sculpture: Greek Sculpture and Modern Art from Winckelmann to Picasso* (London: I.B. Tauris, 2012), 192–4.
27 Pater, 'The Heroic Age of Greek Art', 205–6.
28 'Notes on Art and Archaeology', *The Academy*, 13 March 1880.
29 'Dr Schliemann's Relics of Troy', *North Otago Times*, 30 March 1878.
30 However, Schliemann also describes drab earth tones as 'brilliant' in his work, perhaps indicating a burnished finish. For example: Schliemann, Heinrich, *Troy and Its Remains: A Narrative of Researches and Discoveries Made on the Site of Ilium, and in the Trojan Plain* (London: John Murray, 1875), 296.
31 Richards, 'At Other Times'.
32 For another example which praised the originality of Troy's designs, see: 'Relics of Troy', *The Derby Mercury*, 26 December 1877.
33 Nicholas Thomas, 'Objects: Indigenous Signs in Colonial Design', in *Possessions: Indigenous Art, Colonial Culture* (London: Thames & Hudson, 1999), 106–9.
34 Edward Tregear, *The Aryan Maori* (Wellington, New Zealand: George Didsbury, 1885), 91.

35 Andrea Witcomb, *Re-Imagining the Museum: Beyond the Mausoleum* (London: Routledge, 2003), 24.
36 Sadiah Qureshi, *Peoples on Parade: Exhibitions Empire and Anthropology in Nineteenth-Century Britain* (Chicago: University of Chicago Press, 2011).
37 Richards, 'At Other Times'.

Chapter 7: Laughing at Schliemann

1 'Dr Schliemann's Collection of Trojan Antiquities', *The Manchester Courier and Lancashire General Advertiser*, 21 December 1877.
2 Rachel Bryant Davies, *Troy, Carthage and the Victorians: The Drama of Classical Ruins in the Nineteenth-Century Imagination* (Cambridge: Cambridge University Press, 2018), 103–17.
3 Cornelius Holtorf, *From Stonehenge to Las Vegas : Archaeology as Popular Culture* (Walnut Creek, CA: Altamira Press, 2005), 1.
4 Ibid., 56–7. Norman Levitt 'The Colonisation of the Past and the Pedagogy of the Future', in *Archaeological Fantasies: How Pseudoarchaeology Misrepresents the Past and Misleads the Public*, ed. Garrett G. Fagan (Abingdon: Routledge, 2006), 270–2.
5 'A Correction', *Fun*, 9 May 1877.
6 'Mems from Mycenae', *Funny Folks*, 31 March 1877. 'Archæological Discoveries', *Funny Folks*, 6 January 1877.
7 'The Latest Relics', *Fun*, 21 March 1877.
8 Walter Pater, 'The Heroic Age of Greek Art', in *Greek Studies* (London: Macmillan, 1895), 194–233.
9 'Not a Bad Egg', *Fun*, 5 March 1879, 100.
10 'Archæological Discoveries', *Funny Folks*, 6 January 1877.
11 For the Athena story, see: D.F. Easton, 'Schliemann's Mendacity: A False Trail?', *Antiquity* 58, no. 244 (1984): 197–204. The toads story (so weird that the editors gently refuted it in a footnote): Heinrich Schliemann, *Troy and Its Remains: A Narrative of Researches and Discoveries Made on the Site of Ilium, and in the Trojan Plain* (London: John Murray, 1875), 157.
12 'Archæological Discoveries', *Funny Folks*, 6 January 1877. 'The German Ghoul', *Funny Folks*, 24 March 1877.
13 'A Correction', *Fun*, 9 May 1877.
14 'The German Ghoul', *Funny Folks*, 24 March 1877.
15 Bryant Davies, *Troy, Carthage and the Victorians*, 103–17.
16 'The Hero of Mycenae', *Funny Folks*, 12 May 1877.
17 'Dr Schliemann on the Early Civilization of Greece', *British Architect*, 4 May 1877.
18 'How About Those Buttons?', *Punch or the London Charivari*, 13 January 1877, 3.

19 'Schliemann's Researches in Greece', *Supplement to the Illustrated London News*, 24 March 1877.
20 'Notes', *The Sporting Times*, 19 January 1878.

Chapter 8: Weighing up ancient Troy

1 Susanne Duesterberg, *Popular Receptions of Archaeology: Fictional and Factual Texts in 19th and Early 20th Century Britain* (Bielefeld: Transcript, 2015), 272–80.
2 'A Wonderful Treasure Trove', *Scientific American*, 6 January 1877. Bertram Fulke Hartshorne, 'Dr. Schliemann's Trojan Collection', *The Archaeological Journal* 34 (1877): 291–6.
3 Lesley Fitton, *Heinrich Schliemann and the British Museum* (London: British Museum, 1991), 14, 30.
4 Manfred Korfmann, 'Introduction – Troia and the Natural Sciences', in *Troja and the Troad: Scientific Approaches*, ed. Günther A. Wagner, Ernst Pernicka and Hans-Peter Uerpmann (Berlin: Springer, 2003), 5–6.
5 Fitton, *Heinrich Schliemann and the British Museum*, 21.
6 Francis O'Gorman, '"To See the Finger of God in the Dimensions of the Pyramid": A New Context for Ruskin's "The Ethics of the Dust" (1866)', *The Modern Language Review* 98, no. 3 (2003): 563–73.
7 Heinrich Schliemann, *Troy and Its Remains: A Narrative of Researches and Discoveries Made on the Site of Ilium, and in the Trojan Plain* (London: John Murray, 1875), 359.
8 H.W. Chisholm, 'Ninth Annual Report of the Warden of the Standards on the Proceedings and Business of the Standard Weights and Measures Department of the Board of Trade for 1874–5' (London, 1875), https://books.google.com.hk/books?id=KSxcAAAAQAAJ&printsec=frontcover&hl=zh-TW&source=gbs_ge_summary_r&cad=0#v=onepage&q&f=false, accessed 18 March 2019.
9 E.H.H. Green, 'Gentlemanly Capitalism and British Economic Policy, 1880–1914: The Debate Over Bimetallism and Protectionism', in *Gentlemanly Capitalism and British Imperialism: The New Debate on Empire*, ed. Raymond E. Dumett (London: Longman, 1999), 44–67. P.J. Cain and A.G. Hopkins, 'Gentlemanly Capitalism and Economic Policy: City, Government and the "National Interest", 1850–1914', in *British Imperialism 1688–2015* (Abingdon: Routledge, 2016), 149–64.
10 Schliemann, *Troy and Its Remains*, 328.
11 Barclay Head, 'The Origin and Transmission of Some of the Principal Ancient Systems of Weight, as Applied to Money from the Earliest Times down to the Age of Alexander the Great', *Journal of the Institute of Bankers* 1 (1879): 167–201.
12 'Discussion on Mr Barclay Head's Paper' *Journal of the Institute of Bankers* 1 (1879), p. 189.

Part Four: Troy's place in history

1. 'Troy', *The Times*, 31 March 1875.
2. The idea of a modern Trojan War often comes up when people are arguing about Troy, for a comparable version in the eighteenth century, see: Rachel Bryant Davies, *Troy, Carthage and the Victorians: The Drama of Classical Ruins in the Nineteenth-Century Imagination* (Cambridge: Cambridge University Press, 2018), 67.
3. 'Troy', *The Times*, 31 March 1875.
4. Ibid.

Chapter 9: The other Homeric Question

1. Untitled article ['Troy and the New Archaeology'], *The Times*, 20 December 1877, 9.
2. Rachel Bryant Davies, *Troy, Carthage and the Victorians: The Drama of Classical Ruins in the Nineteenth-Century Imagination* (Cambridge: Cambridge University Press, 2018), 47–67.
3. Untitled article ['Troy and the New Archaeology'], *The Times*, 20 December 1877, 9.
4. 'Troy', *The Times*, 16 August 1877.
5. David Gange and Rachel Bryant Davies, 'Troy', in *Cities of God: The Bible and Archaeology in Nineteenth-Century Britain*, ed. David Gange and Michael Ledger-Lomas (Cambridge: Cambridge University Press, 2013), 39–70. David Gange, *Dialogues with the Dead: Egyptology in British Culture and Religion, 1822–1922* (Oxford: Oxford University Press, 2013), 42–3.
6. Cornelia Pearsall, 'Locating Troy', in *Tennyson's Rapture: Transformation in the Victorian Dramatic Monologue* (Oxford: Oxford University Press, 2008), 1–42.
7. 'Royal Institute of British Architects', *The British Architect and Northern Engineer*, 4 May 1877.
8. Lesley Fitton, *Heinrich Schliemann and the British Museum* (London: British Museum, 1991), 17.
9. Jan Haywood and Naoíse Mac Sweeney, *Homer's* Iliad *and the Trojan War: Dialogues on Tradition* (London: Bloomsbury Academic, 2018), 107–45.
10. Michael Squire, 'Ekphrasis at the Forge and the Forging of Ekphrasis: The Shield of Achilles in Graeco-Roman Word and Image', *Word and Image* 29, no. 2 (2013): 157–91.
11. Alexander Stuart Murray, 'A New View of the Homeric Question', *Contemporary Review* 23 (1874): 219.

12 Frederick Apthorp Paley, *On Post-Epic or Imitative Words in Homer* (London: Norgate, 1879).
13 Murray, 'A New View of the Homeric Question'.
14 Alexander Stuart Murray, 'Dr. Schliemann's Trojan Antiquities', *The Academy*, 22 December 1877.
15 Ibid.
16 'The Trojan Treasure', *The Times*, 20 December 1877.
17 Ibid.
18 First published in the *Fortnightly Review*, February 1880. Walter Pater, 'The Heroic Age of Greek Art', in *Greek Studies* (London: Macmillan, 1895), 219.
19 Elizabeth Prettejohn, 'Pater on Sculpture', in *Pater the Classicist: Classical Scholarship, Reception, and Aestheticism*, ed. Charles Martindale, Stefano Evangelista and Elizabeth Prettejohn (Oxford: Oxford University Press, 2017), 220–38.
20 Homer, *Iliad*, 18.610, 19.380.
21 Elizabeth Prettejohn, *Beauty and Art, 1750–2000* (Oxford: Oxford University Press, 2005), 9–29.
22 'Dr Schliemann's Collection of Trojan Antiquities', *The Manchester Courier and Lancashire General Advertiser*, 21 December 1877.
23 'Dr Schliemann's Excavations in the Troad', *Illustrated London News*, 5 January 1878, 11.
24 T.D. Olverson, *Women Writers and the Dark Side of Late Victorian Hellenism* (Basingstoke: Palgrave Macmillan, 2010). Isobel Hurst, 'Classical Training for the Woman Writer', in *Victorian Women Writers and the Classics: The Feminine of Homer*, ed. Isobel Hurst (Oxford: Oxford University Press, 2007), 52–100.
25 Gange and Bryant Davies, 'Troy'.
26 'List of Fellows', *Transactions of the Royal Historical Society* 8 (1880): i–xxii. See also the brief discussion of Harrison in her daughter's entry in the *ODNB*: Malcolm Todd, 'Toynbee, Jocelyn Mary Catherine (1897–1985)', *Oxford Dictionary of National Biography* (Oxford: Oxford University Press, 2004), https://doi.org/10.1093/ref:odnb/62392, accessed 6 April 2019.
27 'The Household: An Englishwoman's Thoughts About Women', *Michigan Farmer*, 7 March 1882, 7.
28 Fergus Millar, 'Toynbee, Arnold Joseph (1889–1975), Historian', in *Oxford Dictionary of National Biography* (Oxford: Oxford University Press, 2004), https://doi.org/10.1093/ref:odnb/31769, accessed 25 April 2017.
29 'Fine Art', *The Academy*, 11 December 1880, 429–30.
30 Naoíse Mac Sweeney, *Troy: Myth, City, Icon* (London: Bloomsbury Academic, 2018), 32–109.
31 Peter Jablonka, 'Troy', in *The Oxford Handbook of the Bronze Age Aegean*, ed. E.H. Cline (Oxford: Oxford University Press, 2012), 849–61.
32 Susanne Duesterberg, *Popular Receptions of Archaeology: Fictional and Factual Texts in 19th and Early 20th Century Britain* (Bielefeld: Transcript, 2015), 253. Kathrin

Maurer, 'Archeology as Spectacle: Heinrich Schliemann's Media of Excavation', *German Studies Review* 32, no. 2 (2009): 303–17.

Chapter 10: How old was Troy?

1. 'Relics of Troy', *Daily News*, 10 December 1877.
2. Bruce G. Trigger, *A History of Archaeological Thought* (Cambridge University Press, 2006), 290–1.
3. David A. Traill, *Schliemann of Troy: Treasure and Deceit* (London: John Murray, 1995), 167. Schliemann, Heinrich, *Mycenae: A Narrative of Researches and Discoveries at Mycenae and Tiryns* (New York: Charles Scribner's sons, 1880), 63–4.
4. Susan Heuck Allen, *Finding the Walls of Troy: Frank Calvert and Heinrich Schliemann at Hisarlık* (Berkeley: University of California Press, 1999), 171–2.
5. Naoíse Mac Sweeney, *Troy: Myth, City, Icon* (London: Bloomsbury Academic, 2018), 23. Lesley Fitton, *The Discovery of the Greek Bronze Age* (Cambridge MA: Harvard University Press, 1996), 94.
6. 'The Tomb of Agamemnon', *British Architect*, 19 January 1877.
7. Mac Sweeney, *Troy: Myth, City, Icon*, 93. Peter Rowley-Conwy, *From Genesis to Prehistory: The Archaeological Three Age System and Its Contested Reception in Denmark, Britain, and Ireland* (Oxford: Oxford University Press, 2007), 7.
8. Antonis Kotsonas, 'Politics of Periodization and the Archaeology of Early Greece', *American Journal of Archaeology* 120, no. 2 (2016): 239–70.
9. Walter Pater, 'The Heroic Age of Greek Art', in *Greek Studies* (London: Macmillan, 1895), 194–233.
10. Charles Newton, 'Dr Schliemann's Discoveries at Mycenae', in *Essays on Art and Archaeology* (London: Macmillan, 1880), 246–302. See also: 'Dr. Schliemann's Discoveries at Troy', *The Times*, 2 May 1874.
11. Fredric Jameson, *The Political Unconscious: Narrative as a Socially Symbolic Act* (London: Routledge, 2002), 13–19.
12. Heinrich Schliemann, *Troy and Its Remains: A Narrative of Researches and Discoveries Made on the Site of Ilium, and in the Trojan Plain* (London: John Murray, 1875), 85.
13. Ibid.
14. Rowley-Conwy, *From Genesis to Prehistory*, 1–5. Trigger, *A History of Archaeological Thought*, 215–23.
15. Rowley-Conwy, *From Genesis to Prehistory*, 1–2.
16. Ibid., 260.
17. Ibid., 235. Tony Bennett, *Pasts Beyond Memory: Evolution, Museums, Colonialism* (London: Routledge, 2004), 43.

18 James C. Southall, 'XXVI The Ruins of Troy', in *The Recent Origin of Man: As Illustrated by Geology and the Modern Science of Pre-Historic Archaeology* (London: Trübner & Co., 1875), 440–9. David Gange, *Dialogues with the Dead: Egyptology in British Culture and Religion, 1822–1922* (Oxford: Oxford University Press, 2013), 30–1.
19 'Art. II – Recent Origin of Man', *Methodist Quarterly Review*, January 1877, 29–56.
20 Heinrich Schliemann, *Ilios: The City and Country of the Trojans* (London: John Murray, 1880), 237.
21 Rowley-Conwy, *From Genesis to Prehistory*, 245.
22 Schliemann, *Ilios*, 257–8.
23 Lesley Fitton, *Heinrich Schliemann and the British Museum* (London: British Museum, 1991), 9, 20.
24 'The Trojan Treasure' *The Times*, 20 December 1877.
25 'Dr. Schliemann's Discoveries at Troy' *The Times*, 2 May 1874.
26 William Ewart Gladstone, *Juventus Mundi: The Gods and Men of the Heroic Age* (Boston, MA: Little, Brown and Company, 1869), 533–8. Horace Gordon Hutchinson, *Life of Sir John Lubbock, Lord Avebury, Vol. 1* (London: Macmillan and Co., 1914), 96.
27 W. Chandler Roberts-Austen, 'Alloys', *Scientific American Supplement*, 17 February 1894.
28 'Troy', *The Times*, 17 December 1877.
29 'Troy', *The Times*, 18 April 1878, 7.
30 Ian Jenkins, *Archaeologists and Aesthetes in the Sculpture Galleries of the British Museum, 1800–1939* (London: British Museum Press, 1992), 56–74.
31 He was initially known simply as General Lane Fox, but I will refer to him by Pitt Rivers, the name he took in 1880, since this is the name by which he is best known today. Rethinking Pitt Rivers, '"Typological Museums, as Exemplified by the Pitt Rivers Museum at Oxford, and His Provincial Museum at Farnham, Dorset", *Journal of the Society of Arts*, 18 December, 1891, pp. 115–22', http://web.prm.ox.ac.uk/rpr/index.php/article-index/12-articles/189-typological-museums, accessed 28 August 2018.
32 Tony Bennett, *The Birth of the Museum: History, Theory, Politics* (London: Routledge, 1995), 195–201.
33 Rethinking Pitt Rivers, 'Museum Displays at Bethnal Green Museum', http://web.prm.ox.ac.uk/rpr/index.php/article-index/12-articles/281-museum-displays-at-bethnal-green-museum, accessed 28 August 2018.
34 Rethinking Pitt Rivers, 'A Year in the Life: 1878', http://web.prm.ox.ac.uk/rpr/index.php/pitt-rivers-life/42-a-year-in-the-life-1878, accessed 28 August 2018.
35 [A.H.L.F. Pitt Rivers], 'Eastern Excavations', *Nature: A Weekly Illustrated Journal of Science*, 21 March 1878, no. 438, 397–9. Although the review is anonymous, Pitt Rivers's notes for this article are preserved in his papers: Rethinking Pitt Rivers, 'P66 Salisbury and South Wiltshire Museum PR Papers', http://web.prm.ox.ac.uk/rpr/index.php/primary-documents-index/14-general/698-p66-salisbury-and-south-wiltshire-museum-pr-papers, accessed 28 August 2018.

36 [Pitt Rivers], 'Eastern Excavations', 399.
37 'Dr. Schliemann', *The Times*, 12 April 1878.
38 A. Lane-Fox Pitt Rivers, 'On the Evolution of Culture (1875)', in *The Evolution of Culture and Other Essays by the Late Lt.-Gen. A. Lane-Fox Pitt-Rivers*, ed. J.KL. Myres (Oxford: Clarendon Press, 1906), 20–44.
39 [Pitt Rivers], 'Eastern Excavations', 397–9.
40 William Ryan Chapman, 'Arranging Ethnology: A.H.L.F. Pitt Rivers and the Typological Tradition', in *Objects and Others: Essays on Museums and Material Culture*, ed. George W. Stocking (Madison, WI: University of Wisconsin Press, 1985), 15–43.
41 Friedrich Max Müller, *Lectures on the Science of Language*, Vol. 1 (London: Longmans, Green and Co., 1873), 24–6.
42 Pitt Rivers, 'On the Evolution of Culture'.
43 Alison Petch, 'Notes on the Opening of the Pitt Rivers Museum', *Journal of Museum Ethnography* 19 (2006): 101–12.
44 Pitt Rivers, 'On the Evolution of Culture'.

Chapter 11: Who were the Trojans?

1 'Troy', *The Times*, 16 August 1877.
2 Egypt: 'The Collection of Art Objects from the Site of Troy', *The Art Journal*, April 1878. Central America: 'Toltecs and Aztecs', *All the Year Round*, 4 February 1888. Peru: Andrew Lang, 'The Art of Savages', *The Magazine of Art*, January 1882. India: George C.M. Birdwood, 'Handbook to the Indian Court, Paris Universal Exhibition 1878', in *Report of Her Majesty's Commissioners for the Paris Universal Exhibition of 1878* (London: George E. Eyre and William Spottiswoode, 1880). Switzerland: 'Troy', *The Times*, 17 December 1877. Pomerania: Francois Lenormant, 'Antiquities at the Paris Exhibition', *The Contemporary Review*, 1 August 1878. Japan: 'Relics of Troy', *The Derby Mercury*, 26 December 1877. Ohio: William C. Borlase, 'The Schliemann Collection at the South Kensington Museum', *The Academy*, 9 February 1878.
3 Malcolm Quinn, *The Swastika: Constructing the Symbol* (London: Routledge, 1994).
4 Cathy Gere, *The Tomb of Agamemnon* (Cambridge, MA: Harvard University Press, 2006), 121.
5 Susanne Duesterberg, *Popular Receptions of Archaeology: Fictional and Factual Texts in 19th and Early 20th Century Britain* (Bielefeld: Transcript, 2015), 209–328.
6 David Gange, *Dialogues with the Dead: Egyptology in British Culture and Religion, 1822-1922* (Oxford: Oxford University Press, 2013), 142–50.
7 Bruce G. Trigger, *A History of Archaeological Thought* (Cambridge: Cambridge University Press, 2006), 167.
8 Debbie Challis, *The Archaeology of Race: The Eugenic Ideas of Francis Galton and Flinders Petrie* (Abingdon: Bloomsbury Academic, 2013), 1–20. Karen E. Fields and

Barbara J. Fields, 'A Tour of Racecraft', in *Racecraft: The Soul of Inequality in American Life* (London: Verso, 2014).

9   Theodor W. Adorno and Max Horkheimer, *Dialectic of Enlightenment*, trans. John Cumming (London: Verso, 1997).

10 Wiktor Stoczkowski, *Explaining Human Origins: Myth, Imagination, and Conjecture* (Cambridge: Cambridge University Press, 2002), 1–28.

11 Denise Eileen McCoskey, *Race: Antiquity and Its Legacy* (London: I.B.Tauris, 2012), 51–3.

12 Charles Brian Rose, 'Troy and the Historical Imagination', *The Classical World* 91, no. 5 (1998): 405–13.

13 McCoskey, *Race: Antiquity and Its Legacy*, 144. Rachel Kousser, 'Destruction and Memory on the Athenian Acropolis', *Art Bulletin* 91, no. 3 (2009): 263–82.

14 Edith Hall, *Inventing the Barbarian: Greek Self-Definition Through Tragedy* (Oxford: Clarendon Press, 1989), 102. Edward W. Said, *Orientalism* (London: Penguin, 1978), 63.

15 Walter Pater, 'The Heroic Age of Greek Art', in *Greek Studies* (London: Macmillan, 1895), 209–33.

16 Said, *Orientalism*, 56–73.

17 William Ewart Gladstone, *Homeric Synchronism: An Enquiry into the Time and Place of Homer* (New York: Harper, 1876), 41.

18 Gange, *Dialogues with the Dead*, 143–7.

19 Gere, *The Tomb of Agamemnon*, 81–95.

20 Cornelia Pearsall, 'Locating Troy', in *Tennyson's Rapture: Transformation in the Victorian Dramatic Monologue* (Oxford: Oxford University Press, 2008), 1–42.

21 William Ewart Gladstone, *Juventus Mundi: The Gods and Men of the Heroic Age* (Boston, MA: Little, Brown and Company, 1869), 464.

22 David Bebbington, 'The Olympian Religion', in *The Mind of Gladstone: Religion, Homer, and Politics* (Oxford: Oxford University Press, 2004), 178–214.

23 'The Troy Collection at South Kensington', *The Builder*, 5 January 1878.

24 Ibid.

25 'The Heroic Age', *The Times*, 8 January 1878, 10. 'The Heroic Age', *Bury and Norwich Post*, 15 January 1878, 2. 'Varieties', *The Leisure Hour: An Illustrated Magazine for Home Reading*, 2 March 1878, 144. 'Town & Country', *Lyttelton Times*, 49, no. 5377, 17 May 1878, https://paperspast.natlib.govt.nz/newspapers/LT18780517.2.11, accessed 28 August 2018.

26 'Notes', *The Sporting Times*, 19 January 1878. Quoted in Chapter 7.

27 Challis, *The Archaeology of Race*, 1–44. Tony Bennett, *Pasts Beyond Memory: Evolution, Museums, Colonialism* (London: Routledge, 2004).

28 Małgosia Nowak-Kemp and Yannis Galanakis, 'Ancient Greek Skulls in the Oxford University Museum, Part I: George Rolleston, Oxford and the Formation of the

Human Skulls Collection', *Journal of the History of Collections* 24, no. 1 (2011): 89–104. Debbie Challis, 'Skull Triangles: Flinders Petrie, Race Theory and Biometrics', *Bulletin of the History of Archaeology* 26, no. 1 (2016): art. 5, https://www.archaeologybulletin.org/articles/10.5334/bha-556/, accessed 18 March 2019.

29 Challis, *The Archaeology of Race*, 8. Jennifer Ruth, ' "Gross Humbug" or "the Language of Truth"? The Case of the *Zoist*', *Victorian Periodicals Review* 32, no. 4 (1999): 299–323.

30 'Dr. Schliemann, The Merchant-Archaeologist', *The Phrenological Journal and Science of Health*, July 1877, 13.

31 Duesterberg, *Popular Receptions of Archaeology*, 211–26.

32 'Relics of Troy', *The Derby Mercury*, 26 December 1877.

33 For example: 'Relics of Troy', *The Derby Mercury*, 26 December 1877. 'Troy', *The Times*, 18 April 1878, 7. Emile Burnouf, 'Cyprus and Mycenae', *The Athenaeum*, 22 March 1879.

34 Duesterberg, *Popular Receptions of Archaeology*, 267.

35 Challis, *The Archaeology of Race*, 7–8, 40–1.

36 V&A archive, MA/31/7: Register of Loans In, 1878–1937, 5.

37 Heinrich Schliemann, *Ilios: The City and Country of the Trojans* (London: John Murray, 1880), 271–2, 507–12.

38 Peter Rowley-Conwy, *From Genesis to Prehistory: The Archaeological Three Age System and Its Contested Reception in Denmark, Britain, and Ireland* (Oxford: Oxford University Press, 2007), 63–4.

39 Schliemann, *Ilios*, 510.

40 Ibid., 511.

41 Quinn, *The Swastika*, xi.

42 Schliemann, *Ilios*, xv.

43 Gere, *The Tomb of Agamemnon*, 129.

44 Louis Palma di Cesnola, *Cyprus: Its Ancient Cities, Tombs and Temples – A Narrative of Researches and Excavations* (London: John Murray, 1877).

45 [A.H.L.F. Pitt Rivers], 'Eastern Excavations', *Nature: A Weekly Illustrated Journal of Science*, 21 March 1878, no. 438, 397–9.

46 Ibid.

47 Lenormant, 'Antiquities at the Paris Exhibition'.

48 Partha Mitter, 'Greece, India, and Race Among the Victorians', in *African Athena: New Agendas*, ed. Daniel Orrells, Gurminder K. Bhambra and Tessa Roynon (Oxford: Oxford University Press, 2011), 56–70.

49 Martin Bernal, *Black Athena: The Afroasiatic Roots of Classical Civilization – Volume 1: The Fabrication of Ancient Greece, 1785–1985* (London: Vintage, 1991). Challis, *The Archaeology of Race*, 5.

50 Mitter, 'Greece, India, and Race Among the Victorians'. Bennett, *Pasts Beyond Memory*.

51 Heinrich Schliemann, *Troy and Its Remains: A Narrative of Researches and Discoveries Made on the Site of Ilium, and in the Trojan Plain* (London: John Murray, 1875), 101–6. Schliemann, *Ilios*, 348–53.
52 Quinn, *The Swastika*, 1–29.
53 LLewellyn Jewitt, 'A Few Words on the Fylfot Cross', *The Reliquary* (July 1881), 1–10. J.H.R. 'The Vivified Tau', *The Antiquary*, 4 (1881): 83. A.H. Sayce, 'The Early History of the Levant', *The Academy*, 18 August 1883, 119.
54 V&A, 'The Cross, D.127-1906', http://collections.vam.ac.uk/item/O843147/the-cross-drawing-simpson-william-ri/, accessed 28 August 2018.
55 Hodder M. Westropp, 'The Hissarlik Relics', *The Athenaeum*, 12 January 1878. Sayce, 'The Early History of the Levant'.
56 Bertram Fulke Hartshorne, 'Dr. Schliemann's Trojan Collection', *The Archaeological Journal* 34 (1877): 291–6.
57 Friedrich Max Müller, 'The Hissarlik Inscriptions Deciphered', *The Academy*, 16 May 1874.
58 Hartshorne, 'Dr. Schliemann's Trojan Collection'.
59 George Smith, 'On the Reading of the Cypriote Inscriptions', *Transactions of the Society of Biblical Archaeology* 1 (1872), 129–44. Gange, *Dialogues with the Dead*, 136–41.
60 Which he translated into French as 'Puisse la terre faire dix labours dix mille pièces d'étoffes.' Schliemann, *Troy and Its Remains*, 50–1. Schliemann, *Ilios*, 526–7. On Burnouf's influence, see Cathy Gere, *Knossos and the Prophets of Modernism* (Chicago: University of Chicago Press, 2009), 39–42.
61 Schliemann, *Ilios*, 238–43.
62 'Editorial Article 3', *The Manchester Guardian*, 7 February 1881. James Hilton, 'Remarks on Jade', *Archaeological Journal* 45, no. 1 (1888): 187–205.
63 'Editorial Article 3', *The Manchester Guardian*, 7 February 1881.
64 William C. Borlase, 'The Schliemann Collection at the South Kensington Museum', 123.
65 Trigger, *A History of Archaeological Thought*, 158–61.
66 'Museums', *American Antiquarian and Oriental Journal*, 1880, 65.
67 Ignatius Donnelly, *Atlantis: The Antediluvian World* (New York: Harper & Brothers, 1882), 397–400. Garrett G. Fagan, ed., *Archaeological Fantasies: How Pseudoarchaeology Misrepresents the Past and Misleads the Public* (Abingdon: Routledge, 2006), 124–5.
68 William C. Borlase, 'A Visit to Dr. Schliemann's Troy', *Fraser's Magazine*, February 1878.
69 'Workmen and Museums', *The Liverpool Mercury*, 14 February 1887.
70 Debbie Challis, *From the Harpy Tomb to the Wonders of Ephesus: British Archaeologists in the Ottoman Empire 1840–1880* (London: Duckworth, 2008), 40.

Part Five: Troy's legacy

1. Jane Ellen Harrison, 'Reminiscences of a Student's Life', *Arion* 4, no. 2 (1965), 343.

Chapter 12: Jane Harrison's Odyssey

1. 'A Woman's View of the Greek Question: An Interview with Miss Jane Harrison', *The Pall Mall Gazette*, 4 November 1891, 1–2.
2. Annabel Robinson, *The Life and Work of Jane Ellen Harrison* (Oxford: Oxford University Press, 2002), 56–7.
3. Mary Beard, *The Invention of Jane Harrison* (Cambridge, MA: Harvard University Press, 2002), 40. Robinson, *The Life and Work of Jane Ellen Harrison*, 72–3. Stefano Evangelista, 'Lessons in Greek Art: Jane Harrison and Aestheticism', *Women's Studies* 40, no. 4 (2011): 513–36.
4. 'A Woman's View of the Greek Question', 1–2.
5. Robinson, *The Life and Work of Jane Ellen Harrison*, 75–6.
6. Ibid., 75–7.
7. Bruce Robertson, 'The South Kensington Museum in Context: An Alternative History', *Museum and Society* 2, no. 1 (2004): 1–14.
8. Beard, *The Invention of Jane Harrison*, 100. Evangelista, 'Lessons in Greek Art'.
9. Evangelista, 'Lessons in Greek Art'.
10. Ibid.
11. Penelope, 'Our Ladies' Column by One of Themselves', *The Wrexham Advertiser*, 21 November 1885. 'The Man About Town', *The County Gentleman: A Sporting Gazette and Agricultural Journal*, 16 January 1892.
12. Jane Ellen Harrison, *Myths of the Odyssey in Art and Literature* (London: Rivingtons, 1882). Robinson, *The Life and Work of Jane Ellen Harrison*, 57–84.
13. Although Harrison left out some events that were not sufficiently represented in art: Harrison, *Myths of the Odyssey*, xvii–xviii.
14. Harrison, *Myths of the Odyssey*, 1–44.
15. Ibid., 1.
16. Beard, *The Invention of Jane Harrison*, 100. Evangelista, 'Lessons in Greek Art', 519–20.
17. 'Notes on Art and Archaeology', *The Academy*, 23 October 1886, 283.
18. Harrison, *Myths of the Odyssey*, xv.
19. Ibid., xiii.
20. Ibid., xiii–xiv.
21. John Siegel, 'The Public in the Museum', in *The Emergence of the Modern Museum: An Anthology of Nineteenth-Century Sources*, ed. John Siegel (Oxford: Oxford University Press, 2008), 79–82.

22 'A New Employment for Women of Culture and Reliable Information', *The Ladies' Treasury: A Household Magazine*, 1 June 1893.
23 'Dr Schliemann's Excavations in the Troad', *Illustrated London News*, 5 January 1878, 11–13.
24 'A Woman's View of the Greek Question', 1–2.
25 For a more detailed discussion of Harrison's audiences, see Abigail Baker, 'Myths of The Odyssey in the British Museum', *Bulletin of the Institute of Classical Studies* (forthcoming).
26 Harrison, *Myths of the Odyssey*, 27–9.
27 Ibid., vii.
28 Ibid., viii–ix.
29 H.A. Shapiro, *Myth Into Art: Poet and Painter in Classical Greece* (London: Routledge, 1994), 7. Klaus Junker, *Interpreting the Images of Greek Myths*, trans. Annemarie Künzl-Snodgrass and Anthony Snodgrass (Cambridge: Cambridge University Press, 2012).
30 Charles Newton, 'On the Study of Archæology', in *Essays on Art and Archaeology* (London: Macmillan, 1880), 1–38.
31 Harrison, *Myths of the Odyssey*, xii.
32 Charles Newton, 'On the Study of Archæology', 23.
33 House of Commons, *Report of the Select Committee on the National Gallery*, London, 1853, Appendix XII, 776.
34 Mary Beard, 'The Invention (and Re-invention) of "Group D": An Archaeology of the Classical Tripos 1879–1984', in *Classics in 19th and 20th Century Cambridge: Curriculum, Culture and Community*, ed. Christopher Stray (Cambridge: Cambridge Philological Society, 1998), 95 134.
35 Jane Ellen Harrison, 'The Dawn of Greece', *The Quarterly Review* 194 (1901): 218–43. On Harrison as the author of this review, see: Robinson, *The Life and Work of Jane Ellen Harrison*, 139–42.
36 Evangelista, 'Lessons in Greek Art'.
37 Harrison, 'The Dawn of Greece', 221.

Chapter 13: Arthur Evans's Labyrinth

1 'Excavation of Prehistoric Knossos', *The Times*, 10 August 1900.
2 Arthur Evans, *The Ashmolean Museum as a Home of Archaeology in Oxford: An Inaugural Lecture Given in the Ashmolean Museum, November 20, 1884* (Oxford: Parker & Co., 1884). Arthur Evans, 'Introduction', in *Schliemann of Troy: The Story of a Gold-Seeker*, by Emil Ludwig (London: Unwin Brothers, 1931), 9–21. Arthur Evans, 'Review: Troja: Results of the Latest Researches and Discoveries on the Site of

Homer's Troy, and in the Heroic Tumuli and other Sites, made in the Year 1882', *The Academy*, 29 December 1883, 437–9.

3   Evans, 'Review: Troja', 438.

4   J. Alexander MacGillivray, *Minotaur: Sir Arthur Evans and the Archaeology of the Minoan Myth* (London: Pimlico, 2001). Mary Beard, 'Builder of Ruins', in *Confronting the Classics* (London: Profile, 2013), 17–25.

5   Cathy Gere, *Knossos and the Prophets of Modernism* (Chicago: University of Chicago Press, 2009).

6   Andreas Lapourtas, 'Arthur Evans and His Representation of the Minoan Civilisation at Knossos', *The Museum Archaeologist* 22 (1995): 71–82. Donald Preziosi, 'Archaeology as Museology: Re-thinking the Minoan Past', in *Labyrinth Revisited: Rethinking 'Minoan' Archaeology*, ed. Yannis Hamilakis (Oxford: Oxbow Books, 2002), 30–9.

7   W. St. Chad Boscawen, 'The Knossos Exhibition: The "Oldest Masters" in the World', *Globe*, 13 February 1903.

8   Yannis Galanakis, 'Exhibiting the Minoan Past: Oxford to Knossos', in *Minoan Archaeology: Challenges and Perspectives for the 21st Century: Proceedings of the International Ph.D. and Post-Doc Conference at Heidelberg, 23–27 March 2011*, ed. Sarah Cappel, Ute Günkel-Maschek and Diamantis Panagiotopoulos (Louvain-la-Neuve: Presses Universitaires de Louvain, 2015), 17–34.

9   Joan Evans, *Time and Chance: the Story of Arthur Evans and his Forebears* (London: Longmans, Green and Co., 1943), 207.

10 Royal Academy of Arts, *Old Masters, Deceased Masters of the British School, Albert Cuyp and Palace of Knossos in Crete* (London: Royal Academy of Arts, 1903), https://www.royalacademy.org.uk/art-artists/exhibition-catalogue/1903-old-masters-deceased-masters-of-the-british-school-albert-cuyp-and, accessed 28 August 2018.

11 Royal Academy, *Old Masters*, 47, 49.

12 *Modern Society*, untitled article, 24 January 1903, unpaginated.

13 Gere, *Knossos and the Prophets of Modernism*, 98–104, 151–2. Theodore Ziolkowski, *Minos and the Moderns: Cretan Myth in Twentieth-Century Literature and Art* (Oxford: Oxford University Press, 2008), 75.

14 John McWhirter, 'MacWhirter, John (1837–1911), Landscape Painter', *Oxford Dictionary of National Biography* (Oxford: Oxford University Press, 2004), https://doi.org/10.1093/ref:odnb/34826, accessed 26 May 2018.

15 *Modern Society*, 24 January 1903.

16 Gere, *Knossos and the Prophets of Modernism*, 105–39.

17 Royal Academy, *Old Masters*, 51.

18 'Art: The Old Masters Exhibition at Burlington House', *Observer*, 11 January 1903.

19 'Knossos at Burlington House', *The Builder*, 31 January 1903.

20 'The Academy Winter Exhibition', *The Architect & Contract Reporter*, 9 January 1903.

21 Royal Academy, *Old Masters*, 46.
22 Ibid., 47.
23 'Knossos at Burlington House', *The Builder*, 31 January 1903.
24 Susan Sherratt, 'Representations of Knossos and Minoan Crete in the British, American and Continental Press 1900–1930', *Creta Antica* 10, no. 2 (2009): 619–49.
25 'Art: The Old Masters Exhibition at Burlington House', *Observer*, 11 January 1903. 'Knossos at Burlington House', *The Builder*, 31 January 1903.
26 'The Academy Winter Exhibition', *The Architect & Contract Reporter*, 9 January 1903. Boscawen, 'The Knossos Exhibition: The "Oldest Masters" in the World'.
27 H.N.B., 'Minos in Piccadilly', *The Speaker*, 10 January 1903.
28 Galanakis, 'Exhibiting the Minoan Past'.
29 H.N.B., 'Minos in Piccadilly'.
30 'Knossos at Burlington House', *The Builder*, 31 January 1903.

Chapter 14: Dream and reality

1 Susann Wagenknecht, 'Debating Troy in the Mass Media: The Catalytic Impact of Public Controversy on Academic Discourse', in *The Sciences' Media Connection: Public Communication and Its Repercussions*, ed. Simone Rödder, Martina Franzen and Peter Weingart (Dordrecht: Springer, 2012), 291–306.
2 Andreas W. Vetter, *Troia: Traum und Wirklichkeit Ausstellungsführer* (Braunschweig: Braunschweigisches Landesmuseum und Herzog Anton Ulrich-Museum Braunschweig, 2001), 135, 146.
3 Johannes Haubold, 'Wars of *Wissenschaft*: The New Quest for Troy', *International Journal of the Classical Tradition* 8, no. 4 (2002): 564–79.
4 Vetter, *Troia: Traum und Wirklichkeit*, 8.
5 Wagenknecht, 'Debating Troy in the Mass Media'. For a picture of this and a full discussion of the objections, see Dieter Hertel and Frank Kolb, 'Troy in Clearer Perspective', *Anatolian Studies* 53 (2003): 71–88.
6 Perhaps most famously argued by Tennyson. See: Cornelia Pearsall, *Tennyson's Rapture: Transformation in the Victorian Dramatic Monologue* (Oxford: Oxford University Press, 2008), 1–42.
7 D.F. Easton, J.D. Hawkins, A.G. Sherratt and E.S. Sherratt. 'Troy in Recent Perspective', *Anatolian Studies* 52 (2002): 75–109.
8 Haubold, 'Wars of *Wissenschaft*'.
9 Easton et al. 'Troy in Recent Perspective'. Hertel and Kolb, 'Troy in Clearer Perspective'.
10 Easton et al. 'Troy in Recent Perspective', 77.
11 Haubold, 'Wars of *Wissenschaft*'.

12 Antonis Kotsonas, 'Showcasing New Trojan Wars: Archaeological Exhibitions and the Politics of Appropriation of Ancient Troy', in *Aegis: Essays in Mediterranean Archaeology*, ed. Zetta Theodoropoulou Polychroniadis and Doniert Evely (Oxford: Archaeopress Publishing, 2015), 235–42.
13 Johannes Haubold, 'Dream and Reality in the Work of Heinrich Schliemann and Manfred Korfmann' in *Archaeology and Homeric Epic*, ed. Susan Sherratt and John Bennet (Oxford: Oxbow Books, 2017), 19–34.
14 British Museum, 'Babylon: Myth and Reality', http://www.britishmuseum.org/about_us/past_exhibitions/2008/archive_babylon.aspx, accessed 28 August 2018; Louvre, 'Founding Myths: From Hercules to Darth Vader' https://www.louvre.fr/en/expositions/founding-myths-hercules-darth-vader, accessed 28 August 2018; Museo Nazionale Etrusco di Villa Giulia, 'La Sirena: Soltanto un Mito? Nuovi Spunti per una Storia della Medicina fra Mito, Religione e Scienza', http://www.villagiulia.beniculturali.it/index.php?it/21/archivio-news/158/mostra-la-sirena-soltanto-un-mito-nuovi-spunti-per-una-storia-della-medicina-fra-mito-religione-e-scienza, accessed 28 August 2018; Hellenic Museum, Melbourne, 'Gods, Myths and Mortals: Greek Treasures Across the Millennia', www.hellenic.org.au/gods-myths-mortals, accessed 28 August 2018.
15 Roland Barthes, 'Myth Today', in *Mythologies*, trans. Annette Lavers (London: Vintage Books, 2009), 131–87.
16 Hayden V. White, *The Practical Past* (Evanston, IL: Northwestern University Press, 2014), 1–45. White's use of these two terms derives from the work of Michael Oakeshott, but here I am most interested in White's development of these ideas.

References

A.H. Hews and Company, *Price-List and Illustrated Catalogue of Antique Pottery: Known as the Albert Ware Manufactured by A.H. Hews and Company, Inc. North Cambridge Mass*. Available online: https://archive.org/details/pricelistillustr00ahhe (accessed 28 August 2018).

Adorno, Theodor W., and Max Horkheimer. *Dialectic of Enlightenment*, translated by John Cumming. London: Verso, 1997.

All the Year Round. 'Toltecs and Aztecs'. 4 February 1888.

Allen, Lindsay. 'From Silence: A Persepolis Relief in the Victoria and Albert Museum'. *V&A Online Journal* 5 (2013). Available online: http://www.vam.ac.uk/content/journals/research-journal/issue-no.-5-2013/from-silence-a-persepolis-relief-in-the-victoria-and-albert-museum/ (accessed 15 March 2017).

Allen, Susan Heuck. *Finding the Walls of Troy: Frank Calvert and Heinrich Schliemann at Hisarlık*. Berkeley: University of California Press, 1999.

American Antiquarian and Oriental Journal. 'Museums'. 1880, 65.

Arentzen, Wout. 'Frank Calvert, Henry Austen Layard and Heinrich Schliemann'. *Anatolian Studies* 51 (2001): 169–85.

Art Journal. 'The Tale of Troy'. July 1883.

Awdry, Frances. 'Lucy's Romance'. *The Monthly Packet of Evening Readings for Members of the English Church*, 1 December 1881.

Baird, J.A. 'Photographing Dura-Europos, 1928–1937: An Archaeology of the Archive'. *American Journal of Archaeology* 115, no. 3 (2011): 427–46.

Baker, Abigail. 'Myths of The Odyssey in the British Museum'. *Bulletin of the Institute of Classical Studies* (forthcoming).

Baker, Malcolm. 'Bode and Museum Display: The Arrangement of the Kaiser-Friedrich-Museum and the South Kensington Response'. *Jahrbuch Der Berliner Museen* 38 (1996): 143–53.

Barber, Edwin Atlee. 'The Rise of the Pottery Industry'. *Popular Science Monthly* 40, December (1891): 146–70.

Barthes, Roland. 'Myth Today'. In *Mythologies*, translated by Annette Lavers, 131–87. London: Vintage Books 2009.

Batchelor, John. 'Scott, William Bell (1811–1890), Poet and Painter'. *Oxford Dictionary of National Biography*. Oxford: Oxford University Press, 2004. Available online: https://doi.org/10.1093/ref:odnb/24938 (accessed 11 July 2018).

Beard, Mary. 'Builder of Ruins'. In *Confronting the Classics*, 17–25. London: Profile, 2013.

Beard, Mary. 'The Invention (and Re-invention) of "Group D": An Archaeology of the Classical Tripos 1879–1984'. In *Classics in 19th and 20th Century Cambridge:*

Curriculum, Culture and Community, edited by Christopher Stray, 95–134. Cambridge: Cambridge Philological Society, 1998.

Beard, Mary. *The Invention of Jane Harrison*. Cambridge, MA: Harvard University Press, 2002.

Bebbington, David. *The Mind of Gladstone: Religion, Homer, and Politics*. Oxford: Oxford University Press, 2004.

Bennett, Tony. *Pasts Beyond Memory: Evolution, Museums, Colonialism*. London: Routledge, 2004.

Bennett, Tony. *The Birth of the Museum: History, Theory, Politics*. London: Routledge, 1995.

Bernal, Martin. *Black Athena: The Afroasiatic Roots of Classical Civilization – Volume 1: The Fabrication of Ancient Greece, 1785-1985*. London: Vintage, 1991.

Betham-Edwards, M. 'Social Aspects of the Paris Exhibition'. *The Eclectic Magazine of Foreign Literature*, October 1878.

Bilsel, Can. *Antiquity on Display: Regimes of the Authentic in Berlin's Pergamon Museum*. Oxford: Oxford University Press, 2012.

Birdwood, George C.M. 'Handbook to the Indian Court, Paris Universal Exhibition 1878'. In *Report of Her Majesty's Commissioners for the Paris Universal Exhibition of 1878*. London: George E. Eyre and William Spottiswoode, 1880.

Birmingham Daily Post. 'Dr. Schliemann's Collection'. 20 December 1877.

Boardman, Brigid M. 'Introduction'. In *The Poems of Francis Thompson*, edited by Brigid M. Boardman, xxv–xxxiv. London: Continuum in association with Boston College, 2001.

Bohrer, Frederick N. *Photography and Archaeology*. London: Reaktion, 2011.

Borges, Jorje Luis. 'Pierre Menard, Author of the Quixote'. In *Labyrinths: Selected Stories and Other Writings*, translated by JEI. New York: New Directions Publishing Corporation 1964.

Borlase, William C. 'A Visit to Dr. Schliemann's Troy'. *Fraser's Magazine*, February 1878.

Borlase, William C. 'The Schliemann Collection at the South Kensington Museum'. *The Academy*, 9 February, 1878.

Boscawen, W. St. Chad. 'The Knossos Exhibition: The "Oldest Masters" in the World'. *Globe*. 13 February 1903.

Brake, Laurel. '"Time' s Turbulence": Mapping Journalism Networks'. *Victorian Periodicals Review* 44, no. 2 (2011): 115–27.

British Architect. 'Dr Schliemann on the Early Civilization of Greece'. 4 May 1877.

British Architect. 'The Tomb of Agamemnon'. 19 January 1877.

British Museum Collection Online. 'Electrotype/dagger, 1908, 1230.17'. Available online: http://www.britishmuseum.org/research/collection_online/collection_object_details.aspx?objectId=447686&partId=1 (accessed 11 July 2018).

British Museum Collection Online. 'The Treasury of Atreus, column. 1905, 1105.1-3'. Available online: http://www.britishmuseum.org/research/collection_online/

collection_object_details.aspx?objectId=457905&partId=1 (accessed 28 August 2018).

British Museum Collections Online. 'Prof. Athanasios Rhousopoulos (Biographical Details)'. Available online: http://www.britishmuseum.org/research/search_the_collection_database/term_details.aspx?bioId=61758 (accessed 28 August 2018).

British Museum. 'Babylon: Myth and Reality'. Available online: http://www.britishmuseum.org/about_us/past_exhibitions/2008/archive_babylon.aspx (accessed 28 August 2018).

Bryant Davies, Rachel. *Troy, Carthage and the Victorians: The Drama of Classical Ruins in the Nineteenth-Century Imagination*. Cambridge: Cambridge University Press, 2018.

Burgon, Thomas. 'XVI An Attempt to Point out the Vases of Greece Proper Which Belong to the Heroic and Homeric Ages'. *Transactions of the Royal Society of Literature of the United Kingdom*, 2 (2nd series) (1847): 258–96.

Burn, Lucilla. *The Fitzwilliam Museum: A History*. London: Philip Wilson Publishers Ltd, 2016.

Burnouf, Emile. 'Cyprus and Mycenae'. *The Athenaeum*, 22 March 1879.

Burton, Anthony. 'The Uses of the South Kensington Art Collections'. *Journal of the History of Collections* 14, no. 1 (2002): 79–95.

Bury and Norwich Post. 'The Heroic Age'. 15 January 1878, 2.

Butler, Shane, ed. *Deep Classics: Rethinking Classical Reception*. London: Bloomsbury Academic, 2016.

Cain, P.J., and A.G. Hopkins. 'Gentlemanly Capitalism and Economic Policy: City, Government and the "National Interest", 1850–1914'. In *British Imperialism 1688–2015*, 149–64. 3rd edn. Abingdon: Routledge, 2016.

Calder, William M. III, and Justus Cobet, eds. *Heinrich Schliemann Nach Hundert Jahren*. Frankfurt am Main: Vittorio Klostermann, 1990.

Candlin, Fiona. *Art, Museums and Touch*. Manchester: Manchester University Press, 2010.

Cesnola, Louis Palma di. *Cyprus: Its Ancient Cities, Tombs and Temples – A Narrative of Researches and Excavations*. London: John Murray, 1877.

Challis, Debbie. 'Skull Triangles: Flinders Petrie, Race Theory and Biometrics'. *Bulletin of the History of Archaeology* 26, no. 1 (2016): art. 5. Available online: https://www.archaeologybulletin.org/articles/10.5334/bha-556/ (accessed 18 March 2019).

Challis, Debbie. *From the Harpy Tomb to the Wonders of Ephesus: British Archaeologists in the Ottoman Empire 1840–1880*. London: Duckworth, 2008.

Challis, Debbie. *The Archaeology of Race: The Eugenic Ideas of Francis Galton and Flinders Petrie*. Abingdon: Bloomsbury Academic, 2013.

Chapman, William Ryan. 'Arranging Ethnology: A.H.L.F. Pitt Rivers and the Typological Tradition'. In *Objects and Others: Essays on Museums and Material Culture*, edited by George W. Stocking, 15–43. Madison, WI: University of Wisconsin Press, 1985.

Chisholm, H.W. 'Ninth Annual Report of the Warden of the Standards on the Proceedings and Business of the Standard Weights and Measures Department of the Board of Trade for 1874–5'. London, 1875. Available online: https://books.google.com.hk/books?id=KSxcAAAAQAAJ&printsec=frontcover&hl=zh-TW&source=gbs_ge_summary_r&cad=0#v=onepage&q&f=false (accessed 18 March 2019).

Cockerell, C.R. *Travels in Southern Europe and the Levant, 1810–1817*, edited by Samuel Pepys Cockerell. London: Longman, Green and Co., 1903.

Csapo, Eric. 'Max Müller and Solar Mythology'. In *Theories of Mythology*, 18–30. Oxford: Blackwell, 2005.

Daily Arkansas Gazette. 'Schliemann and His Enemies', no. 242. 5 September 1877.

Daily Evening Bulletin. 'Dr. Schliemann'. 6 September 1877.

Daily News. 'Relics of Troy'. 10 December 1877.

Dakers, Caroline. *The Holland Park Circle: Artists and Victorian Society*. New Haven, CT: Yale University Press, 1999.

Delbourgo, James. *Collecting the World: The Life and Curiosity of Hans Sloane*. London: Allen Lane, 2017.

Dewitt, Anne. 'Advances in the Visualization of Data: The Network of Genre in the Victorian Periodical Press'. *Victorian Periodicals Review* 48, no. 2 (2018): 161–82.

Dodgson Collingwood, Stuart. *The Life and Letters of Lewis Carroll*. London: T. Fisher Unwin, 1898.

Donnelly, Ignatius. *Atlantis: The Antediluvian World*. New York: Harper & Brothers, 1882.

Donohue, A.A. *Greek Sculpture and the Problem of Description*. Cambridge: Cambridge University Press, 2005.

Duesterberg, Susanne. *Popular Receptions of Archaeology: Fictional and Factual Texts in 19th and Early 20th Century Britain*. Bielefeld: Transcript, 2015.

Easton, Donald F. 'Priam's Gold: The Full Story'. *Anatolian Studies* 44 (1994): 221–43.

Easton, Donald F. 'Schliemann's Mendacity: A False Trail?'. *Antiquity* 58, no. 244 (1984): 197–204.

Easton, Donald F. 'The First Excavations at Troy: Brunton, Calvert and Schliemann'. In *Studia Troica Monographien 5*, edited by Ernst Pernicka, Charles Brian Rose, and Peter Jablonka, 32–103. Bonn: Dr. Rudolf Habelt GmbH, 2014.

Easton, Donald F., J.D. Hawkins, A.G. Sherratt, and E.S. Sherratt. 'Troy in Recent Perspective'. *Anatolian Studies* 52 (2002): 75–109.

Eatwell, Ann. 'Borrowing from Collectors: The Role of the Loan in the Formation of the Victoria and Albert Museum and Its Collection (1852–1932)'. *Journal of the Decorative Arts Society 1850 to the Present* 24 (2000): 20–9.

'Eleventh Annual Report of the Deputy Master of the Mint, 1880', London: George E. Eyre and William Spottiswoode, 1880.

Evangelista, Stefano. 'Lessons in Greek Art: Jane Harrison and Aestheticism'. *Women's Studies* 40, no. 4 (2011): 513–36.

Evans, Arthur. 'Introduction'. In *Schliemann of Troy: The Story of a Gold-Seeker*, by Emil Ludwig, 9–21. London: Unwin Brothers, 1931.

Evans, Arthur. 'Review: Troja: Results of the Latest Researches and Discoveries on the Site of Homer's Troy, and in the Heroic Tumuli and Other Sites, Made in the Year 1882'. *The Academy*, 29 December 1883, 437–9.

Evans, Arthur. *The Ashmolean Museum as a Home of Archaeology in Oxford: An Inaugural Lecture Given in the Ashmolean Museum, November 20, 1884*. Oxford: Parker & Co., 1884.

Evans, Joan. *Time and Chance: The Story of Arthur Evans and His Forebears*. London: Longmans, Green and Co., 1943.

Fagan, Garrett G., ed. *Archaeological Fantasies: How Pseudoarchaeology Misrepresents the Past and Misleads the Public*. Abingdon: Routledge, 2006.

Fields, Karen E., and Barbara J. Fields. *Racecraft: The Soul of Inequality in American Life*. London: Verso, 2014.

Fitton, Lesley. *Heinrich Schliemann and the British Museum*. London: British Museum, 1991.

Fitton, Lesley. *The Discovery of the Greek Bronze Age*. Cambridge MA: Harvard University Press, 1996.

Fowler, Robert. 'The Homeric Question'. In *The Cambridge Companion to Homer*, edited by R. Fowler, 220–32. Cambridge: Cambridge University Press, 2004.

Frayling, Christopher. *Henry Cole and the Chamber of Horrors: The Curious Origins of the Victoria and Albert Museum*. London: V&A Publishing, 2010.

Fun. 'A Correction'. 9 May 1877.

Fun. 'Not a Bad Egg'. 5 March 1879, 100.

Fun. 'The Latest Relics'. 21 March 1877.

Funny Folks. 'Archaeological Discoveries'. 6 January 1877.

Funny Folks. 'Mems from Mycenae'. 31 March 1877.

Funny Folks. 'The German Ghoul'. 24 March 1877.

Funny Folks. 'The Hero of Mycenae'. 12 May 1877.

Galanakis, Yannis. 'Exhibiting the Minoan Past: Oxford to Knossos'. In *Minoan Archaeology: Challenges and Perspectives for the 21st Century: Proceedings of the International Ph.D. and Post-Doc Conference at Heidelberg, 23–27 March 2011*, edited by Sarah Cappel, Ute Günkel-Maschek and Diamantis Panagiotopoulos, 17–34. Louvain-la-Neuve: Presses Universitaires de Louvain, 2015.

Gange, David. *Dialogues with the Dead: Egyptology in British Culture and Religion, 1822–1922*. Oxford: Oxford University Press, 2013.

Gange, David, and Rachel Bryant Davies. 'Troy'. In *Cities of God: The Bible and Archaeology in Nineteenth-Century Britain*, edited by David Gange and Michael Ledger-Lomas, 39–70. Cambridge: Cambridge University Press, 2013.

Gere, Cathy. *Knossos and the Prophets of Modernism*. Chicago: University of Chicago Press, 2009.

Gere, Cathy. *The Tomb of Agamemnon*. Cambridge, MA: Harvard University Press, 2006.

Gissing, George. *Isabel Clarendon*. London: Chapman and Hall, 1886.
Gladstone, William Ewart. *Homeric Synchronism: An Enquiry into the Time and Place of Homer*. New York: Harper, 1876.
Gladstone, William Ewart. *Juventus Mundi: The Gods and Men of the Heroic Age*. Boston, MA: Little, Brown and Company, 1869.
Green, E.H.H. 'Gentlemanly Capitalism and British Economic Policy, 1880–1914: The Debate Over Bimetallism and Protectionism'. In *Gentlemanly Capitalism and British Imperialism: The New Debate on Empire*, edited by Raymond E. Dumett, 44–67. London: Longman, 1999.
Greene, T.W. 'Old Keys'. *The Magazine of Art*, January 1879.
Grote, George. *A History of Greece: Volume 1*. 1846. Cambridge: Cambridge University Press, 2009.
Grylls, Rosalie Glynn. 'Rossetti and Browning'. *The Princeton University Library Chronicle* 33, no. 3 (1972): 232–50.
H.N.B. 'Minos in Piccadilly'. *The Speaker*. 10 January 1903.
Hall, Edith. *Inventing the Barbarian: Greek Self-Definition Through Tragedy*. Oxford: Clarendon Press, 1989.
Hall, Edith, and Fiona Macintosh. *Greek Tragedy and the British Theatre 1660–1914*. Oxford: Oxford University Press, 2005.
Hammerschlag, Keren Rosa ' "Nature Straight from God" or "Galvanised Mummy"? Resurrecting Classicism in Frederic Leighton's *And the Sea Gave Up the Dead Which Were In It*. *Nineteenth-Century Art Worldwide* 9, no. 2 (2010). Available online: http://www.19thc-artworldwide.org/autumn10/frederic-leightons-and-the-sea-gave-up-the-dead-which-were-in-it (accessed 11 July 2018).
Hänsel, Alix. *Schliemann und Troja: Die Sammlungen Des Museums für Vor- und Frühgeschichte Band 1*. Regensburg: Schnell Steiner, 2009.
Harloe, Katherine. *Winckelmann and the Invention of Antiquity: History and Aesthetics in the Age of Altertumswissenschaft*. Oxford: Oxford University Press, 2013.
Harper's Bazaar. 'Aesthetic, Bridal, and Reception Toilettes'. 19 November 1881.
Harrison, Jane Ellen. 'Reminiscences of a Student's Life'. *Arion* 4, no. 2 (1965): 312–46.
Harrison, Jane Ellen. 'The Dawn of Greece'. *The Quarterly Review* 194 (1901): 218–43.
Harrison, Jane Ellen. *Myths of the Odyssey in Art and Literature*. London: Rivingtons, 1882.
Hartshorne, Bertram F. 'Dr. Schliemann's Trojan Collection'. *The Archaeological Journal* 34 (1877): 291–6.
Haskell, Francis. *The Ephemeral Museum: Old Master Paintings and the Rise of the Art Exhibition*. New Haven, CT: Yale University Press, 2000.
Haubold, Johannes. 'Dream and Reality in the Work of Heinrich Schliemann and Manfred Korfmann'. In *Archaeology and Homeric Epic*, edited by Susan Sherratt and John Bennet, 19–34. Oxford: Oxbow Books, 2017.
Haubold, Johannes. 'Wars of *Wissenschaft*: The New Quest for Troy'. *International Journal of the Classical Tradition* 8, no. 4 (2002): 564–79.

Haywood, Jan, and Naoíse Mac Sweeney. *Homer's* Iliad *and the Trojan War: Dialogues on Tradition*. London: Bloomsbury Academic, 2018.

Head, Barclay. 'The Origin and Transmission of Some of the Principal Ancient Systems of Weight, as Applied to Money from the Earliest Times Down to the Age of Alexander the Great'. *Journal of the Institute of Bankers* 1 (1879): 167–201.

Hellenic Museum, Melbourne. 'Gods, Myths and Mortals: Greek Treasures Across the Millennia'. Available online: www.hellenic.org.au/gods-myths-mortals (accessed 28 August 2018).

Hertel, Dieter, and Frank Kolb. 'Troy in Clearer Perspective'. *Anatolian Studies* 53 (2003): 71–88.

Hilton, James. 'Remarks on Jade'. *Archaeological Journal* 45, no. 1 (1888): 187–205.

Hodgson, Amanda. 'The Troy Connection: Myth and History in Sigurd the Volsung'. In *William Morris: Centenary Essays; Papers from the Morris Centenary Conference Organized by the William Morris Society at Exeter College Oxford, 30 June–3 July 1996*, edited by Peter Faulkner and Peter Preston, 71–9. Exeter: University of Exeter Press, 1999.

Holtorf, Cornelius. *From Stonehenge to Las Vegas: Archaeology as Popular Culture*. Walnut Creek, CA: Altamira Press, 2005.

Hood, Sinclair. 'Schliemann's Mycenae Albums'. In *Archaeology and Heinrich Schliemann: A Century After His Death. Assessments and Prospects. Myth – History – Science*, edited by George S. Korres, Nektarios Karadimas and Georgia Flouda, 70–8. Athens: Aegeus Society, 2012.

Hooper-Greenhill, Eilean. 'Education, Communication and Interpretation: Towards a Critical Pedagogy in Museums'. In *The Educational Role of the Museum*, edited by Eilean Hooper-Greenhill, 3–27. 2nd edn. Abingdon: Routledge, 1999.

Hooper-Greenhill, Eilean. *Museums and the Shaping of Knowledge*. London: Routledge, 1992.

House of Commons. *Report of the Select Committee on the National Gallery*, London, 1853, Appendix XII.

Hurst, Isobel. 'Classical Training for the Woman Writer'. In *Victorian Women Writers and the Classics: The Feminine of Homer*, edited by Isobel Hurst, 52–100. Oxford: Oxford University Press, 2007.

Hutchinson, Horace Gordon. *Life of Sir John Lubbock, Lord Avebury, Vol. 1*. London: Macmillan and Co., 1914.

Illustrated London News, Supplement to the. 'Schliemann's Researches in Greece'. 24 March 1877.

Illustrated London News. 'Dr Schliemann's Researches at Mycenae'. 31 March 1877.

Illustrated London News. 'Dr. Schliemann's Collection'. 29 December 1877.

Illustrated London News. 'Dr. Schliemann's Excavations in the Troad'. 5 January 1878, 11–13.

Illustrated London News. 'The Discoveries at Mycenae'. 24 February 1877.

Independent Statesman. 'Letters from Abroad'. 29 May 1879.

J.H.R. 'The Vivified Tau'. *The Antiquary* 4 (1881): 83.

Jablonka, Peter. 'Troy'. In *The Oxford Handbook of the Bronze Age Aegean*, edited by E.H. Cline, 849–61. Oxford: Oxford University Press, 2012.

Jameson, Fredric. *The Political Unconscious: Narrative as a Socially Symbolic Act*. London: Routledge, 2002.

Jauss, Hans Robert. *Toward an Aesthetic of Reception*, translated by Paul de Man. Minneapolis, MN: University of Minnesota Press, 1982.

Jebb, R.C. ' "Echoes of Hellas" by Prof. George C. Warr, with Illustrations by Walter Crane'. *The Classical Review* 2, no. 8 (1888): 248–9.

Jenkins, Ian. 'Frederic Lord Leighton and Greek Vases'. *Burlington Magazine*, October (1983): 597–605. Available online: http://burlington.org.uk/media/_file/article-11722.pdf (accessed 29 March 2019).

Jenkins, Ian. *Archaeologists and Aesthetes in the Sculpture Galleries of the British Museum, 1800–1939*. London: British Museum Press, 1992.

Jenkyns, Richard. *Dignity and Decadence: Victorian Art and the Classical Inheritance*. London: Harper Collins, 1991.

Jenkyns, Richard. *The Victorians and Ancient Greece*. Oxford: Blackwell, 1980.

Jewitt, LLewellyn. 'A Few Words on the Fylfot Cross'. *The Reliquary* (July 1881): 1–10.

Junker, Klaus. *Interpreting the Images of Greek Myths*, translated by Annemarie Künzl-Snodgrass and Anthony Snodgrass. Cambridge: Cambridge University Press, 2012.

Kenner, Hugh. 'Renaissance II'. In *The Pound Era*, 41–53. Berkeley: University of California Press, 1971.

Knell, Simon. *National Galleries: The Art of Making Nations*. Abingdon: Routledge, 2016.

Korfmann, Manfred. 'Introduction – Troia and the Natural Sciences'. In *Troia and the Troad: Scientific Approaches*, edited by Günther A. Wagner, Ernst Pernicka and Hans-Peter Uerpmann, 1–7. Berlin: Springer, 2003.

Kotsonas, Antonis. 'Politics of Periodization and the Archaeology of Early Greece'. *American Journal of Archaeology* 120, no. 2 (2016): 239–70.

Kotsonas, Antonis. 'Showcasing New Trojan Wars: Archaeological Exhibitions and the Politics of Appropriation of Ancient Troy'. In *Aegis: Essays in Mediterranean Archaeology*, edited by Zetta Theodoropoulou Polychroniadis and Doniert Evely 235–42. Oxford: Archaeopress Publishing, 2015.

Kousser, Rachel. 'Destruction and Memory on the Athenian Acropolis'. *Art Bulletin* 91, no. 3 (2009): 263–82.

Lang, A. 'The Art of Savages'. *The Magazine of Art*. January 1882.

Lang, Andrew. 'The Tale of Troy'. *The Academy*, 9 June 1883.

Lapourtas, Andreas. 'Arthur Evans and His Representation of the Minoan Civilisation at Knossos'. *The Museum Archaeologist* 22 (1995): 71–82.

Latacz, Joachim. *Troy and Homer: Towards a Solution of an Old Mystery*. Oxford: Oxford University Press, 2004.

Leahy, Helen Rees. *Museum Bodies: The Politics and Practices of Visiting and Viewing*. Abingdon: Routledge, 2016.

Lenormant, Francois. 'Antiquities at the Paris Exhibition'. *The Contemporary Review*, 1 August 1878.

Levitt, Norman. 'The Colonisation of the Past and the Pedagogy of the Future'. In *Archaeological Fantasies: How Pseudoarchaeology Misrepresents the Past and Misleads the Public*, edited by Garrett G. Fagan, 270–2. Abingdon: Routledge, 2006.

Llewellyn-Jones, Lloyd. *Aphrodite's Tortoise: The Veiled Woman of Ancient Greece*. Swansea: The Classical Press of Wales, 2003.

Lord, Beth. 'Representing Enlightenment Space'. In *Reshaping Museum Space: Architecture, Design, Exhibitions*, edited by S. Macleod, 146–57. Abingdon: Routledge, 2005.

Louvre. 'Founding Myths: From Hercules to Darth Vader'. Available online: https://www.louvre.fr/en/expositions/founding-myths-hercules-darth-vader (accessed 28 August 2018).

Lyttelton Times 'Town & Country'. 17 May 1878, no. 5377, 49. Available online: https://paperspast.natlib.govt.nz/newspapers/LT18780517.2.11 (accessed 28 August 2018).

Lyttelton Times. 'Artistic Pottery'. 26 May 1882. Available online: https://paperspast.natlib.govt.nz/newspapers/LT18820526.2.35 (accessed 11 July 2018).

Mac Sweeney, Naoíse, *Troy: Myth, City, Icon*. London: Bloomsbury Academic, 2018.

MacGillivray, J. Alexander. *Minotaur: Sir Arthur Evans and the Archaeology of the Minoan Myth*. London: Pimlico, 2001.

Maliszewski, Dariusz. 'Trojan Schematic Idols at Munich'. *Anatolian Studies* 43 (1993): 111–15.

Marchand, Suzanne L. *Down from Olympus: Archaeology and Philhellenism in Germany, 1750–1970*. Princeton, NJ: Princeton University Press, 1996.

Martindale, Charles. 'Introduction: Thinking Through Reception'. In *Classics and the Uses of Reception*, edited by Charles Martindale and Richard F. Thomas, 1–13. Oxford: Blackwell, 2006.

Maurer, Kathrin. 'Archeology as Spectacle: Heinrich Schliemann's Media of Excavation'. *German Studies Review* 32, no. 2 (2009): 303–17.

McClellan, Andrew. *Inventing the Louvre: Art, Politics, and the Origins of the Modern Museum in Eighteenth-Century Paris*. Berkeley: University of California Press, 1994.

McCoskey, Denise Eileen. *Race: Antiquity and Its Legacy*. London: I.B.Tauris, 2012.

McWhirter, John. 'MacWhirter, John (1837–1911), Landscape Painter'. *Oxford Dictionary of National Biography*. Oxford: Oxford University Press, 2004. Available online: https://doi.org/10.1093/ref:odnb/34826 (accessed 26 May 2018).

Methodist Quarterly Review. 'Art. II – Recent Origin of Man'. January 1877, 29–56.

Meyer, Caspar. 'Ancient Vases in Modern Vitrines: The Sensory Dynamics and Social Implications of Museum Display'. *Bulletin of the Institute of Classical Studies*, forthcoming.

Meyer, E. 'Schliemann's Letters to Max Müller in Oxford'. *Journal of Hellenic Studies* 82 (1962): 75–105.

Meynell, Everard. *The Life of Francis Thompson*. New York: Charles Scribner's Sons, 1913.

Michigan Farmer. 'The Household: An Englishwoman's Thoughts About Women'. 7 March 1882, 7.

Miles, Margaret M. *Art as Plunder: The Ancient Origins of the Debate About Cultural Property*. Cambridge: Cambridge University Press, 2008.

Millar, Delia. 'Simpson, William (1823–1899), Watercolour Painter and Journalist'. *Oxford Dictionary of National Biography*. Oxford: Oxford University Press, 2004. Available online: https://doi.org/10.1093/ref:odnb/25597 (accessed 26 May 2018).

Millar, Fergus. 'Toynbee, Arnold Joseph (1889–1975), Historian'. *Oxford Dictionary of National Biography*. Oxford: Oxford University Press, 2004. Available online: https://doi.org/10.1093/ref:odnb/31769 (accessed 25 April 2017).

Mitter, Partha. 'Greece, India, and Race Among the Victorians'. In *African Athena: New Agendas*, edited by Daniel Orrells, Gurminder K. Bhambra and Tessa Roynon, 56–70. Oxford: Oxford University Press, 2011.

Modern Society. Untitled article. 24 January 1903, unpaginated.

Moorehead, Caroline. *The Lost Treasures of Troy*. London: Quality Paperbacks Direct, 1994.

Müller, Friedrich Max, *Lectures on the Science of Language*, Vol. 1. London: Longmans, Green and Co., 1873.

Müller, Friedrich Max. 'The Hissarlik Inscriptions Deciphered'. *The Academy*, 16 May 1874.

Müller, Friedrich Max. *Comparative Mythology: An Essay*. London: George Routledge and Sons, 1909.

Müller, Georgina Adelaide, ed. *The Life and Letters of the Right Honourable Friedrich Max Müller*, Vol. 1. London: Longman Green and Co., 1902.

Munn, Geoffrey C. 'The Archaeologist, the Collector and the Jeweller, 1820–1900'. In *Heinrich Schliemann Nach Hundert Jahren*, edited by William M. Calder III and Justus Cobet, 326–34. Frankfurt am Main: Vittorio Klostermann, 1990.

Murray, Alexander Stuart. 'A New View of the Homeric Question'. *Contemporary Review* 23 (1874): 218–44.

Murray, Alexander Stuart. 'Dr. Schliemann's Trojan Antiquities'. *The Academy*, 22 December 1877.

Museo Nazionale Etrusco di Villa Giulia. 'La Sirena: Soltanto un Mito? Nuovi Spunti per una Storia della Medicina fra Mito, Religione e Scienza'. Available online: http://www.villagiulia.beniculturali.it/index.php?it/21/archivio-news/158/mostra-la-sirena-soltanto-un-mito-nuovi-spunti-per-una-storia-della-medicina-fra-mito-religione-e-scienza (accessed 28 August 2018).

Newton, Charles. *Essays on Art and Archaeology*. London: Macmillan, 1880.

Nichols, Kate. *Greece and Rome at the Crystal Palace: Classical Sculpture and Modern Britain, 1854–1936*. Oxford: Oxford University Press, 2015.

North Otago Times. 'Dr Schliemann's Relics of Troy'. 30 March 1878.

Nowak-Kemp, Małgosia, and Yannis Galanakis. 'Ancient Greek Skulls in the Oxford University Museum, Part I: George Rolleston, Oxford and the Formation of the

Human Skulls Collection'. *Journal of the History of Collections* 24, no. 1 (2011): 89–104.

O'Gorman, Francis. '"To See the Finger of God in the Dimensions of the Pyramid": A New Context for Ruskin's "The Ethics of the Dust" (1866)'. *The Modern Language Review* 98, no. 3 (2003): 563–73.

Observer. 'Art: The Old Masters Exhibition at Burlington House'. 11 January 1903.

Olverson, T.D. *Women Writers and the Dark Side of Late Victorian Hellenism*. Basingstoke: Palgrave Macmillan, 2010.

Paley, Frederick Apthorp. *On Post-Epic or Imitative Words in Homer*. London: Norgate, 1879.

Pater, Walter. 'The Heroic Age of Greek Art'. In *Greek Studies*, 194–233. London: Macmillan, 1895.

Pearce, Susan. 'William Bullock: Collections and Exhibitions at the Egyptian Hall, London 1816–25'. *Journal of the History of Collections* 20, no. 1 (2008): 17–35.

Pearsall, Cornelia D. *Tennyson's Rapture: Transformation in the Victorian Dramatic Monologue*. Oxford: Oxford University Press, 2008.

Penelope. 'Our Ladies' Column by One of Themselves'. *The Wrexham Advertiser*. 21 November 1885.

Penny, H. Glenn. *Objects of Culture: Ethnology and Ethnographic Museums in Imperial Germany*. Chapel Hill, NC: University of North Carolina Press, 2002.

Petch, Alison. 'Notes on the Opening of the Pitt Rivers Museum'. *Journal of Museum Ethnography* 19 (2006): 101–12.

Peter Parley's Annual 1880. 'Dr Henry Schliemann', 82–101. London: Ben George, 1880.

Petersen, Daniel. 'Live from Troy: Embedded in the Trojan War'. In *Return to Troy: New Essays on the Hollywood Epic*, edited by Martin M. Winkler, 27–48. Leiden: Brill, 2015.

[Pitt Rivers, A.H.L.N.]. 'Eastern Excavations', *Nature: a Weekly Illustrated Journal of Science* 21 March 1878, no. 438, 397–9.

Pitt Rivers, A. Lane-Fox. 'On the Evolution of Culture (1875)'. In *The Evolution of Culture and Other Essays by the Late Lt.-Gen. A. Lane-Fox Pitt-Rivers*, edited by J.L. Myres, 20–44. Oxford: Clarendon Press, 1906.

Poole, Lynn, and Gray Poole. *One Passion, Two Loves: The Story of Heinrich and Sophia Schliemann, Discoverers of Troy*. New York: Thomas Y. Crowell Company, 1966.

Porter, James I. 'Homer: The History of an Idea'. In *The Cambridge Companion to Homer*, edited by R. Fowler, 324–43. Cambridge: Cambridge University Press, 2004.

Potter's American Monthly. 'The Art World'. March 1882.

Potts, Alex. 'Introduction'. In *History of the Art of Antiquity*, edited by J.J. Winckelmann and A. Potts, 1–37. Los Angeles: Getty Publications, 2006.

Prettejohn, Elizabeth. 'Pater on Sculpture'. In *Pater the Classicist: Classical Scholarship, Reception, and Aestheticism*, edited by Charles Martindale, Stefano Evangelista and Elizabeth Prettejohn, 220–38. Oxford: Oxford University Press, 2017.

Prettejohn, Elizabeth. *Beauty and Art, 1750–2000*. Oxford: Oxford University Press, 2005.

Prettejohn, Elizabeth. *Rossetti and His Circle*. London: Tate Gallery Publishing, 1997.
Prettejohn, Elizabeth. *The Modernity of Ancient Sculpture: Greek Sculpture and Modern Art from Winckelmann to Picasso*. London: I.B.Tauris, 2012.
Preziosi, Donald. 'Archaeology as Museology: Re-thinking the Minoan Past'. In *Labyrinth Revisited: Rethinking 'Minoan' Archaeology*, edited by Yannis Hamilakis, 30–9. Oxford: Oxbow Books, 2002.
Punch or the London Charivari. 'How About Those Buttons?' 13 January 1877, 3.
Quinn, Malcolm. *The Swastika: Constructing the Symbol*. London: Routledge, 1994.
Qureshi, Sadiah. *Peoples on Parade: Exhibitions Empire and Anthropology in Nineteenth-Century Britain*. Chicago: University of Chicago Press, 2011.
Rethinking Pitt Rivers. 'Museum Displays at South Kensington Museum'. Available online: http://web.prm.ox.ac.uk/rpr/index.php/article-index/12-articles/282-museum-displays-at-south-kensington-museum (accessed 28 August 2018).
Rethinking Pitt Rivers. ' "Typological Museums, as Exemplified by the Pitt Rivers Museum at Oxford, and His Provincial Museum at Farnham, Dorset". *Journal of the Society of Arts*, 18 December, 1891, pp. 115–22'. Available online: http://web.prm.ox.ac.uk/rpr/index.php/article-index/12-articles/189-typological-museums (accessed 28 August 2018).
Rethinking Pitt Rivers. 'A Year in the Life: 1878'. Available online: http://web.prm.ox.ac.uk/rpr/index.php/pitt-rivers-life/42-a-year-in-the-life-1878 (accessed 28 August 2018).
Rethinking Pitt Rivers. 'Museum Displays at Bethnal Green Museum'. Available online: http://web.prm.ox.ac.uk/rpr/index.php/article-index/12-articles/281-museum-displays-at-bethnal-green-museum (accessed 28 August 2018).
Rethinking Pitt Rivers. 'P66 Salisbury and South Wiltshire Museum PR Papers'. Available online: http://web.prm.ox.ac.uk/rpr/index.php/primary-documents-index/14-general/698-p66-salisbury-and-south-wiltshire-museum-pr-papers (accessed 28 August 2018).
Rice, Michael, and Sally MacDonald. 'Introduction – Tea with a Mummy: The Consumer's View of Egypt's Immemorial Appeal'. In *Consuming Ancient Egypt*, edited by Sally MacDonald and Michael Rice, 1–22. Walnut Creek, CA: Left Coast Press, 2010.
Richards, David. 'At Other Times: Modernism and the "Primitive" '. In *The Cambridge History of Modernism*, edited by Vincent Sherry, 64–82. Cambridge: Cambridge University Press, 2017.
Roberts-Austen, W. Chandler. 'Alloys'. *Scientific American Supplement*, 17 February 1894.
Robertson, Bruce. 'The South Kensington Museum in Context: An Alternative History'. *Museum and Society* 2, no. 1 (2004): 1–14.
Robinson, Annabel. *The Life and Work of Jane Ellen Harrison*. Oxford: Oxford University Press, 2002.
Rose, Charles Brian. 'Troy and the Historical Imagination'. *The Classical World* 91, no. 5 (1998): 405–13.

Rose, Charles Brian. *The Archaeology of Greek and Roman Troy*. Cambridge: Cambridge University Press, 2013.

Ross, Iain. 'Archaiologia'. In *Oscar Wilde and Ancient Greece*, 97–126. Cambridge: Cambridge University Press, 2012.

Rossetti, Dante Gabriel. 'Troy Town'. In *Poems*, 16–20. 1870. Cambridge: Cambridge University Press, 2013.

Rowley-Conwy, Peter. *From Genesis to Prehistory: The Archaeological Three Age System and Its Contested Reception in Denmark, Britain, and Ireland*. Oxford: Oxford University Press, 2007.

Royal Academy of Arts. *Old Masters, Deceased Masters of the British School, Albert Cuyp and Palace of Knossos in Crete*. London: Royal Academy of Arts, 1903. Available online: https://www.royalacademy.org.uk/art-artists/exhibition-catalogue/1903-old-masters-deceased-masters-of-the-british-school-albert-cuyp-and (accessed 28 August 2018).

Royal Cornwall Gazette. 'Treasures from Troy'. 24 August 1877, 2.

Ruth, Jennifer. ' "Gross Humbug" or "the Language of Truth"? The Case of the *Zoist*'. *Victorian Periodicals Review* 32, no. 4 (1999): 299–323.

Saherwala, Geraldine, Klaus Goldmann and Gustav Mahr. *Heinrich Schliemanns 'Sammlung Trojanischer Altertümer': Beitrage Zur Chronik Einer Grossen Erwerbung Der Berliner Museen*. Berlin: Spiess, 1993.

Said, Edward W. *Orientalism*. London: Penguin, 1978.

Sayce, A.H. 'The Early History of the Levant'. *The Academy*, 18 August 1883, 119.

Schliemann, Heinrich. *Atlas Trojanischer Alterthümer*. Leipzig, 1874. Available online: http://digi.ub.uni-heidelberg.de/diglit/schliemann1874/0001 (accessed 28 August 2018).

Schliemann, Heinrich. *Ilios: The City and Country of the Trojans*. London: John Murray, 1880.

Schliemann, Heinrich. *Mycenae: A Narrative of Researches and Discoveries at Mycenae and Tiryns*. New York: Charles Scribner's Sons, 1880.

Schliemann, Heinrich. *Troy and Its Remains: A Narrative of Researches and Discoveries Made on the Site of Ilium, and in the Trojan Plain*. London: John Murray, 1875.

Science and Art Department of the Committee of Council on Education, South Kensington Museum. *Drawings of Glass Cases in the South Kensington Museum, with Suggestions for the Arrangement of Specimens*. London: Vincent Brooks, Day & Son, 1876.

Science and Art Department of the Committee of Council on Education, South Kensington Museum. *Twenty Fifth Report of the Science and Art Department of the Committee of Council on Education, with Appendices*. London: Parliamentary Papers, 1878.

Scientific American. 'A Wonderful Treasure Trove'. 6 January 1877.

Scott, William Bell. 'The Hissarlik Antiquities at the South Kensington Museum'. *The Academy*, 16 February 1878.

Scott, William Bell. *Autobiographical Notes of the Life of William Bell Scott: and Notices of His Artistic and Poetic Circle of Friends, 1830–1882*, Vol. 2, edited by William Minto. London: James R. Osgood, McIlvaine & Co., 1892.

Shanks, Michael, and Christopher Y. Tilley. *Re-Constructing Archaeology: Theory and Practice*. London: Routledge, 1992.

Shanower, Eric. 'Twenty-First-Century Troy'. In *Classics and Comics*, edited by George Kovacs and C.W. Marshall, 195–206. Oxford: Oxford University Press, 2014.

Shapiro, H.A. *Myth into Art: Poet and Painter in Classical Greece*. London: Routledge, 1994.

Sherratt, Susan. 'Representations of Knossos and Minoan Crete in the British, American and Continental Press 1900–1930'. *Creta Antica* 10, no. 2 (2009): 619–49.

Sherratt, Susan, and John Bennet. 'Introduction'. In *Archaeology and Homeric Epic*, edited by Susan Sherratt and John Bennet, vii–xvi. Oxford: Oxbow Books, 2017.

Siapkas, Johannes, and Lena Sjögren. *Displaying the Ideals of Antiquity: The Petrified Gaze*. New York: Routledge, 2013.

Siegel, Jonah, ed. *The Emergence of the Modern Museum: An Anthology of Nineteenth-Century Sources*. Oxford: Oxford University Press, 2008.

Simpson, William. 'Mycenæ, Troy and Ephesus'. In *The Autobiography of William Simpson*, edited by G. Eyre-Todd, 273–5. London: T. Fisher Unwin, 1903.

Simpson, William. 'The Schliemannic Ilium'. *Fraser's Magazine*. July 1877.

Smith, George. 'On the Reading of the Cypriote Inscriptions'. *Transactions of the Society of Biblical Archaeology* 1 (1872): 129–44.

Snodgrass, Anthony. 'Homer, the Moving Target'. In *Archaeology and Homeric Epic*, edited by Susan Sherratt and John Bennet, 1–9. Oxford: Oxbow Books, 2017.

South Kensington Museum. *A Guide to the Art Collections of the South Kensington Museum: Illustrated with Plans and Wood Engravings*. London: Spottiswoode & Co., n.d.

Southall, James C. 'XXVI The Ruins of Troy'. In *The Recent Origin of Man: As Illustrated by Geology and the Modern Science of Pre-Historic Archaeology*, 440–9. London: Trübner & Co., 1875.

Springall, Jill. 'Collier, John (1850–1934), Portrait Painter'. *Oxford Dictionary of National Biography*. Oxford: Oxford University Press, 2004. Available online: https://doi.org/10.1093/ref:odnb/32499 (accessed 11 July, 2018).

Squire, Michael. 'Ekphrasis at the Forge and the Forging of Ekphrasis: The Shield of Achilles in Graeco-Roman Word and Image'. *Word and Image* 29, no. 2 (2013): 157–91.

Stoczkowski, Wiktor. *Explaining Human Origins: Myth, Imagination, and Conjecture*. Cambridge: Cambridge University Press, 2002.

Swain, Hedley. *An Introduction to Museum Archaeology*. Cambridge: Cambridge University Press, 2007.

The Academy. 'Fine Art'. 11 December 1880, 429–30.

The Academy. 'Notes on Art and Archaeology'. 13 March 1880.

The Academy. 'Notes on Art and Archaeology'. 23 October 1886, 283.

The Architect & Contract Reporter. 'The Academy Winter Exhibition'. 9 January 1903.
The Art Journal. 'The Collection of Art Objects from the Site of Troy'. April 1878.
The Athenaeum. 'Dramatic Gossip'. 26 May 1883.
The Athenaeum. 'The Tale of Troy'. 2 June 1883.
The British Architect and Northern Engineer. 'Royal Institute of British Architects'. 4 May 1877.
The Builder. 'Knossos at Burlington House'. 31 January 1903.
The Builder. 'The Troy Collection at South Kensington'. 5 January 1878.
The Citizen. 'Dr Schliemann's Collection'. 26 December 1877.
The County Gentleman: A Sporting Gazette and Agricultural Journal. 'The Man About Town'. 16 January 1892.
The Derby Mercury. 'Relics of Troy'. 26 December 1877.
The Graphic. 'Dr. and Madame Schliemann'. 20 January 1877.
The Graphic. 'Dr. Schliemann's Discoveries at Mycenae'. 20 January 1877.
The Graphic. 'Our Illustrations'. 16 June 1877.
The Graphic. 'The Court'. 15 December 1877.
The Ladies' Treasury: A Household Magazine. 'A New Employment for Women of Culture and Reliable Information'. 1 June 1893.
The Leeds Mercury. 'Special Correspondence (by Private Telegraph)'. 21 December 1877.
The Leisure Hour: An Illustrated Magazine for Home Reading. 'Varieties'. 2 March 1878, 144.
The Lichfield Mercury. 'Dr Schliemann's Excavations'. 15 March 1878.
The Liverpool Mercury. 'Workmen and Museums'. 14 February 1887.
The Manchester Courier and Lancashire General Advertiser. 'Dr Schliemann's Collection of Trojan Antiquities'. 21 December 1877.
The Manchester Guardian. 'Editorial Article 3'. 7 February 1881.
The Manchester Weekly Times. 'Dr. Schliemann's Collection'. 29 December 1877.
The Pall Mall Gazette. 'A Woman's View of the Greek Question: An Interview with Miss Jane Harrison'. 4 November 1891, 1–2.
The Pall Mall Gazette. 'Summary of This Morning's News'. 7 December 1877.
The Phrenological Journal and Science of Health. 'Dr. Schliemann, The Merchant-Archaeologist'. 13 July 1877.
The Saturday Review. 'The Tale of Troy'. 9 June 1883.
The Sporting Times. 'Notes'. 19 January 1878.
The Times. 'Agricultural Hall'. 27 December 1877, 9.
The Times. 'Dr. Schliemann'. 12 April 1878.
The Times. 'Dr. Schliemann's Discoveries at Troy'. 2 May 1874.
The Times. 'Excavation of Prehistoric Knossos'. 10 August 1900.
The Times. 'Excavations at Troy'. 27 November 1878, 4.
The Times. 'Industries at the Manchester Exhibition'. 27 May 1887.
The Times. 'South Kensington Museum'. 27 December 1877, 9.
The Times. 'The Gold Masks of Mycenae'. 20 December 1877, 6.

The Times. 'The Heroic Age'. 8 January 1878, 10.
The Times. 'The Trojan Treasure'. 20 December 1877, 6.
The Times. 'Troy – Mr. Bertram F. Hartshorne Writes to Us'. 21 August 1877.
The Times. 'Troy'. 16 August 1877.
The Times. 'Troy'. 17 December 1877.
The Times. 'Troy'. 18 April 1878, 7.
The Times. 'Troy'. 31 March 1875.
The Times. 'Troy'. 6 December 1877.
The Times. Untitled article ['Troy and the New Archaeology']. 20 December, 1877, 9.
The Western Daily Press. 'The Schliemann Treasures'. 21 December 1877.
Thomas, Nicholas. 'Objects: Indigenous Signs in Colonial Design'. In *Possessions: Indigenous Art/Colonial Culture*, 95–125. London: Thames & Hudson, 1999.
Thompson, Francis. 'Sister Songs (1895)'. In *The Poems of Francis Thompson*, edited by Brigid M. Boardman, 59–94. London: Continuum in association with Boston College, 2001.
Todd, Malcolm. 'Toynbee, Jocelyn Mary Catherine (1897–1985)'. *Oxford Dictionary of National Biography*. Oxford: Oxford University Press, 2004. Available online: https://doi.org/10.1093/ref:odnb/62392 (accessed 6 April 2019).
Tolstikov, Vladimir, and Mikhail Treister. *The Gold of Troy: Searching for Homer's Fabled City – Catalogue of an Exhibition 'Priam's Treasure' Held in April 1996 at the Pushkin State Museum of Fine Arts in Moscow*. New York: Harry N. Abrams Inc., 1996.
Traill, David A. ' "Priam's Treasure": Clearly a Composite'. *Anatolian Studies* 50 (2000): 17–35.
Traill, David A. 'Schliemann and His Academic Employees'. In *Heinrich Schliemann Nach Hundert Jahren*, edited by William M. Calder III and Justus Cobet, 237–55. Frankfurt am Main: Vittorio Klostermann, 1990.
Traill, David A. *Schliemann of Troy: Treasure and Deceit*. London: John Murray, 1995.
Transactions of the Royal Historical Society. 'List of Fellows', 8 (1880): i–xxii.
Tregear, Edward. *The Aryan Maori*. Wellington, New Zealand: George Didsbury, 1885.
Trigger, Bruce G. *A History of Archaeological Thought*. Cambridge: Cambridge University Press, 2006.
V&A Archive. MA/4/37-8: Abstracts of Correspondence, 1864 to 1914.
V&A Archive. MA/31/7: Register of Loans In, 1878–1937.
V&A Collections Online. 'Candlestick: Palissy, Bernard, born 1510 – died 1590'. Available online: http://collections.vam.ac.uk/item/O86254/candlestick-palissy-bernard/ (accessed 15 January 2019).
V&A. '1858 Exhibition of the Photographic Society of London'. Available online: http://www.vam.ac.uk/content/articles/0-9/1858-exhibition-of-the-photographic-society-of-london/ (accessed 28 August 2018).
V&A. 'Architectural History of the V&A 1862–1863: The North and South Courts – A Double-Sided Showpiece'. Available online: https://web.archive.org/web/20130419072739/http://www.vam.ac.uk/content/articles/a/architectural-

history-of-the-v-and-a-1862-1863-the-north-and-south-courts-a-double-sided-showpiece (accessed 21 March 2019).

V&A. 'Colour Sketch for Spirit Fresco "The Arts of Industry as Applied to War"'. Available online: http://collections.vam.ac.uk/item/O133138/colour-sketch-for-spirit-fresco-oil-painting-leighton-frederic-lord/ (accessed 28 August 2018).

V&A. 'The Cross, D.127-1906'. Available online: http://collections.vam.ac.uk/item/O843147/the-cross-drawing-simpson-william-ri/ (accessed 28 August 2018).

Vetter, Andreas W. *Troia: Traum und Wirklichkeit Ausstellungsführer*. Braunschweig: Braunschweigisches Landesmuseum und Herzog Anton Ulrich-Museum Braunschweig, 2001.

Vickers, Michael. 'Value and Simplicity: Eighteenth-Century Taste and the Study of Greek Vases'. *Past & Present* 116, no. 1 (1987): 98–137.

Wagenknecht, Susann. 'Debating Troy in the Mass Media: The Catalytic Impact of Public Controversy on Academic Discourse'. In *The Sciences' Media Connection: Public Communication and Its Repercussions*, edited by Simone Rödder, Martina Franzen and Peter Weingart, 291–306. Dordrecht: Springer, 2012.

Walford, Edward. 'West Brompton, South Kensington Museum, &c.'. *Old and New London: Vol. 5*. London: Cassell, Petter & Galpin, 1878. Available online: http://www.british-history.ac.uk/old-new-london/vol5/pp100-117 (accessed 28 August 2018).

Warr, George C., and Walter Crane. *Echoes of Hellas: The Tale of Troy and the Story of Orestes from Homer and Aeschylus with Introductory Essay and Sonnets by George C. Warr*. London: Marcus Ward and Co., 1887.

Westropp, Hodder M. 'The Hissarlik Relics'. *The Athenaeum*, 12 January 1878.

White, Hayden V. *The Practical Past*. Evanston, IL: Northwestern University Press, 2014.

Whitehead, Christopher. *Museums and the Construction of Disciplines: Art and Archaeology in Nineteenth Century Britain*. London: Duckworth, 2009.

Wilde, Oscar 'The Truth of Masks'. In *Intentions*, 235. London: Osgood McIlvaine & Co., 1894.

Winsbury, Rex. *Zenobia of Palmyra: History, Myth and the Neo-Classical Imagination*. London: Duckworth, 2010.

Witcomb, Andrea. *Re-Imagining the Museum: Beyond the Mausoleum*. London: Routledge, 2003.

Woodson-Boulton, Amy. *Transformative Beauty: Art Museums in Industrial Britain*. Redwood City, CA: Stanford University Press, 2012.

Ziolkowski, Theodore. *Minos and the Moderns: Cretan Myth in Twentieth-Century Literature and Art*. Oxford: Oxford University Press, 2008.

Index

Achilles 81, 111, 146
  'barbaric' 166
  shield 143–4, 146
  tumulus 20
Aeneid 92–3, 171
Agamemnon 152
Ajax 75
Alexander the Great 17
Alma-Tadema, Lawrence 106
Andromache 80, 105, 145–6
archaeology
  anachronism 129
  context 10–11, 58–9, 78, 83
  dating 4, 47–8, 138–9, 151–60, 188
  deep time 139, 153–4, 166–7, 193
  epistemology 23–4, 201, 204
  everyday life 66, 126–7, 200–1
  imagination 24–7, 195
  interdisciplinary 185
  political 162–3, 170, 199, 201
  popular culture 96, 125–6, 129–30, 197
  relationship to literature 182–3, 185, 189, 194–5
  stratigraphy 26, 47–8, 54, 148–9, 154–9, 202
  three-age system 70, 153–6, 203
  unrepeatable 23
Argive Heraion 92
Aristotle 81
art 96, 99–113
  idealized beauty 64–5
  modern art 121, 123, 190–1
  old masters 190–1
Aryan theory
  explaining Homer 20
  global connections 123, 173–5
  language origins 171–5
  swastika 66–9, 138, 161–2, 172–3
  Trojans 71–4, 161–2, 168–9
Ashmolean Museum 190
Assyria 111, 144–5, 170, 185

Athena
  in Homer 64
  owl-headed 15, 63–4, 66, 68, 74–5, 92
Atlantis 174

banks 36–8, 128, 131–5
Barthes 200–1
Bell Scott, William 115–17, 159
Berlin Royal Museum 7, 61–2
Bible 19–21, 133, 142
bimetallism 133–5
Borges, Jorge Luis 25–6
Borlase, William 35–6, 173–4
Braunschweigisches Landesmuseum 198
British Museum
  ancient weights 132–3
  artistic inspiration 103, 107
  comparing objects with Troy 64–5, 86
  display style 46
  interest in Mycenae 37–8
  lack of space 37, 41–2
  lectures 181–3
  staff *see* Head, Barclay; Merlin, Charles; Murray, Alexander Stuart; Newton, Charles
Browning, Elizabeth Barrett 148
Burgon, Thomas 19
Burlington House, London 190
Burnouf, Émile 161, 173

Calvert, Frank 18, 23, 35
Carroll, Lewis 97
Cesnola, Luigi Palma di 86, 170
China 173
Chisholm, H. W. 132–3
Choiseul-Gouffier, Compte de 17
classical reception 8, 26, 198
Clytemnestra 106–9
Cole, Henry 46
Collier, John 106–9
Cyprus 86, 170
  syllabary 69, 71, 172–3

Darwin, Charles 116, 154, 157, 162, 166, 174
Department of Science and Art 38
Department of Standards 132–3
depas amphikupellon 80–2, 90, 104–5, 197
diadems *see* jewellery
Donnely, Ignatius 174

Eastern Question 165–6, 169–71, 199
Egypt
    comparison with Troy 159, 161
    Egyptomania 96
    influence on Troy 69, 170–1
    in paintings 109
    textual evidence for Troy 133–4
ekphrasis 143–6
electrotype 100–1
Etruscans 92–3
Evans, Arthur 108, 178–9, 189–95, 201
Evans, John 155
evolution 156–60, 171, 174, 203
    social darwinism 115–17, 166–7

fashion 100–2, 129
Flaxman, John 4
Frazer, Sir James George 187

Gladstone, William Ewart
    copper age 155
    ethnicity of Trojans 164–5, 170
    interpretation of Homer 21, 162
    location of Troy 79
    naming headdress 79
    request for exhibition 14, 37–8
    support for Schliemann 8–9, 187
Grote, George 18–19

Harrison, Jane Ellen 110, 178–9, 181–8, 200
Hartshorne, Bertram Fulke 13
Head, Barclay V. 133–5
Hector 80
Helen
    humour 127
    images 4, 100, 103–4, 112
    jewellery 53, 78, 110–11, 147
Hera 92
Herakles 88
Herzog Anton Ulrich-Museum 198

Hew's and Co., Cambridge Massachusetts 101–2
Hisarlık 17–18, 23, 138, 198 *see also* Troy
Hittites 18, 133–5, 172, 199
Homer 2
    Assyrian art 144–5, 185
    'Bible of the Greeks' 24
    education 96
    guide to exhibition 144–5
    history 18–19, 139–40, 141, 199
    Homeric Question 2, 19–20, 141–3, 178, 182–7
    rarity of tin 155
    as second-hand knowledge 142–3
    as strange 129–30
    style 121
    terms from 64, 75–82, 90, 92, 143, *see also depas amphikupellon, glaukopis* vase
human remains *see* skulls
humour 13, 125–30, 147

idols 64–5, 69, 73–5, 159, 166
    headdress 78, 106
    net sinkers 174
    psi figurines 92
Iliad
    archaeological finds 26, 70, 75–81, 90, 131, 145–9
    date written 144
    ethnic identity in 163–6
    evidence of early Greece 18–21
    illustrations 4
    landscape 16–17, 52
    performance 110–13
    religion 64–5
    shield of Achilles 143–4
    uneducated readings 147–8
    violence 71, 77, 129, 166–7
Ilium Novum 21
India 20, 66, 109, 161, 171–2
industrial production 118–20, 129
inscriptions 66, 85, 172–3
Institute of Bankers 133–4

jade 173
jewellery
    ancient wearers 71–2, 80, 145–7
    concealment 78–80

depiction in art 105–9
fashion 100–1
iconography 78
reconstruction by wearing 52–4
Jones, Sir William 171
Julius Caesar 19

key 82–4
Knossos 179, 189–95, 201
Kolb, Frank 199–202
Korfmann, Manfred 197–202

Lang, Andrew 86, 111
Layard, Austen Henry 37–8
Leighton, Sir Frederick 103, 105, 110
Lubbock, Sir John 133, 155
Lucan 17, 141
Lydians 92–3

Manchester Royal Jubilee Exhibition 100
Māori 122–3
maps 52, 58, 191–2, 198–9
Marshall, Sarah Edith 148
Merlin, Charles 37
Modernism 97, 122, 182, 189
Morris, William 121
Müller, Friedrich Max
    arranging exhibition 46–7, 151, 172
    aryan theory 172
    interpretation of Homer 20
    linguistic theories 159
    support for Schliemann 13
Murray, Alexander Stuart 144–6, 184
museums
    chronological display 46, 156–7
    classical reception 4
    context 58, 191
    facilities for scholars 185
    grand narratives 61
    historical reconstruction 31, 54, 76, 145, 198
    histories of 6–7, 30–2
    interpretation 45–59, 62, 68, 190–1, 201
    lectures 181–6
    museology 6–8, 30–3
    sunday opening 174–5
    temporary exhibitions 7, 41–2
    typological display 86, 157–9
    visitors as active 6–7

visitor experiences 36–7, 62–5, 93–4, 183–4
Mycenae
    architecture 103, 110, 184
    beauty 120–1
    better known than Troy 12
    connections to Troy 88–9, 90–2, 161
    dating 151–2
    display at Athenian Bank 36–7
    excavations 22, 170
    finds from 36–8
    humour 127–30
    objects in Trojan exhibition 90–2
    photography 49, 52
    representations in art 103, 106–8
    travellers to 16–19

Native Americans 174
Newton, Charles Thomas 37, 86, 110, 152, 181, 185
New Zealand 63, 102, 122–3, 173

Odyssey 18, 79, 110, 181–4
Orientalism 52, 70–1, 108–9, 163–5

Parthenon 115–17, 163
Paley, Frederick Apthorp 144
Pater, Walter
    ethnicity of Trojans 164
    heroic age 120–2, 127, 146–7, 152, 201
    influence on Jane Ellen Harrison 181–2
Persian Wars 163
Peru 161, 173–4
photography 36, 49–59, 110, 190–1, 202
    archaeological 49–52, 58–9
Pınarbaşı 20
Pitt Rivers, Augustus Henry Lane Fox 42, 157–60, 162, 170–1
Pliny the Elder 19, 103–4
Poseidon 88
pottery 85–93
    depas amphikupellon 90
    double-necked jugs 86–7
    glaukopis vase 63–5, 71–5, 115, 120
    Greek vases 118, 185
    Hanging vessels 88–9
    large vessels 65, 70–1, 84
    modern replicas 101–3
Poynter, Sir Edward 100, 110

Pre-Raphaelite Brotherhood 115, 121
press, the 22, 30, 52-3, 77, 97, 125-7, 192-4
Priam's Palace 13, 71, 142
Priam's treasure *see* treasure

Quatremere de Quincy, Antoine Chrysostome 58

race 160, 161-75
    art 115, 122-3
    human remains 74
    major question raised by Troy 138, 187-8
    science 162
religion
    Christianity 104-5, 132, 154-5, 174-5, *see also* Bible
    at Troy 63-4, 66-9, 73-5, 78-9, 92-3
replicas 100-3, 190-1
Rhousopoulos, Athanasios 36
Roberts-Austen, William Chandler 134, 155
Romans 2, 171
Rossetti, Dante Gabriel 103-4
Royal Academy 190
Royal Mint 134

Sandys, Frederick 103, 109
Sanskrit 171-2
Sarpedon 75
Schliemann, Heinrich
    announcements to press 1-2, 15, 45
    biography 21-3, 167, 178
    circular reasoning 18, 64
    excavations 22-4, 52, 154, 198
    house in Athens 36
    outsider 24, 45, 56, 61
    popular 23-4, 96-7, 200
    possible forgeries 83
    response to criticism 13, 36, 47, 56, 83
    self-promotion 23, 37, 52-3
    untrustworthy 21-5, 127, 197, 202
Schliemann, Sophia 22, 53, 100
Schmalz, Herbert Gustave 105
scientific analysis 24, 58, 202
    geology 173
    human remains *see* skulls
    metals 82, 127-8, 131-5, 155-6

Sellers, Eugenie 110
shield 75-7
Simpson, William 13-14, 15, 24-5, 37, 172
skulls 71-4, 165-9
    Camper's angle 168
    collections 166
    phrenology 129, 167-8
Smith, George 172
social class
    ancient Troy 120, 128-30
    museum visitors 38-9, 46, 97, 174-5
    popular culture 125
    taste 120
Society of Antiquaries 52, 155
South Kensington Museum 30, 37-43, 61
    Bethnal Green branch 157
    display style 39-41, 46, 56-7
    educational priorities 38-9, 118-19
    lack of space 42
    lectures 181
    other collections 41-2, 118, 157
    photographic exhibitions 49
    staff 46
Southall, James Cocke 154-5
spindle whorls 66-9
stone sculpture 84-5, 105
Stuttgart 197
swastika 66-9, 161-3, 172-3
symbols 66-9

Tale of Troy 110-13, 181
talents 128, 133-4, 84
taste 99-100, 118-19
Temple of Athena at Lindos 104
temporary exhibitions 5, 39
Tennyson, Alfred Lord 21, 147
theatre 109-13
Thompson, Francis 104-5
Thomson, E. Gertrude 97
Tiryns 88-9, 185
tools 66, 69-71, 152-6
treasure 42, 126
    comparison with pottery 74-5
    deposition 77-8, 82-3
    discovery 22, 75, 35
    display 77-84
    rediscovery 7
    value 127-8, 131-2
Tregear, Edward 123

Troad 19–20
Troia: Traum und Wirklichkeit 179, 197–202
Trojan exhibition
 announcements 15, 161
 arrangement 45–7, 53, 62, 155–7, 171–2
 collaboration 46–7
 dates 30, 61
 evidence for Troy 5, 14–15, 56–9
 labels 47–9, 54, 77–82, 85, 145
 photographs and plans 49–59
 plan 62–3
 royal visits 97
 selection of objects 42
 sketching at 105, 116
 social hub 97
 visitor numbers 30
Trojan War 71–4, 77
 artistic representations 102–4, 163
 dating 23, 155–6
 European identity 139–40, 163
 extermination 170
 historical event 18–21, 142–5, 152
 Hittite sources 18–19, 199
 literature 26, 144
 new Trojan wars 138, 204
Troy
 architecture 14, 65
 between Asia and Europe 139
 contested 17–18, 197–201
 contradictory 139–40
 depictions 4–5, 100–13
 everyday life 42
 excavation at 17, 22, 48, 52
 fall 16–17, 73, 77–8, 82–3, 152
 'first city' 65, 72, 88
 Homer's Troy 13–14, 65, 72, 82, 152
 landscape 51–8
 materiality 5, 15, 97, 103, 129, 163
 popular culture 199–201
 'primitive' 65, 115–23, 144–5, 166
 religion 64–5, 166
 small finds 65–6
 travellers to 13, 16–20, 35
 'tell' 148–9, 151

V&A *see* South Kensington Museum
Virchow, Rudolf 74, 168–9

Watts, George Frederick 110
White, Hayden 201
Wilde, Oscar 113
Winckelmann, Johann Joachim 116–20
Wolf, Friedrich August 2, 19–20, 141, 148
women
 craft 102
 education 147–8, 184
 museum visitors 100, 147
 readers of Homer 147–8
 scholarship 148, 181–2
 subjects for paintings 103–9
Wood, Robert 20
World War II 6

Xerxes 19
Xoana 111

Zenobia 105

www.ingramcontent.com/pod-product-compliance
Lightning Source LLC
Chambersburg PA
CBHW070024010526
44117CB00011B/1696